Netscape Navigator

Netscape Navigator

Jason J. Manger

McGRAW-HILL BOOK COMPANY

London · New York · St Louis · San Francisco · Auckland · Bogotá
Caracas · Lisbon · Madrid · Mexico · Milan · Montreal
New Delhi · Panama · Paris · San Juan · São Paulo
Singapore · Sydney · Tokyo · Toronto

Published by
McGRAW-HILL Book Company Europe
Shoppenhangers Road, Maidenhead, Berkshire, SL6 2QL, England
Telephone 01628 23432
Fax 01628 770224

British Library Cataloguing in Publication Data
The CIP data of this title is available from the British Library, UK

ISBN 0–07–709190–6

Library of Congress Cataloging-in-Publication Data
The CIP data of this title is available from the Library of Congress,
Washington DC, USA

12345   CL   98765

Typeset by Ian Kingston Editorial Services, Nottingham
and printed and bound in Great Britain at Clays Ltd, St Ives plc

Printed on permanent paper in compliance with the ISO Standard 9706

Contents

Introduction

Much has been written about the Internet, the Web and *Cyberspace*, and I'm not about to bore you to death with yet another barrage of historical facts, pie charts and network diagrams. Here are the main concepts in a nutshell. It comes as a surprise to many people that the Internet is in fact a very old network that has been in operation for over a quarter of a century. Now vastly revamped, it is set to become a commercial entity – the forerunner of the *Information Superhighway* that will eventually link every home in the land for business and leisure purposes. The Internet is not *vastly* different from many existing types of electronic media in concept, although it is very different in many other respects. It is not (yet) controlled by any single company or individual, but is rather a cooperative structure where information is allowed – indeed encouraged – to pass through as many parts of the Internet as possible – all of the information on the Internet is shared among its users. Via the Internet you can browse a newspaper, read the sonnets of Shakespeare, order goods and services, listen to music, consult a dictionary, and even chat to friends. These are run-of-the-mill things of course, things we can do *without* the Internet. If, however, you also take into account that you can talk (and see) friends in *real-time* irrespective of their geographical distance, make audio/visual phone calls to anywhere in the world for the price of a local phone call, gain twenty-four hour access to just about any fact known to humanity, and consult a pool of unrestricted information that is uncontrollable by any government on the planet, then the Internet may just appeal to you.

This book is mainly concerned with publishing and publicizing information via the Internet. In essence the Internet is really one large publishing house. Everything on the Internet is immediately accessible to anybody with a telephone and some basic computer hardware. The World-Wide Web (or the *Web*) is the tool that has revolutionized access to the Internet. The Web is set to become the new publishing phenomenon, a system borne out of the world's largest computer network known as the Internet. The Web *is* publishing, albeit in electronic form – allowing information to be stored, distributed and published to a global audience. Designed by Tim Berners-Lee at CERN (the famous particle physics laboratory in Switzerland) the Web has also made the Internet a far more accessible entity. It has itself been described as a *very large hard disk*, where all of the Internet's resources can be brought to you in an instant.

In order to *explore* the Internet, a host of graphical tools known as *browsers* have been developed, and are now in widespread use. Netscape is one such tool, and represents a milestone in the development of Internet software. Netscape is what is known as a *graphical Web browser*, a software tool that offers an alternative interface to the Internet – an interface that is intuitive and visually attractive to the end user. Many alternative Web browsers are available, notably Mosaic (Netscape's main predecessor), although Netscape's enhancements and features have made it the *de facto* standard Web browser in the Internet community.

Readership and audience

Businesses interested in publishing their goods and services on the Internet will be particularly attracted to Netscape now that secure transaction support is available. In fact, the Web has probably done more for the commercialization of the Internet than any other individual factor. Thousands of companies and organizations now have a presence on the Internet using the Web as their publishing and communications tool.

Novice Internet users (or *newbies*, to use that horrible netphrase) will want to examine Netscape because it allows the entire Internet to be accessed through a common interface, and without the need to learn any esoteric or cryptic commands – a problem that plagued the Internet prior to the Web's arrival. Readers interested in using the World-Wide Web as a publishing medium will want to examine the new enhancements to the HTML (HyperText Mark-up Language) standard, which has now reached version 3.0. HTML is the key to publishing on the Internet and is the topic of an extensive chapter of this book. Netscape has also brought many other new features with it. *Dynamic documents* and *secure transaction* support are two significant new features, and coverage is given to both of these important topics.

Book contents

This book is mainly concerned with two things, namely the Netscape program/interface, and the underlying hypertext language that Netscape understands, namely HTML. Many different HTML examples are provided, along with screen extracts of the visual effects that they achieve, so that you can understand how the hypertext area of the Web is put together. Details of how Netscape interfaces to other Internet resources, such as USENET (Network News), FTP (File Transfer Protocol) servers and Gopher servers, are also dealt with in detail. The liberal use of screenshots from the Netscape program will quickly allow you to see how the package works, and there are hints and tips scattered throughout the book. Just about any subject known can be found on the Web, and we'll show you where and how. As for appendices, you can expect to find a newly re-vamped 'Web resource list', which first appeared in McGraw-Hill's *The World-Wide Web, Mosaic and More*, and much more besides.

What will I learn using this book?

Chapter 1 introduces the Netscape program itself, and tells you how to acquire and install the system on your computer. Every menu and option in the Netscape package is then examined in detail, and screenshots accompany each description. You will also learn how to install and configure third-party programs, known as *helper applications*. These programs are used to assist Netscape when it needs to view different file formats, such as still images, audio files and motion video. In Chapter 2 you will learn about uniform resource locators (or URLs). URLs have been one of the keys to the success of the Web – a compact notation for specifying the unique type and location of a resource located on the Internet. When you supply a valid URL to Netscape you pull information from the Internet into your computer, which then renders any visual effects that are required. In Chapter 3 you will learn how to converse in HTML, the Web's HyperText Mark-up Language. You must learn a smattering of HTML in order to publish your own work on the Internet. Chapter 4 covers an area of the Internet known as USENET – a truly massive collection of over ten thousand forums in which you will find discussions on every subject from Alchemy to Zen-Buddhism. Locating information from the Internet can be a most difficult task, given its size and ever-changing nature. For this purpose Chapter 5 concentrates on a number of *search engines* – tools that can be used to locate information from the Internet.

Ultimately, by reading this book, you will be fully conversant with the Netscape package. You will also know how to undertake further configurations, and will have learned how to publish your own information using HTML.

Version information

Just like any item of software, Netscape is a continually evolving product. The research for this book has been based upon the original version of Netscape, version 1.0N, or

Mosaic Communications Corporation's version of Netscape, although version 1.1b1 (the first beta version from the newly formed Netscape Communications Corporation) was also used, as were versions 1.1b2 and 1.1b3 leading up to the full version 1.1N release of Netscape. At the time of writing, Netscape 1.1N understands many of the proposed features of the HTML 3.0 standard, although it also has introduced some of its own *extensions* – and these are documented where relevant. One of Netscape's undoubted strengths lies in the richness of its features, and its willingness to experiment with new facilities (many of which are in use all over the Web). Netscape is the dominant Web browser at the time of writing, with some 6 million users, making up 75% of the Web-browser community.

Just before this book went to press, Netscape Corporation released version 1.2b1. See Appendix I for more details.

System requirements

This book is based upon the Personal Computer (PC) version of Netscape running in a Microsoft Windows/Windows for Workgroups environment (versions 3.1 or 3.11 respectively). In order to use Netscape 1.1N in this environment you will need the following hardware and software configuration.

Hardware

■ Computer: a personal computer (e.g. IBM clone), for example an IBM-compatible 486-based machine. Netscape is a demanding application that requires a fast computer. A 486SX would be an adequate entry-level machine, although a DX 33 model (or higher) would be better suited. Your computer must also have a hard disk (fixed disk) on which to store the Netscape program (and other utilities). Netscape 1.1N occupies around 1.5 Mbyte of disk space. The Netscape program also requires at least 4 Mbyte of memory (RAM). Netscape 1.1N will run with a *minimum* specification of a 386SX machine with 4 Mbyte of memory.

■ Screen: VGA or Super VGA graphics capability. Netscape will run in a VGA or SVGA graphics mode, although SVGA is better suited in order to show a larger screen area (Netscape screens are also best viewed at their maximum size).

■ Navigation: a mouse, e.g. Microsoft or other serial mouse. Netscape is a Windows-based application and makes extensive use of the mouse in order to allow the user to click on hypermedia objects. While it is possible to navigate without a mouse, it will be impossible to click on hyperlinks. Netscape does not allow the user to 'tab' through successive hyperlinks on a screen so that one may be chosen.

Software

■ A copy of the Netscape browser (version 1.1N). Netscape is available as freeware and soon as a fully supported commercial product (license details are included with the program).

Expect software companies to start licensing versions of the Netscape browser so that they can bundle them as part of future hardware and software deals etc. Netscape also requires a piece of software known as WinSock, even if you are not intending to access the Internet (see below).

■ Helper software applications (*viewers*). In order that Netscape can deal with a wide variety of media types, you should get hold of as many helper applications as possible. These exist as freeware and shareware (as well as commercial) software packages which can be configured to work with Netscape – typically to view audio, video and textual material stored in a range of different file formats.

For Internet access (from home)

■ A modem and telephone line. A modem is a hardware device that sits between your computer and the telephone system in order that you can dial into an Internet service provider to gain Internet access (via the TCP/IP protocol). A modem that supports 14,400 bps is adequate for Web browsing, although a V34/VFAST modem that supports speeds of 28,800 bps can make a significant improvement, and many service providers now support such higher speeds.

■ A suitable WinSock software package. A WinSock package runs the Internet Protocol (IP) on your computer, allowing connection into the Internet. One of the most ubiquitous WinSocks is the Trumpet WinSock shareware package. Many other commercial WinSocks are also available (and Windows 95 will have a WinSock built into it as standard). Refer to the appendices for the location of the Trumpet WinSock package.

■ A subscription to an Internet service provider (supporting the SLIP protocol).

Book conventions

All *computerese* text is set in the `Courier` font: for example Internet host names (e.g. `www.quad-ralay.com`) and URLs (*uniform resource locators* – a method of specifying where a resource of information actually resides on the Internet, and which is common to all graphical Web browsers). For example, `http://www.mcgraw-hill.com` is one example of a URL that makes Netscape download a hypertext page from McGraw-Hill's Web Server `www.mcgraw-hill.com` and then display it on your screen. The `http://` prefix stands for HyperText Transfer Protocol, the communications protocol that is used to move hypertext (text, images and sound) around over the Web. Needless to say, you will learn all about URLs later on in the book.

Jason Manger (`wombat@spuddy.mew.co.uk`)
Surrey
June 1995

C H A P T E R

1

An introduction to Netscape

1.1 Introduction

Netscape is a navigational tool that allows users to explore the Internet in a graphical environment. It is one of many graphical browsers, although it is by far the most important. Why? Well, because Netscape is the commercial successor to Mosaic, the Internet's first *killer application*. Many of the original Mosaic team now work for Netscape Corporation, and, since leaving NCSA (the National Centre for Supercomputing Applications) – Mosaic's birthplace – have ploughed their efforts into the development of the Netscape Web browser.

Then we have the World-Wide Web (WWW, or just the *Web*). The Web is a rather strange entity in many respects, for it is a protocol specification and application rolled into one. It was initially conceived at CERN, the famous particle physics laboratory in Switzerland, in order to make the Internet a more accessible and altogether organized entity by linking together files and other documents using a system known as *hypertext*. Put simply, hypertext is a way of linking and cross-referencing documents. The early WWW browsers were text-based programs – that is to say that they had no graphical user interface (GUI). The concept of *hypermedia* is now upon us, and graphical browsers such as Netscape can deal with many different media, rather than just *plain text*. Netscape facilitates hypermedia by embedding textual and graphical information into a document. Links to other media types, such as audio and video files, are also possible. In addition, Netscape facilitates access to the vast majority of Internet resources through just a single graphical interface (in this book we consider the popular Microsoft Windows graphical user interface) by simply pointing and clicking on objects that appear on the *page*. It is already possible to read newspapers, order goods and services, watch films, and listen to music, all by using the World-Wide Web and a graphical browser such as Netscape.

1.2 **Netscape and Mosaic: which should I use?**

One immediate question that commonly arises when discussing the two main browsers, Netscape and Mosaic, is which is the best package? It should be said that while Netscape and Mosaic share a common graphical interface, the underlying behaviour of each package is quite different. Netscape has been completely rewritten, unlike some Web browsers that share the same core Mosaic code. On the whole, Netscape operates much more quickly than Mosaic. It is also more stable and offers some *enhanced* features not found in other browsers. Whether or not it is *better* than Mosaic is left for you, the end user, to decide.

Netscape's *enhancements* are numerous. The most important features are detailed below. More detailed explanations of these new features are examined throughout the book where relevant.

■ *Modem speed optimization*
Netscape Corporation has made access speed a major priority with Netscape. Multimedia is a demanding environment and so performance using 14,400 baud modems has been optimized, allowing access via standard telephone lines to be as quick as possible. Netscape is very *usable* at such speeds, and coupled with its multi-threading activity (to be discussed) it is a much quicker browser than Mosaic. Access at higher speeds will also be significantly faster. Netscape also works with 9600 baud modems.

■ *Security considerations*
Netscape has built in encryption support in the form of the RSA scheme. Netscape Corporation offers a Netscape Server program (*NetSite*) which, when used in connection with the Netscape browser, will facilitate secure transmissions over the Internet. This single improvement allows sensitive information, such as credit card details, to be passed safely over the Internet.

■ *Document and image-handling performance*

Netscape has many new document loading improvements that will be immediately noticeable to the end user. In particular, it offers multiple simultaneous image loading, continuous document streaming, improved document and image caching, and JPEG image decompression. JPEG is a ubiquitous image format used widely on the Internet, mainly for compressing images to reduce their size.

Netscape also offers a range of new image-loading features. It can now load interlaced images, that is to say images that are built up as a series of layers. With this mode enabled, you can see Netscape loading each layer and the image gradually building up until it is completely visible.

Since Netscape is also enhanced to *multi-thread* document loading, it can also display an image while marking-up some HTML text, so it is possible to move around a document and even select a new hyperlink while the current document is still being loaded.

■ *New user interface features*

Netscape has an enhanced user interface, including an extended *toolbar* and an enhanced *bookmark* facility (for saving the names of Web sites that you visit). The new *bookmark* facility is now organized hierarchically and can be indexed and searched. Mosaic users will also be pleased to learn that there is now a *Stop!* button that halts the loading of the current HTML page.

File downloading is also handled much more efficiently via a dedicated menu function that does away with the need for Mosaic's older (and clumsy) *Record to File* feature. Netscape also has features for printing Web pages and viewing the current HTML source file.

USENET users (USENET is the Internet's USErs' NETwork – a global news system comprising well in excess of ten thousand forums) can even use Netscape as a fully fledged *newsreader*, and this is examined in greater depth within Chapter 4.

Progress monitoring is also improved. Netscape will show you how much of a document is being loaded and will give you a progress check as the document is loaded so that you can see how long you will have to wait for the entire document to be transferred to your machine.

■ *Helper applications*

Helper applications are external programs that act as *filters* – allowing Netscape to deal with documents and images that are stored in proprietary formats. File formats can now be configured within Netscape, which saves editing the appropriate initialization (`.ini`) file by hand – although this is of course possible for the more experienced and confident user, and we show you how in Appendix E. Helper applications allow Web documents to interface to other tools in order to show still images, animations and many other file formats for which there is a *viewer* available (*viewer* is an older Mosaic term, incidentally, which is now referred to as a helper application in Netscape parlance).

No actual helper applications arrive with Netscape (apart from a new audio player with version 1.1), although there are dozens of freeware and shareware applications that can be used, and Appendix D shows you where they reside on the Internet. Many of the standard Microsoft Windows tools can be used as helper applications as well.

■ *HTML enhancements*

All Web authors will want to examine the latest additions to the version of Netscape HTML. Netscape now incorporates some HTML 3.0 features, and has additional *tags* which allow Web documents to contain more complex document and image layout formats. Chapter 3 examines the HTML language and the Netscape *extensions* (non-standard HTML tags).

Netscape 1.1 adheres to parts of the HTML 3.0 specification (in draft at the time of writing), which means that HTML authors can now have access to many new text layout features, such as *tables* and *backgrounds*, as well as colour control for text, hyperlinks and backgrounds.

1.3 Installing Netscape

All versions of Netscape arrive as self-extracting (compressed) archive. The main versions of Netscape used in the writing of this book were 1.0N and the final beta (April 1995) release of Netscape, version 1.1b3. Netscape 1.1N has now been released and is available as both 16-bit and 32-bit applications. These files reside on Netscape Corporation's machine `ftp.netscape.com`, as shown below:

```
ftp.netscape.com      /windows/n16e11n.exe (16-bit version)
ftp.netscape.com      /windows/n32e11n.exe (32-bit version)
```

You can download these files using a suitable FTP (File Transfer Protocol) client program, or by using an existing Web browser, such as Netscape 1.0N or Mosaic by prefixing the above filenames with the URL `ftp://`. For example:

```
ftp://ftp.netscape.com/windows/n16e11n.exe
```

would download the file to your computer.

The 16-bit version of Netscape will run natively in a Microsoft Windows 3.1 environment. It is likely that you will be using the full version of Netscape (v1.1) by the time you are reading this. The 32-bit version of Netscape 1.1 will run in 32-bit environments, such as Windows NT and Windows 95. If you are running Windows 3.x you must use the 16-bit version of Netscape, even if you are running the Win32s software (32-bit extensions to Windows 3.1) because the 32-bit version makes use of some 32-bit features that are not supported by Win32s. A suitable TCP/IP stack, such as the ubiquitous Trumpet WinSock can be used in order to gain an Internet connection via Netscape, although Windows 95 users have a TCP/IP stack built in as standard. The Trumpet WinSock program is covered briefly later in this chapter.

Figure 1.1 The first Netscape dialog box (`setup.exe`).

After downloading the appropriate Netscape archive place this in a directory by itself (create a temporary directory for this purpose) and run the self-extracting file. If you are unpacking Netscape version 1.1 (16-bit), the decompression does *not* constitute a proper installation. Unlike earlier versions of Netscape, version 1.1 has a `setup.exe` program that must be run in order to complete the installation process. Netscape 1.0 users can use Netscape immediately by creating an icon for the `netscape.exe` file that has been uncompressed – although it is unlikely that this version of the package will still be in general use by the time you are reading this, and an upgrade would make sense in any event, since the later versions of Netscape are superior in terms of system performance and features. Netscape version 1.1 users should run `setup.exe` from the Windows Program Manager or File Manager. The setup program performs two main tasks: (i) it extracts and installs all of the Netscape executable files into a new directory; and (ii) it creates a group file and icon for Netscape 1.1. Figure 1.1 illustrates the first dialog box that the Netscape setup program displays.

After clicking on the *Continue* button, Netscape asks you for a directory into which you want to install the main program, as shown in Figure 1.2.

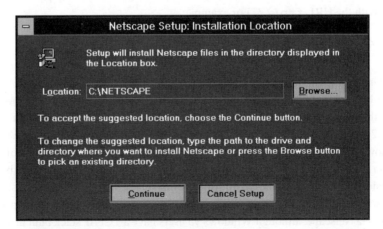

Figure 1.2 Choosing a directory in which to install Netscape.

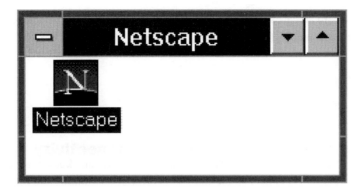

Figure 1.3 A typical Netscape group window and icon.

Netscape recommends the \NETSCAPE directory for the installation, although you can choose any valid directory location. You may well already have an existing version of Netscape already installed. If this is the case, the older version will simply be overwritten, although it makes sense to keep both versions if possible (if disk space permits, that is). After you have chosen a valid directory, Netscape extracts all of its files and installs them in the directory specified. A progress indicator is given as the installation takes place. Netscape then asks you to choose a group name (i.e. a separate Program Manager window) under which to install a Netscape icon so that you can run the package. Netscape will list all of the group windows that are currently valid on your system, and will highlight the group name *Netscape* by default (this group will be created if you choose this name). After choosing a group name Netscape creates a new window for the group and inserts an icon for Netscape 1.1, as shown in Figure 1.3. The *Browse* button allows you to navigate your hard disk for a suitable directory in which to install the main Netscape program and system files.

Before you continue...

Some minor *housekeeping* tasks you may want to consider before running Netscape include ensuring that a temporary directory on your hard disk exists. By default, Netscape looks for a directory called \TEMP. You may also consider backing up the original Netscape archive and then deleting the files from the old installation directory (the directory into which you first copied the archive – you can tell this because the files all end with an underscore (_): for example, netscape.ex_). These files are of no use now, mainly because they are duplicated in the original archive and are thus wasting disk space.

You will also have to acquire a WinSock package if you are to connect to and use the Internet. Alternatively, you can use a null-Winsock package, as described below, to use

Netscape locally. In all cases, it is important to note that you will *not* be able to use Netscape without a suitable WinSock (or null-WinSock) package. Windows 95 has a WinSock built in as standard.

Acquiring a WinSock for Internet connectivity

When Netscape is first run it searches for a piece of software known as a *WinSock*. A WinSock allows you to connect to the Internet – effectively running the Internet Protocol (IP) on your personal computer so that information can flow back and forth between your computer and the rest of the network. Without an Internet connection you can only browse files *locally*, that is to say that you can emulate the World-Wide Web in so far as you are accessing hypertext pages from your local hard disk, or from a disk on a local area network etc. You will not of course be able to connect to any remote Internet systems without a modem and suitable Internet connection. Fundamentally, a WinSock is a communications program. It will interface to a modem via your computer and will facilitate the *log-in* process with your service provider's gateway machine in order to gain access to the Internet. The 'sock' in WinSock comes from the word *socket* – a communications mechanism used by the TCP/IP protocol, which all Internet hosts must 'speak' in order to communicate with one another.

Netscape 1.1 will operate *without* a WinSock program, however, since Netscape Corporation provides the `mozock.dll` file for this purpose (read the tip below for the location of this file) which replaces the normal `winsock.dll` that most Web browsers look for when they are initially started. This piece of software is known as a *null-WinSock*, since it has no network functionality. A null-WinSock will allow you to use Netscape locally, saving you time by making the program discard any network requests (alternatively, you can acquire a real WinSock package and just not use it). When using `mozock.dll`, make sure that you rename the file to `winsock.dll` first. For example, from DOS type:

```
REN mozock.dll winsock.dll
```

The file `winsock.dll` and its associated files must either reside in the same directory as the Netscape program (e.g. `C:\NETSCAPE`), or can be pointed to in a separate directory by using the DOS `PATH` statement in the standard DOS startup file `autoexec.bat` that resides in your hard disk's root directory (`C:\`). One of the most popular *de facto* standard WinSocks is Peter Tattam's offering – the Trumpet WinSock. This shareware WinSock is ubiquitous on the Internet and most home computer users will be using this piece of software to gain their Internet connectivity. At the time of writing the most recent version of the Trumpet WinSock is version 2.x. If you are a Windows 95 user, a suitable WinSock is already built into your software, and this can be used instead. Other commercial WinSocks are also available, e.g. FTP software's IP stack and NetManage *Chameleon*.

▶TIP

Running Netscape without an Internet connection can be achieved in one of two ways: (i) obtain the Trumpet WinSock package, allowing Netscape to find `winsock.dll` (via the DOS `PATH`), and then configure WinSock *not* to dial into your Internet provider's gateway machine (thus ignoring the WinSock completely); or (ii) obtain the special Netscape DLL file `mozock.dll` from the Netscape FTP server at the URL below:

ftp://ftp.mcom.com/pub/unsupported/windows/mozock.dll

and then place this in the Netscape main directory. This will allow local usage without an Internet (i.e. modem-based) connection.

If you are not already a member of the Internet community, getting hold of a suitable WinSock can be a slight problem, since, clearly, you cannot gain access to the network in order to obtain a copy. To overcome this problem your Internet service provider will most probably provide you with a copy, or at least *access* to a copy when you join their system, e.g. via a bulletin board system (BBS). Some service providers may even supply you with the necessary software on a disk. Then of course there are books and CD-ROMs that contain such software. *The Essential Internet Starter Kit CD-ROM* by McGraw-Hill contains the entire text and graphics from my previous two Internet books (*The Essential Internet Information Guide* and *The World-Wide Web, Mosaic and More)* and the CD also contains many useful Internet tools, such as the shareware Trumpet WinSock TCP/IP stack, which is described below.

1.4 **Installing and using the Trumpet WinSock**

This section will be of use to those who already have an Internet service provider, and who thus want to use Netscape to gain access to the information stored on the Internet. The Trumpet WinSock has been chosen since it is a ubiquitous piece of software and is made available as shareware, so you can try it out first before registering it. Trumpet International also has a site on the Web which you may want to look at – see Appendix B for its location. Here are the main concepts involved in using the WinSock program.

■ Upon starting Netscape the file `winsock.dll` is searched for. If Netscape cannot find the file from the current `PATH` statement, or if it is not in the same directory as the

Figure 1.4 The fatal Netscape error that occurs when a WinSock cannot be found.

Netscape program, Netscape terminates with an error message, as shown in Figure 1.4. Netscape will not start until a WinSock or null-WinSock is properly installed.

■ If a suitable `winsock.dll` file is found, the WinSock software is loaded and normally appears as a minimized icon on the user's screen. The WinSock software can be configured to dial into your Internet service provider automatically upon starting (as the Trumpet WinSock is capable of doing). Alternatively, you can log in manually. The WinSock software should be left running in the background for the duration of your Netscape session. Closing down the WinSock program while Netscape is running may cause a system crash (harmless to your system, although it will probably terminate the Netscape program abruptly).

■ As soon as the WinSock software is running Netscape is run, and the Netscape window appears on your screen. Whether or not the WinSock software dialled your service provider's machine will depend on its configuration. If it does dial in, and has established a valid connection, you can now access the Internet using Netscape. Try clicking on the Netscape logo for starters.

Configuring the Trumpet WinSock

Before you can use the Trumpet WinSock package you will have to tell the program a few things about your hardware configuration, such as modem speed, communications port and some additional Internet details that your service provider will make available to you. You can install the WinSock package in any directory you like, just as long as Netscape can find it. To do this ensure that the PATH statement includes the name of the directory in which you installed the WinSock package. Alternatively, you can place it in the same directory as the Netscape program itself, although this does tend to clutter up the files for both packages. PATH is a DOS command and a variable of the same name. Your `autoexec.bat` file will contain the PATH setting that you will need to change. Once you have placed the software on your hard disk, install an icon for the package (`tcpman.exe` – the Trumpet WinSock TCP Manager) under Windows, and then run the `tcpman.exe` program by double-clicking

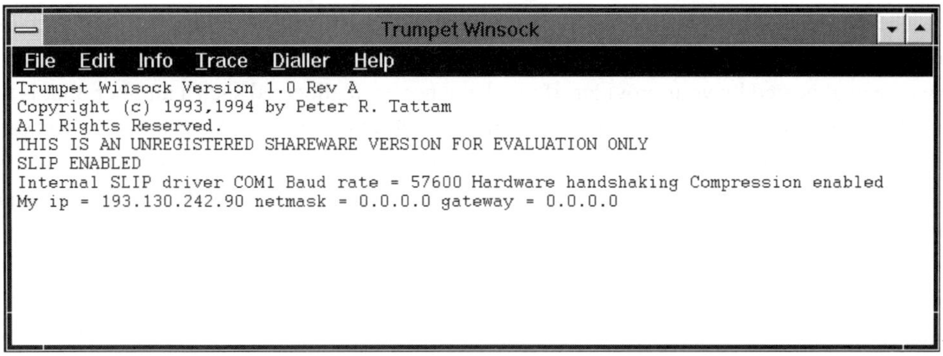

```
─                          Trumpet Winsock                        ▼ ▲
 File  Edit  Info  Trace  Dialler  Help
Trumpet Winsock Version 1.0 Rev A
Copyright (c) 1993,1994 by Peter R. Tattam
All Rights Reserved.
THIS IS AN UNREGISTERED SHAREWARE VERSION FOR EVALUATION ONLY
SLIP ENABLED
Internal SLIP driver COM1 Baud rate = 57600 Hardware handshaking Compression enabled
My ip = 193.130.242.90 netmask = 0.0.0.0 gateway = 0.0.0.0
```

Figure 1.5 The WinSock 1.0 interface (start-up screen).

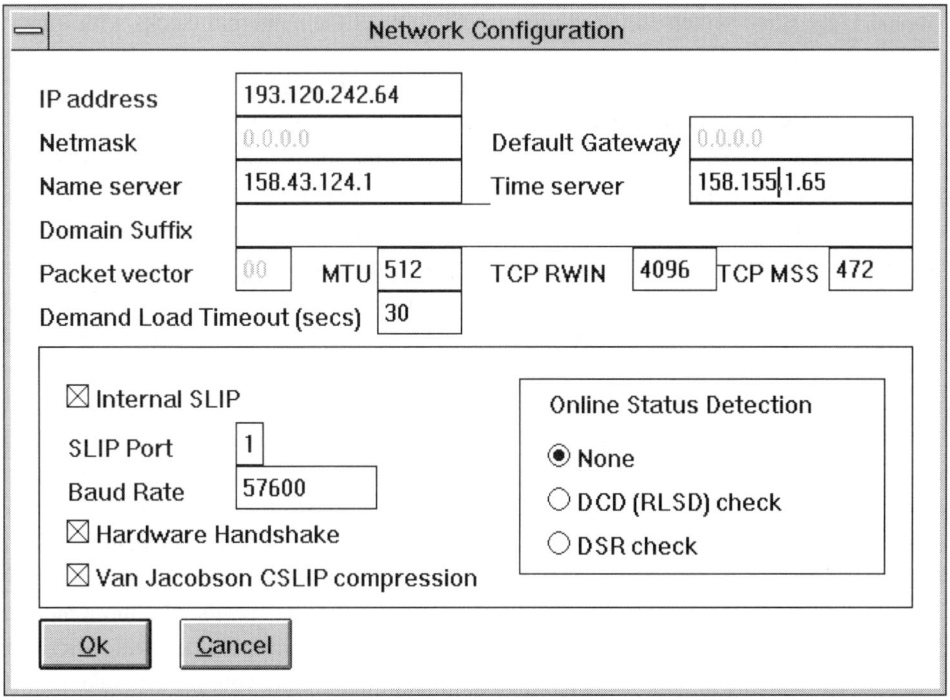

```
─                      Network Configuration

  IP address        193.120.242.64

  Netmask           0.0.0.0          Default Gateway   0.0.0.0

  Name server       158.43.124.1     Time server       158.155 1.65

  Domain Suffix

  Packet vector   00    MTU  512     TCP RWIN  4096    TCP MSS  472

  Demand Load Timeout (secs)  30

  ┌─────────────────────────────┐   ┌───────────────────────────┐
  │  ☒ Internal SLIP            │   │   Online Status Detection │
  │                             │   │                           │
  │  SLIP Port     1            │   │   ⦿ None                  │
  │  Baud Rate    57600         │   │   ○ DCD (RLSD) check       │
  │  ☒ Hardware Handshake       │   │   ○ DSR check              │
  │  ☒ Van Jacobson CSLIP compression │                         │
  └─────────────────────────────┘   └───────────────────────────┘

  [  Ok  ]   [  Cancel  ]
```

Figure 1.6 The WinSock setup screen (File/Setup option).

on the icon provided. The main interface resembles that shown in Figure 1.5, which uses WinSock 1.0 (WinSock version 2.0 is also available, incidentally).

If you click on the File menu you will see an option labelled Setup. Click on this option to configure the WinSock program. Figure 1.6 illustrates a typical WinSock configuration.

The WinSock setup screen consists of a number of fields in which you must provide details of your setup. The *IP Address* field contains the numeric Internet Protocol address that you have been allocated by your provider. If you have not been allocated such a number, that is to say if your service provider allocates a dynamic IP address from a *pool* of addresses, you can leave this field blank – the field will be automatically updated when you access your provider's machine in this case, and will in fact change each time you use their machine. Check with your provider's technical support service that this is the case. Another fundamental IP address that is required is for a *name server*. A name server is basically a computer that resolves addresses so that they can be located on the Internet. Your service provider will supply you with an IP address for their name server (or Domain Name Server – DNS – to use the full name) Alternatively, you can use another host's DNS if you have its IP number (and it is configured to allow *ad hoc* requests from other hosts, as many are, luckily). The *Netmask* and *Default Gateway* fields can be left blank if you are using the Internet from home – these are mainly used in networked environments, e.g. local area networks. The *Time Server* field is another optional entry (time servers allow your machine to reset their internal clocks with a more accurate time at periodic intervals).

All the other WinSock defaults can be kept. Be sure to click on the *Internal SLIP* option in order to use the SLIP protocol – this may in fact already be selected. WinSock 2.x supports the newer PPP as well, although version 1.0 only supports the SLIP protocol (SLIP is supported by the vast majority of Internet service providers and is a popular protocol for modem access to the Internet via Netscape). The *Slip Port* setting is a number that represents the communications port (known as a COM port) on which your modem answers. All personal computers have such ports for devices such as a mouse, printer or modem. Ensure that the COM port on which your modem answers is entered. For example, enter 1 for COM1 or 2 for COM2. The *Baud Rate* setting determines how fast your actual modem connection with the service provider's machine will be. The actual speed will of course depend on your own modem's capabilities. Netscape supports a minimum baud rate of 9600 bps (bits per second – 8 bits being one character). Faster modems use the more common 14,400 baud rate, although many have a *turbo* capability that allows speeds of 19,200 bps. Speeds of 38,400 and 57,600 bps are also possible, although your modem will need to be in the VFAST or V34 class of modem to achieve such speeds, and your computer's serial port must use a UART 16550A interface which is capable of allowing the computer to handle such communication speeds. The more modern PCs, such as 486s, have such a capability. The `msd.exe` utility provided with Microsoft Windows will tell you if your COM port has such an interface, and your modem manual will tell you what baud rates are supported; you can enter a figure on this basis. The remaining defaults can be kept.

Next you should decide whether or not you want the WinSock program to start dialling your service provider's machine when it is initially started. Do this by clicking on the Dialler menu option, and then select Options. You will then see the options *No automatic login* (which prevents WinSock from dialling your provider's machine when it starts); *Automatic login on start up only* (which makes WinSock start dialling when it is started); and *Automatic login and logout on demand* (which allows you to dial in as and when required, and also automatically when WinSock starts). If you choose the first or last options here, you will have to dial into your provider's machine manually using the Dialler menu and then the Login option. The Login option starts the dialling process, whereas the Bye command logs you out by disconnecting the modem. In order to use these facilities, please read the section below. Personally, I like to keep dialling manual, since it is sometimes necessary to make some configuration changes to the WinSock program (at the precise moment which you do not actually want to dial into your provider's machine).

Configuring the Trumpet WinSock to dial into an Internet provider

In order to gain dial-up access to the Internet your service provider will supply you with a means of identification to their system. Principally, this will include a username and password (perhaps of your own choosing), although some other items of information are also sometimes supplied. An Internet Protocol number (IP number) is commonly supplied to you also. This takes the form `n.n.n.n` (e.g. `158.152.8.68`) and is your unique identity on the Internet. Every Internet host has an IP number allocated to them. Many service providers operate a scheme whereby a IP number is allocated *dynamically* from a 'pool' of IP numbers pre-allocated to them. In such cases you will not be specifically allocated an IP number; instead the WinSock program will update itself with this information automatically when you log in. In addition to an IP number you will also normally be allocated a communications protocol. The two most widely used protocols for dial-up Internet access are SLIP (Serial Line Internet Protocol), which is basically the TCP/IP protocol being run over a standard serial communications line, such as your modem uses, and PPP (Point to Point Protocol). SLIP and PPP are both popular, PPP being the more modern and robust implementation, with in-built error correction. You will also have to provide some further information to the WinSock program itself, such as modem speed and your computer's communication port that your modem answers on, as described earlier.

Gaining access to a service provider's machine involves a brief *conversation* between the WinSock program on your computer and the communications software (at the provider's gateway machine) that is answering your telephone call. This initial conversation is handled by a *script*. In essence, a script is a sequence of commands that match responses that come from the provider's machine. Each response involves the WinSock sending some information to the provider's machine, so for example the provider's machine may ask for a username and password, and the WinSock program would then intercept these responses and send the required information. Many Internet providers supply you with a script for their own particular service, although if such a script is not made available (which, unfortunately, is very often the case) you will have to create a script yourself. The Trumpet WinSock uses two scripts, named `login.cmd` and `bye.cmd`, the first for logging in and the second for logging out. Both of these scripts are run by using the Dialler menu with the Login or Bye commands. *Logging in* is the process you undertake when gaining access to your Internet provider's machine, and *logging out* is the process of disconnecting your call to their machine, thus ending communications. Here is the `login.cmd` script (a plain ASCII file, note) that dials my own service provider's machine.

```
output ATN1%C0\13
input 10 OK\13
output atdt14101715379757\13
input 60 CONNECT
input 30 login:
output myname\13
input 30 password:
output mypass\13
input 30 protocol:
output SLIP\13
input 30 address:
address 30
```

This script looks pretty cryptic, but it is straightforward in concept once you understand what each of the lines is actually doing. As mentioned, the script's purpose is basically to match responses from the provider's machine that you are dialling into, and then to provide the correct responses.

The key point to bear in mind is that you have to match the provider's machine prompts exactly, and supply the correct information at the correct time and in the correct order. The `output` command sends some text from the WinSock program to your modem, while the `input` command waits a specified number of seconds for a response sent to your modem from the system being dialled into, i.e. the provider's machine. Trumpet WinSock 2.0 has expanded its scripting language quite significantly, incidentally. If you are upgrading from version 1.0 to 2.0 and are confused about any new commands, simply copy the older `login.cmd` file that you used previously, and this will also function.

The first line in the script normally configures your modem before dialling into the service provider's *gateway* machine. Such commands, while all starting with AT, can be highly system-specific. My own modem, for example, is a Supra 288 fax modem, and the AT command `ATN1%C0\13` is in fact telling the modem to connect to the destination speed at the highest rate (or *baud*) possible (`N1`) and to disable data compression (`%C0`). Data compression is used to make the actual information transmitted over a link more compact, thus carrying more information in the same time. Such compression schemes, such as MNP5, which your modem may support, actually tend to decrease throughput for an Internet Protocol (IP) link, and should ideally be disabled before logging in.

The `\13`s are in fact ASCII codes that are sent to the modem. The number 13 is the ASCII code for the carriage return key, and is thus responsible for sending the command to the modem.

The second line (`input 10 OK\13`) waits 10 seconds for the word OK from the modem. Nearly all modern modems answer a valid command with the word OK. It is important to quote the `\13` code again, since the OK command actually outputs OK and a blank line, i.e. a carriage return (so `input 10 OK` by itself would not work correctly and the command would abort after 10 seconds, thus halting the entire script). Once the modem has accepted the initial (and optional) configuration command you can dial into your provider's machine. This is done by the command `output atdt14101715379757\13` which uses the command ATDT (*Attention, Dial Tone this number*) to dial the number of the provider's gateway machine. This telephone number will have been supplied to you when you joined your provider. Remember to quote the final `\13` code to send the command to the modem. The modem will then dial the number and will answer with a connection code that contains the word CONNECT (this is normally shown along with a connection speed, although just the word CONNECT is enough for the script to match the response – note the case of all matched responses also) and the script waits 60 seconds (`input 60 CONNECT`) for this response to arrive – a bit of overkill perhaps, since most modems connect within three to five seconds. From this stage onwards you will be communicating with the provider's machine (no further OK responses will be given once you dial a number, note). All responses from the provider's machine are now prompts that authenticate you in order to gain access to their service.

The next sequence of `input`/`output` commands is self-explanatory:

```
input 30 login:
output myname\13
```

will make your script wait 30 seconds for the prompt `login:` and then send the word *myname* as a username (this will be your own pre-allocated username). Notice how the `input` command does not include a `\13` code – it must therefore output the prompt `login:` on a single line.

```
input 30 password:
output mypass\13
```

This does the same again, except that a password is now sent after the provider's machine requests it with the `password:` prompt. The fictitious password *mypass* is then sent.

```
input 30 protocol:
output SLIP\13
```

Next, the provider's machine wants to know which protocol to use. This provider supports the SLIP protocol, therefore the word `SLIP` is sent at the `protocol:` prompt.

```
input 30 address:
address 30
```

Finally, the provider needs to know my IP (Internet Protocol) address. This particular service provides a dynamic IP number which changes each time I use their service. So, rather than outputting a literal IP number I use the special command `address`, which makes Trumpet WinSock simply output the address allocated on this occasion. If you have a dedicated IP number, place it after the `output` command; for example, use `output 158.152.8.68\13` (the `\13` is not required when outputting an internally allocated address) instead of the `address` command.

A key tip to remember is to dial your service provider's machine using the WinSock package in *manual* mode. This way you can see the prompts from the system, and then jot these down, remembering to note whether they require a carriage-return etc. You can then, by trial-and-error, try to establish a connection.

Remember to configure the `bye.cmd` script file as well. This file may already be configured satisfactorily, in fact, since it is a very simple script file. It can consist of just three lines, as shown below:

```
output +++
sleep 3
output atz\13
```

All Hayes-compatible modems understand the command +++ which returns the modem to command mode during a communications session. Once these three plus signs have been typed the modem will accept any standard AT command once again. It is also worth using the `sleep` command, which makes the modem wait a pre-specified number of seconds before issuing the next command – this is required for many modems, since they can take a second to respond to the +++ command. The final command shown (`ATZ`) resets the modem and ends the connection, thus terminating your Internet connection on this occasion. The `\13` code is the carriage return keystroke code, as mentioned earlier, that commits the command to the modem. `ATZ` is sometimes replaced by `ATH0`, which *hangs up* the modem, rather than re-setting it (`ATZ` resets can sometimes erase any new settings that are in the modem's memory, but have not yet been saved). Thus `ATH0`, if supported on your modem, is a safer choice, and one that I would recommend.

The information in this section should enable you to get connected into your service provider's machine, although there are no concrete rules that determine the logging in procedure for every machine. The key facts to ascertain concern the exact prompts from the gateway machine. Once you know the order of these, and the information required, you can construct a log-in script quite easily. Luckily, configuration files do not change that often, although a good tip to employ is to get into the habit of constructing multiple `.CMD` (script) files to allow access to a variety of Point-of-Presence (POP) gateways. Many service providers have such POP machines scattered about in order to allow their customers to dial into their service without engaging in a long-distance telephone call. Bear in mind that server machines do become congested, do break down and do disappear for maintenance. Prepare for such eventualities by having multiple script files for different machines, i.e. by dialling into a different POP machine. You can invoke an alternative script file by using the Other option in the Dialler menu.

A few other tips: if you cannot seem to resolve any addresses and see messages such as *Cannot Resolve* or *DNS Failure*, the DNS server on your provider's machine is probably down (i.e. not functioning). You can resolve this (no pun intended) yourself by entering the numeric address of an alternative DNS server (rare to come by, although many Internet magazines let a few slip by in various screen-dumps!). Alternatively you can enter just numeric IP addresses, rather than textual addresses e.g. `193.145.43.3` instead of `myhost.somewhere.com`. This is a horrible solution to say the least, although one that will work, since you do not need a DNS server to resolve the hostname (i.e. turn the textual address into a numeric IP address). Finally, if your service provider's machine seems to die and nothing happens, use the Info menu in WinSock to get some protocol details – if you see *Orphan socket* and not much other activity, the provider's machine is having problems communicating with the outside world. Try a different POP after confirming that this is indeed the case in order to save further time.

1.5 **The Netscape interface**

The remainder of this chapter discusses the Netscape interface, its menu structures and features. A selection of screenshots from Netscape help illustrate the various interface features. As can be seen from Figure 1.7, the main Netscape screen consists of two toolbars, a text area in which all hypertext documents are loaded, and a status bar. The only input

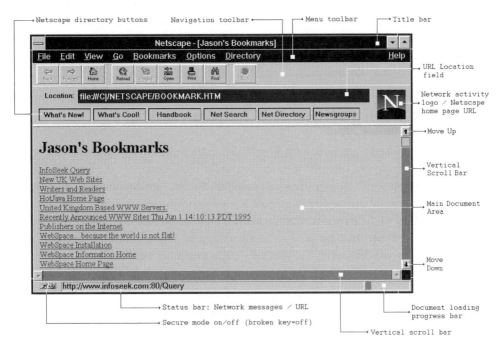

Figure 1.7 The main Netscape screen seen on startup (version 1.1b1).

field on the screen is the URL (uniform resource locator) input field. This field allows the location of a Web resource to be entered, upon which Netscape will attempt to connect to that host and read in the contents of the file specified.

Hypertext pages are the most common documents that you will load with Netscape, although it is possible to connect to other Internet resources. Upon starting, Netscape (by default) will attempt to load a *home page*. If your configuration has enabled Netscape to automatically load such a home page you will see that document loaded accordingly. Netscape versions 1.0N and 1.1 have eight options within the *File* menu, shown horizontally along the top of the window. Along the bottom of the window is a status line showing the progress of various Netscape actions, and a security indicator that informs you whether or not the current page has been sent across the Internet in a *secure* manner (e.g. whether or not the page has been encrypted). All of these options and menus are examined more closely below.

As mentioned, the use of encryption (encoding of data to stop *wire-tappers* viewing your data) support in Netscape has led to the introduction of a small key icon in the lower left-hand corner of the screen.

When a ▩ is shown, Netscape is viewing a hypertext document in *secure mode*, which means that the document was served to you from a secure Web Server, i.e. a server running the Netscape NetSite software. Most of the documents you will see on your travels will be unprotected, however (secure documents tend to be served from companies offering on-line transactions etc.), and thus the icon will appear as ▩ accordingly.

A progress indicator is also provided by Netscape. This consists of a red bar that increases in size as a document is fetched from the Internet (or from a local disk for that matter). Thus you can tell how much of a document has been loaded at any time, and how much there is still to fetch. The main Netscape logo animates as your network connection is active, i.e. as a file is being downloaded (alternatively, in Netscape version 1.0N, which uses the 'N' logo shown in Figure 1.7 rather than the new Netscape 1.1N *Comet Logo*, the logo will pulsate).

1.6 Web navigation: the fundamentals

On the Web, documents are linked via *hyperlinks*. Such links are contained within documents and (by default) are coloured blue and are underlined, as shown (in monochrome) in Figure 1.8. Hyperlinks allow you to move around on the Internet, loading new documents in the main, but also allowing you to contact a large variety of other different services on the Internet. Many of the hypertext documents you load via Netscape will have many such hyperlinks. Most hyperlinks are used to transport you to places with information that is relevant to the current document. These *places* are in fact other computers on the Internet,

This is an example hyperlink

Figure 1.8 A typical hyperlink as viewed through Netscape.

Figure 1.9 A typical URL on Netscape's status line.

just like your own computer in many cases. On the Web, computers that allow you to access hypertext documents are known as Web servers.

You can learn how to create hyperlinks in Chapter 3, which examines HTML (HyperText Mark-up Language). The vast majority of hyperlinks used in Web documents load other hypertext documents from Web servers located all over the world, although it also possible to interface with almost any Internet-based resource, of which there are many.

As you move the mouse pointer over a hyperlink, Netscape changes the arrow cursor into a small hand, and the bottom left-hand corner of the status bar shows the actual address that is associated with that hyperlink. This address is known as a URL, or uniform resource locator. Hyperlinks are thus ways of invoking URLs. A URL specifies the location of a resource, including the name of an Internet host, followed by the actual information resource, commonly a file. So, for example, the hyperlink shown in Figure 1.9 points to Netscape Corporation's home page at the URL `http://www.netscape.com`. Many hyperlinks may of course say where they are taking you, but frequently you will want to examine the status bar to see the exact (Internet) location of a particular resource.

▶TIP

If you ever see a URL that interests you, although it is not a *selectable* hyperlink, you can *cut* the URL out of the current hypertext document and then *paste* it into the main Netscape *Location:* (URL) field in order to invoke it. To mark some text, simply move to the start of the text you want to copy, hold down the left mouse key and highlight the area. When the area is highlighted you can invoke the Copy option in the Edit menu to save the text to the Windows clipboard. Now you should move to the main Netscape URL *Location:* field, delete any existing URL, and then invoke the Paste command from within the Netscape Edit menu.

All pages of information on the Internet resemble one another very closely, although some pages are indexes known as *home pages*. A home page is the first page that you see when contacting a particular Web server on the Internet. Typically, if it is a company, it will have a logo, or in the case of a university, or other academic site, a crest of that institution (shown as an embedded image). A home page will also have many hyperlinks that point to other services that can be called from that page. To all intents and purposes, a home page is a contents page – a main page that advertises particular resources of information. Of course, in structure it is really no different from any other hypertext page on the Internet.

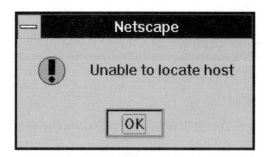

Figure 1.10 *Host not found* error message (Netscape 1.0N).

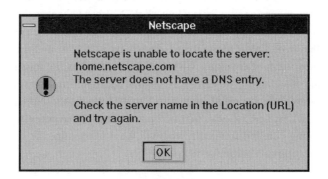

Figure 1.11 *Host not found* error message (Netscape 1.1N).

Netscape does not validate the URLs placed within hyperlinks; indeed, all URLs that specify the name of a remote Internet resource must be *resolved* first by a domain name server (DNS) after you click on a hyperlink. DNS servers are usually configured via your WinSock package (for example, the Trumpet WinSock has a file called `trumpwsk.ini` that contains the IP (Internet Protocol) address of the DNS server of your (or another) Internet service provider. In the case that a particular host on the Internet cannot be resolved (i.e. located), Netscape issues an error message (as illustrated in Figures 1.10 and 1.11). The actual error messages shown differ in Netscape versions 1.0N and 1.1N, so the two figures illustrate both messages for completeness. You will also receive this error message if you try to connect to an Internet host without a suitable modem connection.

Hyperlinks are always associated with a uniform resource locator of one kind or another, whether they link to remote sites (for resources such as FTP sites, Web servers for hypertext files, USENET news servers or Gophers) or local resources (for items such as hypertext files or images). After clicking on a hyperlink, Netscape examines the URL and then attempts to load the resource into the current window. If the hyperlink leads to another hypertext page, it is loaded while you wait. If a URL is not a hypertext page (these URLs end with the letters

.html or .htm), such as a news server, Gopher or FTP site, Netscape creates a structured hypertext document that represents the resource in question, for example the files on an FTP (File Transfer Protocol) server will be rendered as individual hyperlinks and icons (in fact, an entire file system of hyperlinks) so that you can click on a file to download it. Remember that Netscape works in a purely graphical environment, so every resource must eventually be represented in this way. It is not really true to say that some resources are not 'Web-based', since everything rendered by Netscape is made up of an underlying hypertext language (the HTML dialect – see Chapter 3).

▶ TIP

If you click the *right* mouse button on any part of the active Netscape screen you can obtain some basic navigation commands. Better still, if you click the right mouse button while over a hyperlink, Netscape allows you to save the hyperlink into a file (only hypertext files can be saved). You can also save images – a most useful feature in the case where you do not want to make Netscape load and display an image (which may be too time-consuming).

A new feature found in Netscape 1.1 is the use of the right mouse button to bring up a menu list of file saving and navigation options. Many users have expressed the need for a feature that will allow them to save images and hypertext files quickly and easily, *without* loading them. Clicking on the right mouse button when in the Netscape document window brings up the window shown in Figure 1.12. URLs are covered in greater detail in Chapter 2.

As shown in Figure 1.12, the basic *Back* and *Forward* options are provided for simple navigation through pages previously visited. The *Link* and *Image* sections refer to hyperlinks

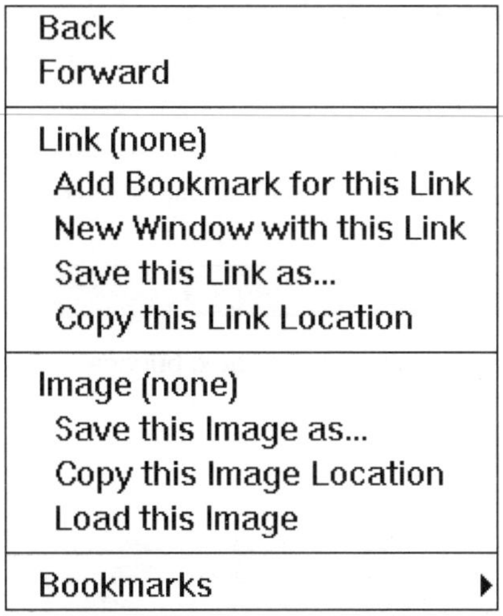

```
Back
Forward

Link (none)
  Add Bookmark for this Link
  New Window with this Link
  Save this Link as...
  Copy this Link Location

Image (none)
  Save this Image as...
  Copy this Image Location
  Load this Image

Bookmarks                    ▶
```

Figure 1.12 Extended save/navigation options (right mouse button).

and in-line images. Activating this menu when on a hyperlink or image allows that link or image to be saved to your local disk (in the case of hyperlinks to other hypertext documents you do not have to load the document first using this feature). Other options include *Add Bookmark for this Link*, which adds the URL selected to a list of URLs that you have visited using Netscape, and *New Window with this Link*, which simply makes Netscape load the current URL into a completely new window. The last option, *Bookmarks*, simply loads a list of URLs that you have created bookmark entries for in past Netscape sessions (bookmarks are examined later in this chapter).

▶TIP

There is also a technique known as *shift-clicking* in Netscape, whereby you hold down the SHIFT key and click on a hyperlink. This allows the file in the hyperlink to be downloaded immediately (Netscape will suggest a filename), i.e. without actually *activating* the hyperlink. This can be useful to capture HTML files directly to your hard disk. It is also used in many other hyperlinks, including FTP file downloads.

1.7 **The Netscape toolbars**

Netscape has two sets of *toolbars*, the first of which (as shown in Figure 1.13) controls the basic screen navigation and document loading features of the package. Depending on your personal configuration, Netscape may also show the toolbar using a series of *icons* rather than text buttons. Figure 1.14 shows the icon button version of Figure 1.13 (you can choose the type of toolbar shown via the Options menu).

The *Back* and *Forward* buttons control the movement back and forth between hypertext pages that have already been loaded into Netscape as you *surf* the Net (sorry – I just had to say this somewhere). Netscape keeps track of all the pages you visit in a buffer, or *cache*. As new pages are loaded into Netscape, the appropriate button becomes highlighted, thus allowing its selection. For example, when you first load Netscape with the URL of a particular Web site, you cannot move backwards or forwards to other pages since none have yet been loaded into

Back	Forward	Home	Reload	Images	Open	Print	Find	Stop

Figure 1.13 The document navigation toolbar (text buttons – v1.1N).

Figure 1.14 The document navigation toolbar (iconized buttons – v1.1N).

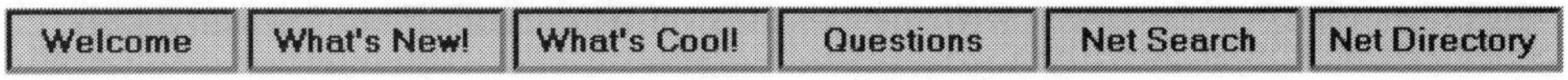

Figure 1.15 The Netscape help button toolbar (Netscape 1.0N).

Figure 1.16 The Netscape help button toolbar (Netscape 1.1N).

the buffer. Netscape will also cache pages to disk, so that pages can be retrieved from past Netscape sessions.

The *Home* button is used to load a default home page if one is defined in Netscape's Options/Preferences/Styles menu option, that is. By default, the home page specification:

```
http://home.netscape.com/home/welcome.html
```

is supplied, although this can be altered if required.

A completely new toolbar is the *Netscape help button toolbar*, as shown in Figures 1.15 and 1.16. All of these buttons link into Netscape Communications Corporation's (NCC) Web server to provide help on various topics. Each button, and the screens they eventually load, are detailed below. You can expect these pages to change over time, as new additions are made to Netscape's server.

Figure 1.17 illustrates the page returned after clicking on the Netscape *What's New* button. Netscape 1.0N used to call a URL based on Mosaic Corporation's home page at site `home.mcom.com`, although this has altered to reflect the change of name from Mosaic Corporation to Netscape Corporation, as have all the buttons in this toolbar now. As the name suggests, the *What's New* page keeps up to date with the latest developments in the Netscape world.

The next button, *What's Cool?*, loads information pertaining to new Web server sites that Netscape thinks are worth a visit. Figure 1.18 illustrates the page returned after clicking on the *What's Cool?* button, which loads in the URL `http://home.netscape.com/whats-cool.html`.

The third directory toolbar button, *Handbook* (Figure 1.19), is a new button that arrived with beta 1.3. It links into the Netscape handbook, an on-line manual that provides in-depth help with all the Netscape features. This is the only manual you will get with the freeware version of Netscape, so read it well.

The fourth button, *Net Search* (Figure 1.20), links to a page that has many links to searching tools on the Web. Many such tools now exist, a good example being *Yahoo*. New tools are being added to this page on a regular basis, so keep visiting this page frequently. Searching tools act in a variety of ways, and can use different methods to find the information you require. Some search URLs for keywords, while others index the contents

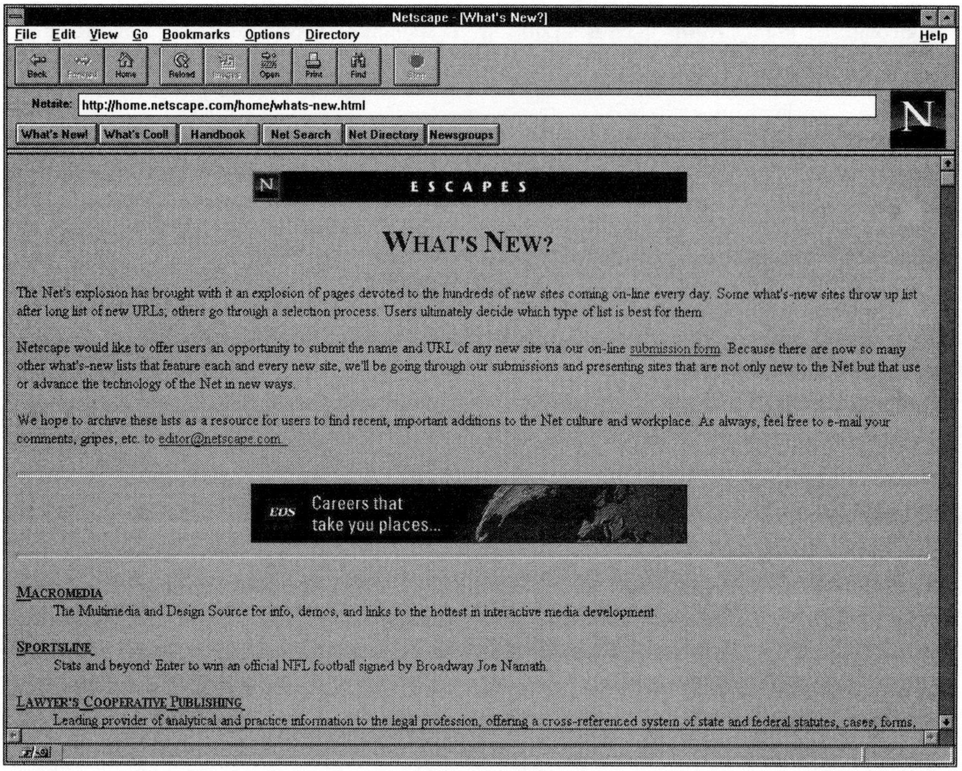

Figure 1.17 Button 1: The Netscape *What's New* page (v1.1N).

of Web page titles etc. Chapter 5 examines a number of search engines that can be found on the Web.

The next button, *Net Directory*, provides a list of directory resources, i.e. lists of resources organized in an A-Z fashion (unlike the *Net Search* option where you have to provide a topic to locate). Currently this points back to the *Yahoo* Web server, which is one of the best Web-searching tools available on the Internet. Many other entries (hyperlinks) are also included at this location that point to subject-based indexes, e.g. the *GNN Subject Index*. Figure 1.21 illustrates a screen extract from this option.

Finally, we have the *Newsgroups* button. USENET, or *NetNews*, is the Internet's messaging forum, containing over 15 000 individual forums that discuss just about every topic. Netscape can link into a news server in order to read and post articles, and this is discussed in Chapter 4. Figure 1.22 illustrates a typical newsgroups screen as seen through Netscape. In the screenshot two newsgroups have been subscribed to, namely `alt.books.technical` and `uk.jobs.offered`. When you click on one of them Netscape will load all the messages available and allow you to read and respond to them accordingly.

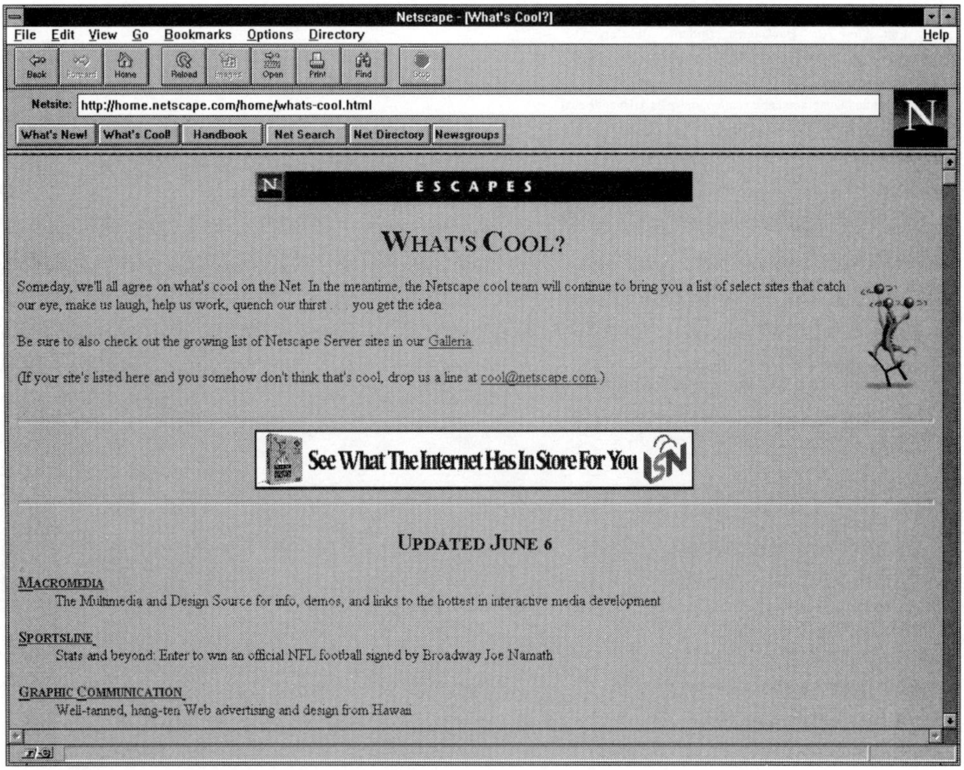

Figure 1.18 Button 2: The Netscape *What's Cool?* page (v1.1N).

1.8 **The Netscape menus**

Netscape has eight main menu options, which are organized horizontally along the top of the screen. Menus control screen navigation, file loading and Netscape's internal configuration and on-line help, among other things.

The File menu

The File menu is shown in Figure 1.23. In all it has ten options, all of which are examined below.

Opening a new window

A useful new feature that has been introduced with Netscape is the ability to have more than one active window open. Since Netscape *multi-threads* multiple Internet connections, it is

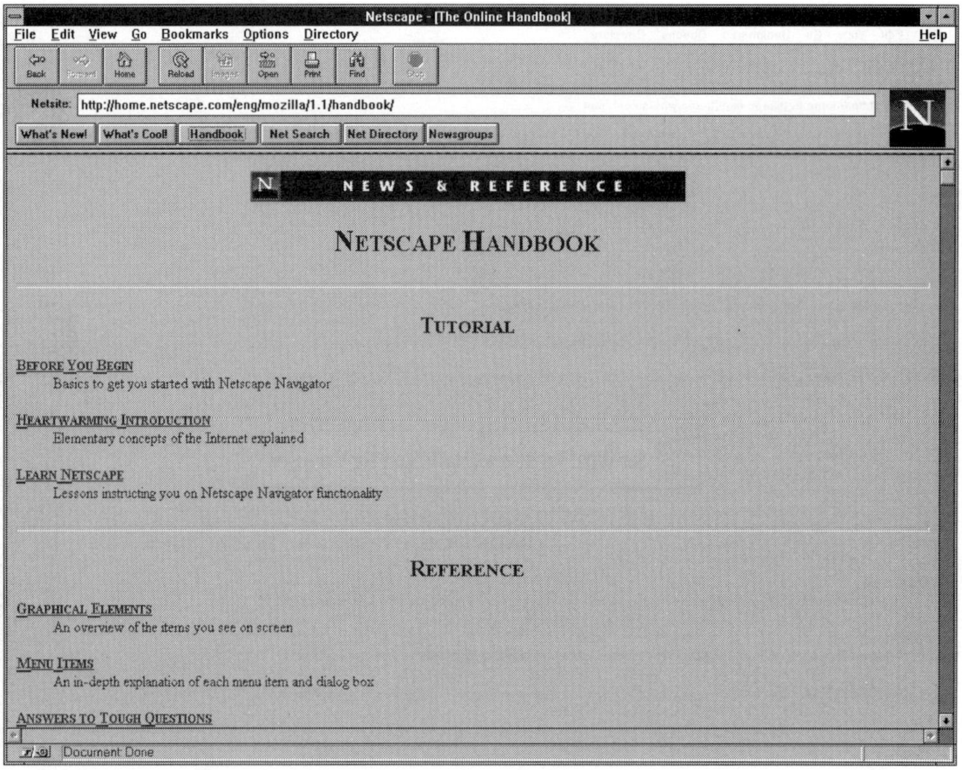

Figure 1.19 Button 1: The Netscape *Handbook* page (v1.1N).

possible to engage in more than one Web session. For example, one window could be downloading a hypertext page, while at the same time another window could be conducting an FTP (file transfer protocol) file download request. When you select the New Window option (CTRL+N), Netscape opens another window and cascades it just below the original window. You can then re-size the new window accordingly. Alternatively, you can double-click on an empty region of the screen to call up the Windows Program Manager, from which you can choose the Tile or Cascade options in the Window menu to align the windows more neatly.

When you come to shut down a window, watch out that you do not press Exit from the File menu, since this will shut down the complete Netscape application – very annoying to say the least, especially if you are in the middle of a large FTP file transfer request. Instead, use the Close option from the File menu to shut down a newly opened window (from within that window of course, and not the main Netscape window, which if closed will also close all other windows in the process). Netscape 1.1N provides the keystroke CTRL+W to shut down the current window.

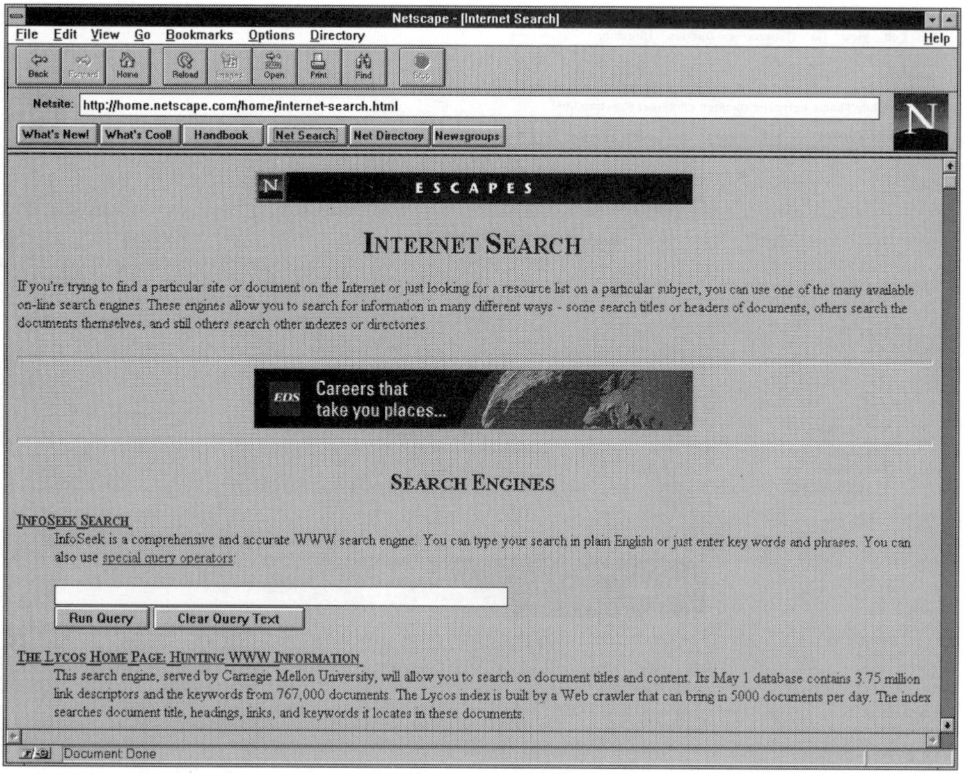

Figure 1.20 Button 4: The Netscape *Net Search* page (v1.1N).

Opening a new Web location

The next option, Open Location (CTRL+L), allows an Internet resource to be called and loaded into the current screen to browse. In order to specify the type of resource, a special prefix code must be specified when mentioning the address of the resource in question. In fact, the term *resource* is very loosely defined and need not be a hypertext page. An Internet resource could be any of the following:

- A hypertext page using the `http://` prefix, e.g. `http://www.easynet.co.uk`

- A Gopher menu using the `gopher://` prefix, e.g. `gopher://gopher.brad.ac.uk`

- A USENET news server using the `news:` prefix, e.g. `news:comp.infosystems.www.misc`

- An FTP (File Transfer Protocol) archive using the `ftp://` prefix, e.g. `ftp://ftp.netscape.com`

On the Web, Internet resources are specified using a *Uniform Resource Locator*, or URL.

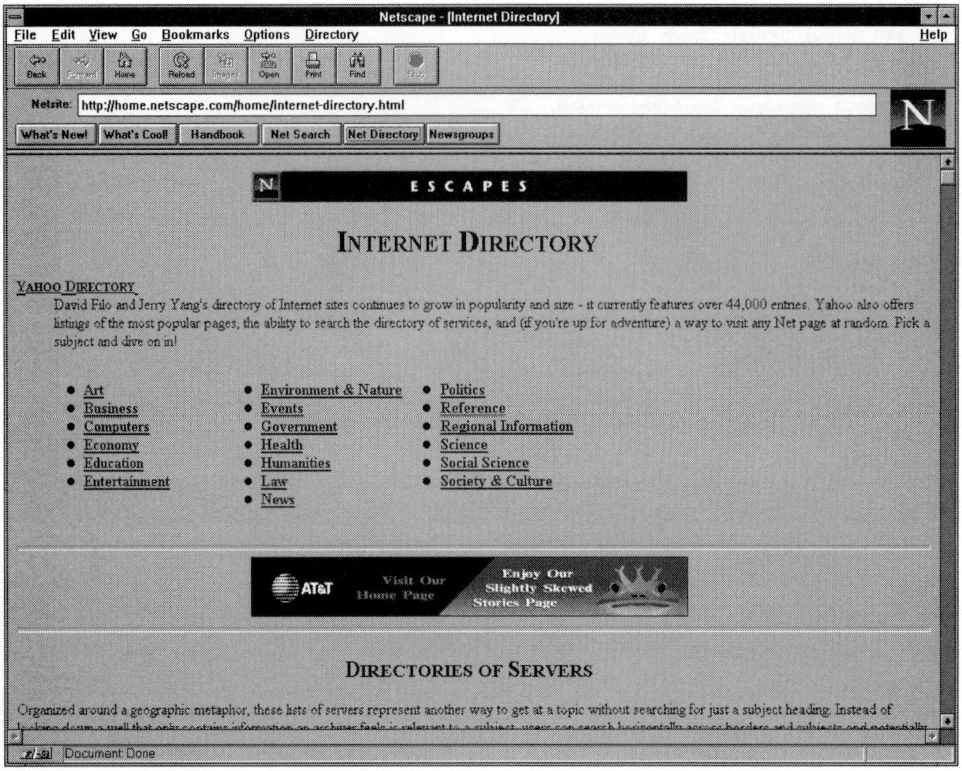

Figure 1.21 Button 5: The Netscape *Net Directory* page (v1.1N).

A URL is a way of specifying where a resource *is* on the Internet and *what* type of resource it actually is. The most common resources on the Internet are *files*. URLs are covered in detail within Chapter 2.

Everything on the Internet is a file, or at least becomes a file at one stage or another. Hypertext pages loaded using the `http://` prefix refer, by default, to HTML files. In fact, `http://` prefixed URLs can load images as well: for example, the URL format: `http://somehost.com/images/image.gif` would also work (loading the picture `image.gif`), as would the loading of a plain ASCII text file. The `ftp://` URL is the most file-intensive resource. This URL constructs a graphical representation of a remote computer's file system, allowing you to browse through its files and directories (via the appropriate hyperlinks) in order to download file(s) of information to your computer.

Once you have clicked on the Open Location option, Netscape provides the dialog box shown in Figure 1.24, into which you can type the URL of a site you want to visit.

You can now type in a URL of your choice. If you don't have any at hand, simply refer to Appendix B for an exhaustive list of the best sites on the Web. Alternatively, type in `home.netscape.com` to move to Netscape Corporation's home page, and press the Enter

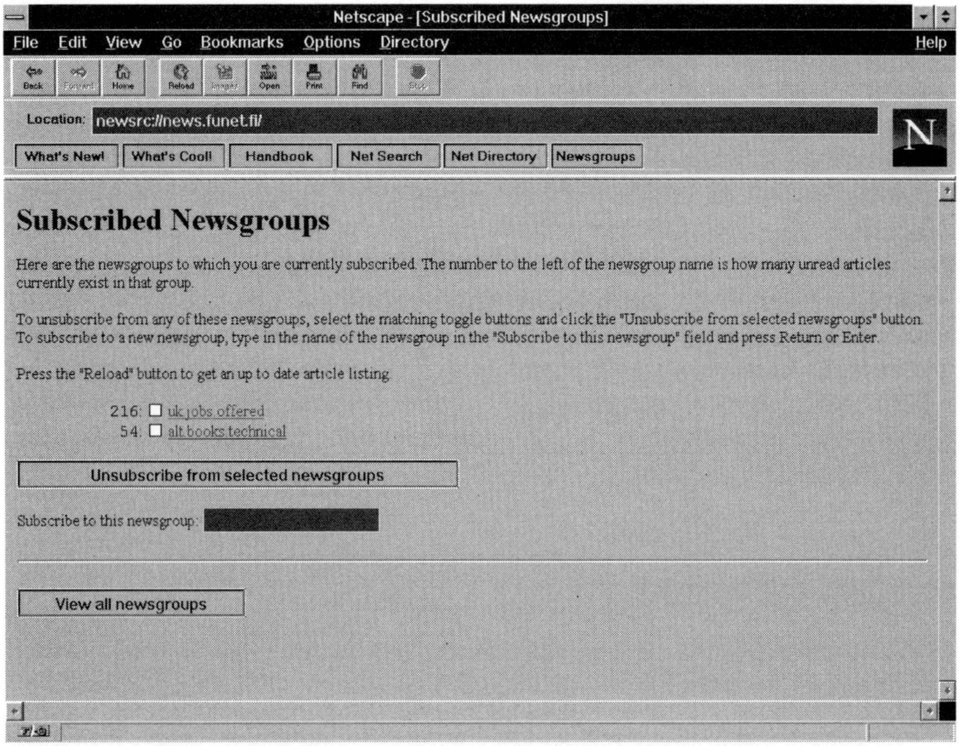

Figure 1.22 A typical Netscape *Newsgroups* page (v1.1N).

key to commit the action. Using the File menu to open a new location is not the fastest way of opening a new URL, however, since the main Netscape screen has a dedicated field for this purpose. This is entitled the *Location:* field when a URL has been entered and you have arrived at a particular site, although when this field is empty its title changes to the words *Go To:* in order to indicate that you are about to move to a new location, i.e. a new Web site on the Internet. The *Open* button works in the same way as pressing the Return key on the keyboard to commit the entry, while the *Close* button terminates this attempt and returns you to your current session.

Once you enter the name of a site you want to visit, that site is then *resolved* by a name server. A name server (or Domain Name Server to use the full name) should be up and running on your Internet provider's machine – it will also be mentioned in the software used to dial into the Internet initially (in the Trumpet WinSock software, for example). In the case that a name cannot be resolved, you will be shown the error message in Figure 1.25.

▶**TIP**

If you have installed Netscape for the first time and you receive the error shown in Figure 1.25, you are probably using Netscape locally while specifying the

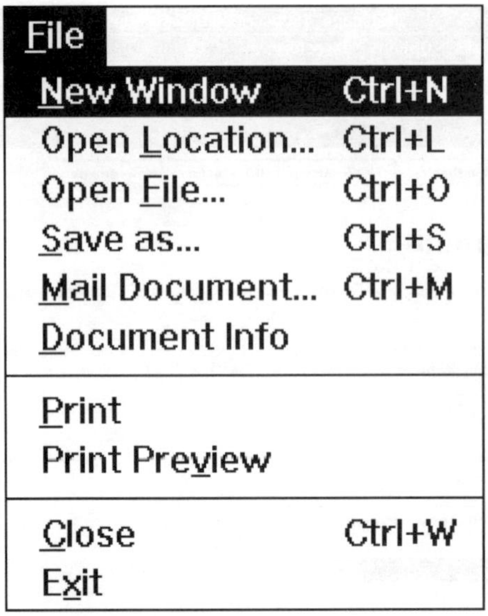

```
 ┌─────────────────────────────────┐
 │ File                            │
 ├─────────────────────────────────┤
 │ New Window           Ctrl+N     │
 │ Open Location...     Ctrl+L     │
 │ Open File...         Ctrl+O     │
 │ Save as...           Ctrl+S     │
 │ Mail Document...     Ctrl+M     │
 │ Document Info                   │
 ├─────────────────────────────────┤
 │ Print                           │
 │ Print Preview                   │
 ├─────────────────────────────────┤
 │ Close                Ctrl+W     │
 │ Exit                            │
 └─────────────────────────────────┘
```

Figure 1.23 The Netscape File menu (v1.1N).

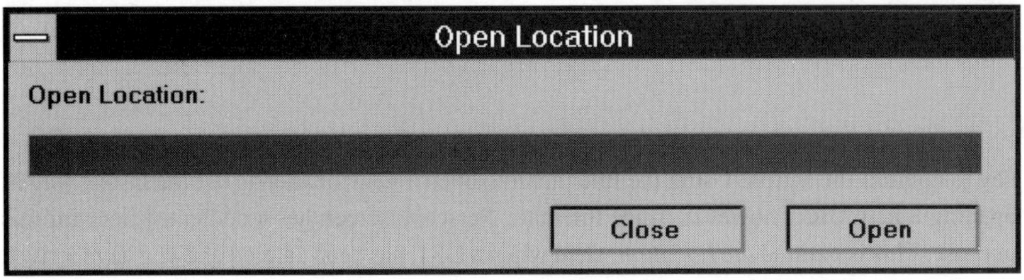

```
 ┌─────────────────────────────────────────────────────┐
 │ ─                   Open Location                    │
 ├─────────────────────────────────────────────────────┤
 │ Open Location:                                       │
 │                                                      │
 │ ████████████████████████████████████████████████████ │
 │                                                      │
 │                          ┌─────────┐   ┌─────────┐   │
 │                          │  Close  │   │  Open   │   │
 │                          └─────────┘   └─────────┘   │
 └─────────────────────────────────────────────────────┘
```

Figure 1.24 The Open Location dialog box in the Netscape File menu.

loading of a default home page from the Internet. Clearly this will not work; hence the error message. If this is not the case, you may have specified an incorrect URL in the default home page that is loaded. You can disable automatic home page loading through Netscape's Options/Preferences/Styles menu option. You can of course load *local* pages automatically – see Chapter 2 for more information on such URLs.

If the URL specified is valid, Netscape will attempt to connect to the host and load the page or service that you have specified. URLs can be tricky things to get right. Make sure

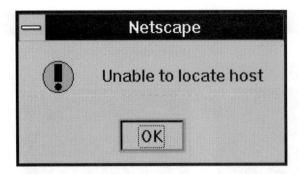

Figure 1.25 An unresolved URL warning.

404 Not Found

The requested URL /fred.html was not found on this server.

Figure 1.26 An invalid path and/or filename.

that the case of letters is adhered to and that the pathnames of all directories are correct. Most URL lookup failures happen because the file and/or directory name is incorrectly specified. In such a case, the Web server being contacted will return a warning message similar to that shown in Figure 1.26, in which the URL:

    http://www.demon.co.uk/fred.html

is in fact invalid because the file `/fred.html` did not exist in this instance, i.e. it did not exist in the root directory (/) of the host specified. You would know whether or not the hostname was valid because Netscape would show the earlier error message otherwise (Figure 1.25).

▶TIP

As a shortcut, you do not have to quote the `http://` prefix when loading a Web page from the Internet, since this is automatically implied when using Netscape. All other URL prefixes must be quoted, however. Netscape will alter the URL in the main *Location:* field by prefixing it with `http://` in the case that you omitted this (as soon as the page in question is loaded).

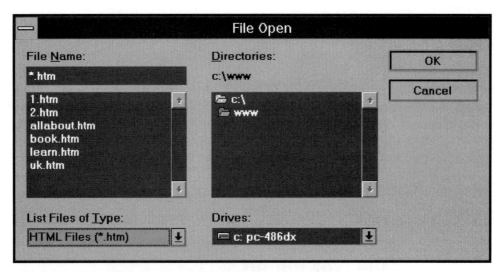

Figure 1.27 Opening a local file (HTML files in this instance).

Opening an existing file (locally)

The next option in the File menu is Open File (CTRL+O). This is a useful option that allows a local file to be opened. Hypertext documents (`.htm` and `.html`) and images (`.gif` and `.jpg`) are loaded into the current window when they are opened. All other file formats are loaded courtesy of an appropriate *helper application*. Helper applications allow Netscape to load a variety of file formats, such as proprietary text and image file formats and full-motion video clips, and are covered later in this chapter. Figure 1.27 illustrates the window displayed when clicking on the Open File option. By default, Netscape attempts to open a hypertext page – notice the `*.htm` wildcard to match such files in the *File Name* field. To change the directory location simply click on the relevant entry in the *Directories* window to find the directory and the file you require.

Netscape supplies a list of file types in the bottom left-hand corner of the window, although you can of course display any file type simply by changing the wildcard expression (e.g. to `*.gif` to show all the GIF (graphics interchange format) images in the current directory). You can also change disk drives to locate the files you require via use of the *Drives* field in the lower right-hand corner of the window.

You may often find that a particular file cannot be viewed because an appropriate helper application has not been installed. In such a case you will see the warning message shown in Figure 1.28. Netscape keeps track of all its helper applications and file types via the `netscape.ini` file. Netscape is more flexible than Mosaic in terms of viewer configuration, since all programs and filename extensions can now be configured within Netscape. Older browsers, such as some versions of Mosaic, relied on the user to hand-edit the appropriate initialization file. Manual editing of the `netscape.ini` file is still possible, and is covered in detail in Appendix E.

Returning to Figure 1.28, we can see that Netscape allows us to proceed using one of three

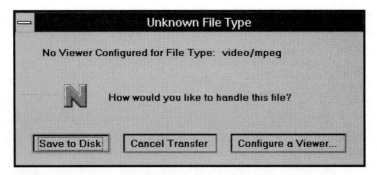

Figure 1.28 *Undefined viewer* message.

options, namely to save the file to disk, cancel the transfer, or configure a viewer for the file. Saving the file to disk allows you to keep the file without viewing it – a slightly strange option given that the file already exists on disk. The configuration option brings up Netscape's helper configuration screen, as shown in Figure 1.29. Configuring helper applications is the subject of a later section of this chapter.

Saving the current file to disk

The next option in the File menu is Save As (CTRL+S) – a most welcome addition which is new to Netscape, and which was rather clumsily implemented in earlier versions of the Mosaic browser. On your trips through the Web you will often want to save various hypertext files and images to your local hard disk in order that you can read them or use them at a later date. The Save As option will do this, and you can even make Netscape remove all of the HTML tags from a file, using the Save File As Type option. Netscape is intelligent enough to save other formats as well, so if you load a GIF or JPEG image, for example, the Save As option will also save these files to disk in their native formats. As illustrated earlier, you can also right-click on a hyperlink or image to save it to disk. Figure 1.30 illustrates the window displayed by Netscape when prompting you to save the file requested. By default, Netscape suggests that the name of the file you wish to save is the same as the file currently used within the active URL, that is to say that if you were accessing a hypertext page on the Internet identified by the URL (my own home page in this example):

`http://www.cityscape.co.uk/users/ag17/index.htm`

then Netscape would automatically provide the name `index.htm` as a suggested name under which to save the file on your local hard disk (this name is taken from the Web server currently being accessed).

▶TIP

Be aware that filenames differ between operating systems. DOS-based Web servers are still quite rare on the Internet – most are UNIX-based servers. UNIX

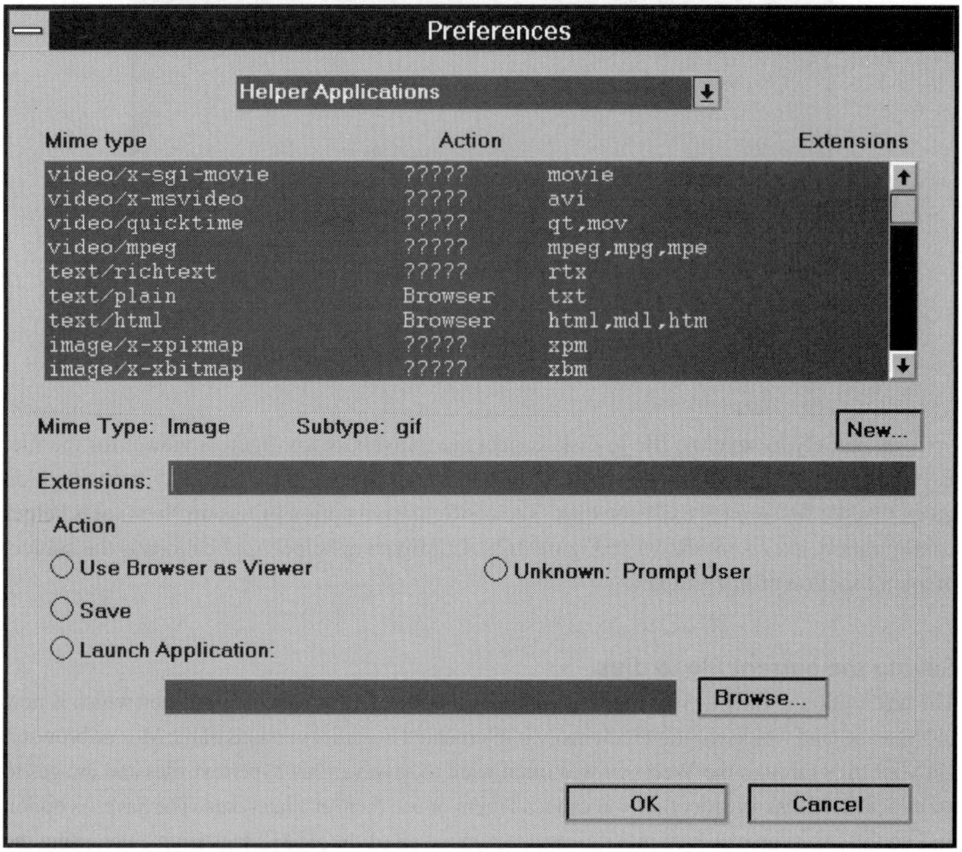

Figure 1.29 Configuring a helper application (*viewer*) for use with Netscape.

will allow more than 12 characters in a filename, so Netscape may truncate (i.e. shorten) filenames that exceed this (DOS-imposed) limit when you use the Save As option. You may therefore want to change the name that Netscape suggests to something more suitable.

Mailing a document to a user

Once Netscape has been configured for use with a mail server you can mail the contents of a file to any user on the Internet, or bordering network, as long as you know their email address, by using the Mail Document option (CTRL+M). Email addresses take the form *user@domain* where *user* is the person's name or alias (nickname), and *domain* is a standard Internet hostname and top-level domain e.g. netscape.com – the commercial company Netscape Communications Corporation. So we could construct an email name such as

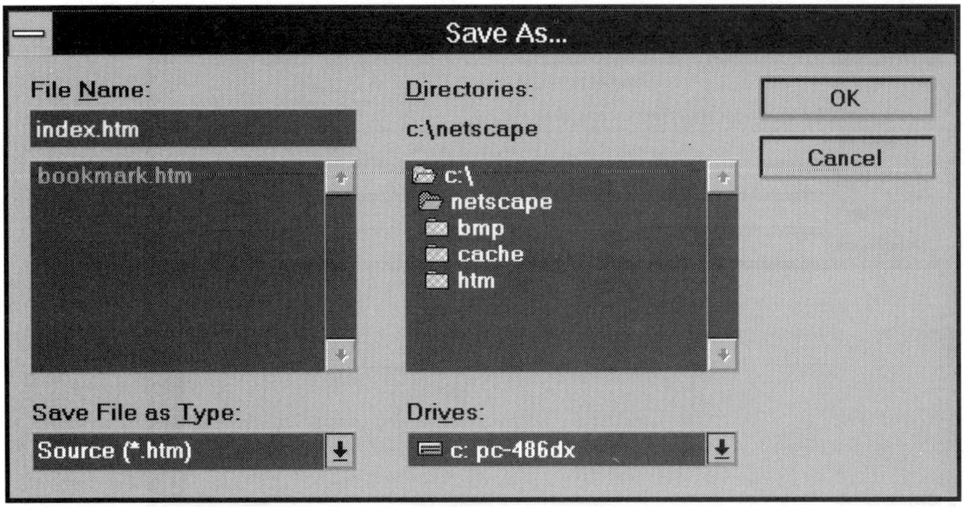

Figure 1.30 The Save As... window when saving a file to disk.

`postmaster@netscape.com`, for example (*postmaster* is in fact a nickname for the person in charge of electronic mail at that Internet site, e.g. an email administrator). Many sites also have a *Webmaster* – a person in charge of Web-related activities at a particular site, e.g. `webmaster@netscape.com`.

When you initially select the Mail Document option, Netscape presents a blank window (Figure 1.31) into which you either type some new text or include the text of the current file loaded into Netscape. Hypertext pages that contain images and hyperlinks will be converted when a file is imported. For a start, any image references (i.e. HTML `<img src>` tags) are replaced with the string `[image]`, and all hyperlinks (i.e. HTML `<a href>` tags are removed completely). In addition, all horizontal rules (HTML `<hr>`) are converted to a line of plain hyphens. Only plain ASCII text can be stored in a mail document.

File attachments

Netscape 1.1 (beta 1) introduced file *attachments* that comply with the MIME standard, which allows binary files to be included in ASCII documents, such as email messages. The *Attach* button allows you to specify a file to include, and this will be encoded into a suitable ASCII code (similar to *UU-encoding* which converts binary files to an ASCII equivalent). When a file is attached in this way, the recipient should ideally have access to a MIME-compliant email program, so that all of the file(s), or *attachments*, can be properly extracted when received.

Including the text from the current hypertext document

In order to pull in the text from the hypertext file that is currently loaded into Netscape, simply click on the *Quote Document* button, as shown in Figure 1.32. (Earlier versions of Netscape had a similar button called *Include Document Text*.)

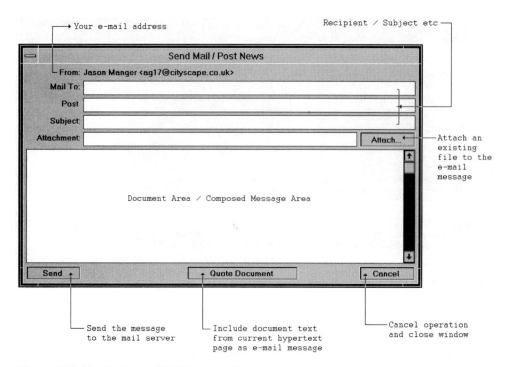

Figure 1.31 The Netscape Mail/News posting screen.

Netscape will then read the current hypertext file into the mail window. Netscape places a series of left-facing chevrons (>) into the resulting message. These are used extensively within Internet email to indicate that a document is being forwarded. The recipient's name (*To:* field) and mail subject field (*Subject:*) are also standard fields in the headers of all Internet email messages. The *Subject:* field is simply changed to the name of the current file that is loaded into Netscape i.e. the URL of the current file in this case, although the *To:* field is left empty and must be filled in with the email address of the recipient of this message. The *From:* line is automatically filled in by Netscape, as set in the Options/Preferences menu.

A valid email name is not actually required, and you could quite easily send outgoing mail anonymously, or of course quote a valid (perhaps anonymous) email address (you may want to email the Internet address `help@anon.penet.fi` to be allocated one of these). Make sure that you include something for an email name, otherwise the email feature will be disabled. Use the Options/Preferences/Mail menu to supply these details.

Quote Document

Figure 1.32 The *Quote Document* button.

When you click on the *Send* option a channel is opened to your Internet provider's mail server (although any valid mail server can be used in theory, just as long as you have permission to access it). Mail servers are configured in Netscape's Options/Preferences menu. The content of your message is then uploaded to the server and distributed across the Internet to the target host. If you enter an invalid email name your mail server will notify you as soon as possible by sending back an email to the person named as the sender. This notification (known as a *bounced* message) will arrive back as an email message itself, although Netscape cannot (yet) be used as a fully-fledged email program. Other programs, such as *Mail-it* and *Eudora*, and many others besides, can be used for receiving email. Netscape currently supports one-way email, for outgoing messages. To abort a message while you are composing (i.e. writing) it click on *Cancel*. Mail that has been sent cannot be stopped, so always check your outgoing email before committing it.

▶TIP

If you want to include part of the text from an existing screen within a mail message, simply highlight the area of text in the current Netscape window by holding down the left mouse button while marking the area on screen, and then click on the Edit menu and select Copy (or press CTRL+C). You can then invoke the Mail Document option, and when in the main text window press SHIFT and INSERT together to insert the text. This is a good technique to use when mailing yourself some text snippets while you are using another machine.

When Netscape starts to send your email message you will see a *Contacting Host* message (followed by the name of your mail server) shown at the bottom of the screen in the Netscape status bar. When the email has been successfully sent the message composing window will simply disappear. No other indication is given. You can use Netscape in the foreground when email is being sent, since both services will be allocated their own separate channel.

Obtaining document information

The Document Info option in the File menu does just what is says: it tells you the current document's title (as defined internally within the document's HTML <title> tag), its location (i.e. the URL of the document), and when the document was last modified. In addition, Netscape will also tell you whether or not the current document is *secure*, that is to say whether or not the Web server that you are currently accessing has the necessary encryption mechanism enabled (you can tell this simply by looking at the Netscape *Location:* field on the screen, which will start https://, indicating a secure hypertext page (the little key on the status line will also be coloured blue and will not be broken in half)). Figure 1.33 illustrates a typical screen displayed when using the Document Information feature.

The Document Information window has changed slightly with the new 1.1 release of Netscape. In the older version of Netscape (1.0N) the details of a document's security were shown in a separate text window – now they appear outside in a more permanent fashion. Also

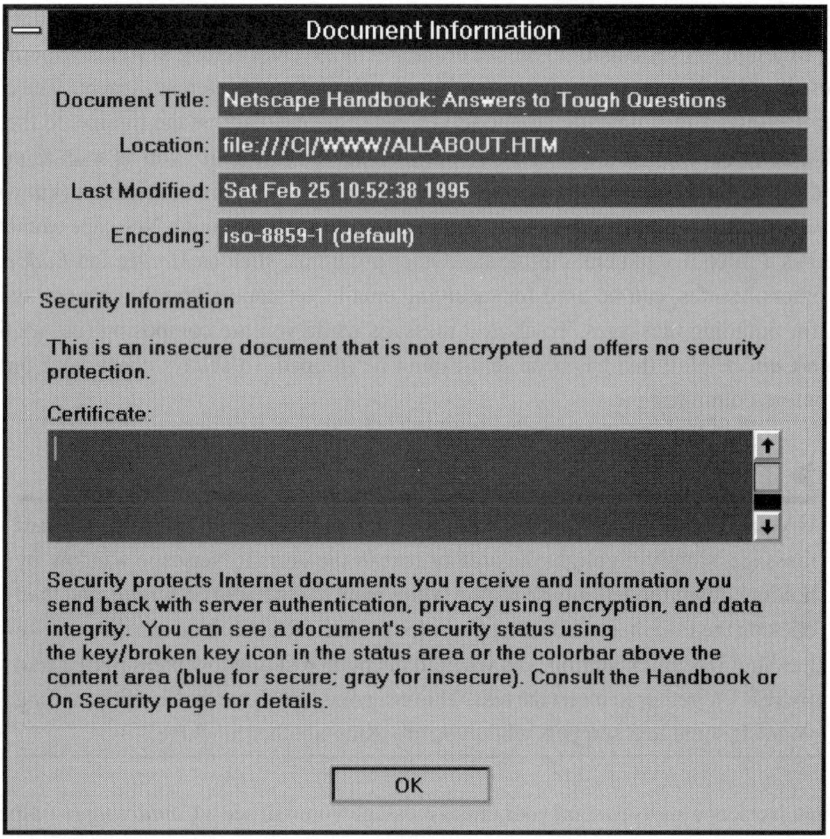

Figure 1.33 The Document Information window (v1.1N).

new is the *Encoding* field, which specifies the character set used for all text within the hypertext document. Multiple character set support is a new feature of Netscape 1.1.

Printing options

The next two options in the File menu concern the printing of the Web document that is currently loaded into Netscape. By invoking the Print option Netscape will use the printer currently installed for Windows as an output device, and will send an as-near-as-possible WYSIWYG version of the current hypertext page to the printer. The next option in the menu, Print Preview, will display a complete page on the screen as it will appear when printed – a useful feature that could allow you to alter the hypertext page before printing to ensure that the printed version of the hypertext document meets your requirements. Depending on the size of the hypertext file currently loaded (and of course its complexity in terms of image content etc.) the time Netscape actually takes to reproduce the image will vary quite dramatically. A lack of disk space can also be a problem when rendering large hypertext files. While Netscape is making the required image it displays a progress monitor. Unfortu-

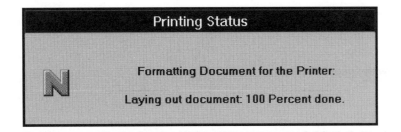

Figure 1.34 Netscape's Print Preview progress window.

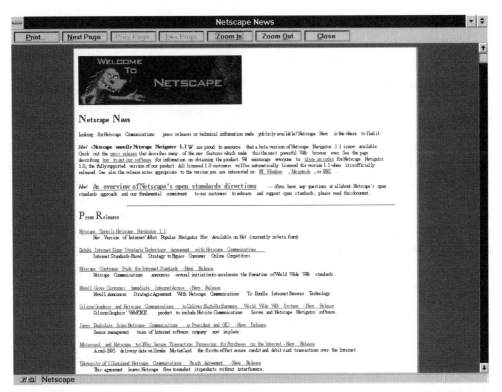

Figure 1.35 A typical screen from Netscape's Print Preview mode.

nately, this progress count cannot be interrupted and you must wait until the image has been constructed (or at least until system resources, such as memory and/or disk space have been exhausted). Figure 1.34 illustrates the progress window displayed by Netscape.

Once Netscape has completed the construction of the image the screen will change to *Print Preview* mode, as shown in Figure 1.35.

In Print Preview mode the mouse cursor also changes to a small magnifying glass, allowing you to zoom in on different portions of the page by simply pressing the left mouse key. Additional buttons are also provided to zoom out, print the image and quit preview mode, as

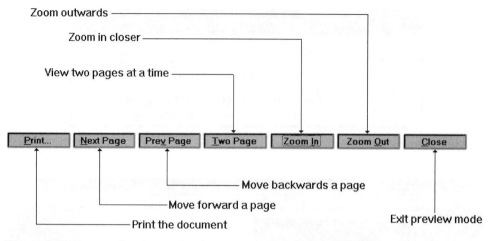

Figure 1.36 Netscape's print preview buttons.

shown in Figure 1.36. If your hypertext document extends beyond a single page (as many of course will), Netscape gives you the option of previewing two pages at once. The *Next Page* and *Prev Page* options will both be available in this case, allowing you to move back and forth between pages. Please note that in preview mode HTML items such as forms and check/radio-boxes will not appear. Hyperlinks – i.e. `<a href>` tags – appear underlined, as in normal hypertext pages. Only images and text are rendered, and only the borders of an HTML table are shown. Users with colour printers can make use of any colour used in the original hypertext page. You will also have noticed that a white background is used in when printing, instead of Netscape's default grey background.

Closing windows and exiting Netscape
The last two options in the File menu are the Close (CTRL+W) and Exit options, both of which are very similar, depending on how they are used. The Close option closes the current window. Since Netscape can handle multiple windowed sessions this option can be used to shut down such a session. Alternatively, you can double-click on the button supplied by Windows on the very top left-hand corner of the current window. The Exit option closes down Netscape, and will perform the same function as the Close option if only one window is open. Note that Netscape 1.1N will not ask you for confirmation when shutting down.

The Edit menu
The next menu in Netscape is the Edit menu. This is concerned mainly with text-editing functions, such as *cutting and pasting* text between Netscape and other applications. A feature new to Netscape is the ability to highlight portions of a hypertext page by dragging the mouse over the required area. By doing this, it is possible to copy parts of a page from

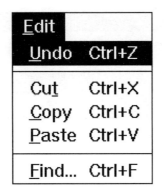

Figure 1.37 The Netscape Edit menu.

Netscape and paste them into another application, perhaps a word processing package. Netscape's URL (*Location:/Go To:* field) can also have text pasted into it, so for example you could highlight a URL in one document (e.g. Windows Notepad), or from a hypertext document loaded into Netscape, and then paste this into the *Location:* field accordingly. Figure 1.37 illustrates the Edit menu as it appears in Netscape version 1.1. Any field into which data can be entered while in Netscape can have text cut, copied or pasted into or from other sources that can save information to the Windows clipboard.

As can be seen from Figure 1.37, the Edit menu consists of five options. The Undo option simply undoes the last edit operation; for example, if you pasted some text into the *Location:* field in Netscape, clicking on Undo would reinstate the text in the field prior to the pasting operation. The Cut option simply takes some text from the *Location:* field (or for that matter from any field within Netscape, such as in an email field or within a fill-out-form which is part of an HTML document), and puts it on the Windows clipboard, while at the same time removing the original text. Text cannot be cut from an existing hypertext document, only copied. The Copy command allows highlighted text to be copied into the Windows clipboard area – which includes both text in fields and text within the current hypertext page (just as long as the areas of text are highlighted beforehand, remember). The Find command allows the user to search for a string within the current hypertext document. Note that this is not an Internet search feature. Figure 1.38 illustrates a typical window when invoking the Find option.

The Find Next command is self-explanatory; it simply makes Netscape search for the next occurrence of a string. The case of letters can be made to be sensitive also. Whenever Netscape performs a search, it is done in a substring manner. For example, entering the search string '*net*' would find words such as Inter**net** and Cyber**net**, as well as just the word **net** itself, of course. You can also change the direction of the search by clicking on the appropriate radio-button. By default, Netscape searches from top to bottom, although once the bottom of a document has been reached it is quicker to change the search direction than moving to the top of the document and then re-searching.

```
┌─────────────────────────────────────────────────────┐
│ ▢                          Find                       │
│                                                       │
│  Find What:  │internet                │  ┌──────────┐ │
│                                         │ Find Next │ │
│                                         └──────────┘ │
│                            Direction    ┌──────────┐ │
│                                         │  Cancel  │ │
│  ▢ Match Case            ○ Up  ● Down   └──────────┘ │
│                                                       │
└─────────────────────────────────────────────────────┘
```

Figure 1.38 The Find option at work.

The View menu

The View menu is the third menu in Netscape, resembling that shown in Figure 1.39. It consists of just four options. The Reload option makes Netscape reload the current hypertext page – a useful feature if you have interrupted a page while it was being downloaded, although Netscape also provides a dedicated icon for this as well in its main toolbar (also entitled Reload). The Load Images option toggles on and off image loading. A dedicated option in Netscape's toolbar is also available for this option. Unless some images actually appear in the current hypertext document Netscape will not allow you to select this option. Next we have the Refresh option, which simply refreshes the current Netscape screen – clearing any screen corruption that other applications may have caused, such as overlapping windows that do not clear properly.

The final option, Source, allows the HTML source text to be viewed. As you may know already, all hypertext pages seen in Netscape are in fact made up of a *tag language* called HTML, and this option allows you to see the actual structure of the current hypertext document. Figure 1.40 illustrates the Source option in action with a hypertext document.

The output from the View/Source option can be copied into the Windows clipboard by highlighting the appropriate area and using the Netscape Edit menu accordingly. If you look in Netscape's File menu you will also notice that you can save the current hypertext file (including HTML tags) to a local file. Read Chapter 3 for more information on using HTML to create your own Web pages.

```
┌────────────────────────────┐
│ View                       │
├────────────────────────────┤
│  Reload        Ctrl+R      │
│  Load Images   Crtl+I      │
│  Refresh                   │
│  Source...                 │
└────────────────────────────┘
```

Figure 1.39 The Netscape View menu.

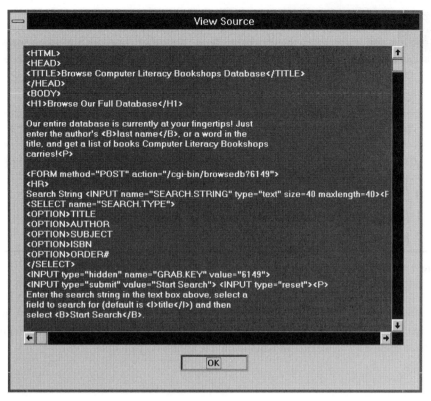

Figure 1.40 The View/Source option in Netscape.

The Go menu

The fourth Netscape menu, entitled Go, allows basic document navigation functions to be undertaken. The most fundamental navigation commands in Netscape are Back, Forward and Home, which move you back a page, forward a page and back to your home page respectively. A home page is a Web term that defines the first page that is loaded when you start Netscape (or when you contact a Web server on the Internet without specifying a particular hypertext page to load). Home pages are defined in the `netscape.ini` file, and can be configured in the Netscape Options/Preferences menu (so there is no need to manually edit `netscape.ini`). Figure 1.41 illustrates the Netscape Go menu.

The Stop Loading option, as the name suggests, interrupts the loading of the current hypertext page (either from a local disk or from the Internet), although a much easier way of doing this is simply to press the Escape key located in the top left-hand corner of most keyboards. Next we have the View History command, which simply presents a list of all the hypertext pages (and other Web services) visited during the current Netscape session. Lastly, Netscape keeps track of the most recent resources loaded – a tick marks the current resource loaded into Netscape, in this case a local file `C:\WWW\UK.HTM` (notice how Netscape formats the URL for this local file as `file:///C|/WWW/UK.HTM` – see Chapter 2 on URLs for

Go	Bookmarks	Options	Directory	
Back				Alt+<-
Forward				Alt+->
Home				
Stop Loading				<Esc>
View History...				Ctrl+H
0 Browse Computer Li...y Bookshops Database				
√ 1 file:///C|/WWW/UK.HTM				
2 Netscape Handbook:...s to Tough Questions				

Figure 1.41 The Netscape Go menu.

more information). Clicking on an alternative selection in this section of the menu makes
Netscape load that resource. Since these pages have been previously loaded, they should also
have been cached by Netscape, and thus should reappear very quickly.

The Bookmarks menu

Bookmarks are useful as an *aide-mémoire* for all the sites you visit on the World-Wide Web.
All of the coverage in this section is relevant to Netscape 1.1, which has significantly
improved this feature. As the name suggests, bookmarks are reminders of places that you
may want to return to at a later date, or perhaps that which you want to return to during your
next Netscape session. You add a new bookmark by clicking on the Add Bookmark option
(or by pressing CTRL+A). When this is done, Netscape adds the current URL and title as a
new bookmark entry. Click on the Bookmarks menu option to see (or move to) the new
entry. You can view any existing bookmarks using the View Bookmarks option. By default,
Netscape keeps all bookmark entries in a file called `bookmark.htm`, which is itself stored
as an HTML-formatted file. The file should not really be edited by hand. Figure 1.42
illustrates the Bookmarks menu in Netscape, showing a few sample sites. Netscape does not
show the URL of the place visited, rather the *title* of the page visited (as set within the page
visited using the HTML tag `<title>` – see Chapter 3 for more on the HTML language).

In order to add a bookmark a document must first be loaded. If no document is loaded,
Netscape simply issues a warning, as shown in Figure 1.43.

▶TIP

You will find that you accumulate many hundreds of URLs over time. It is

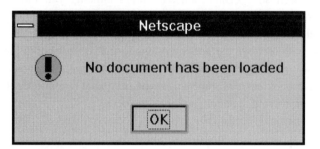

Figure 1.42 The Bookmarks menu in Netscape.

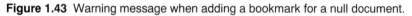

Figure 1.43 Warning message when adding a bookmark for a null document.

possible to see all of the URLs you have visited with Netscape by examining the plain text file `netscape.hst` (Netscape URL history file), which resides in the same directory as the main Netscape program.

Importing URLs from HTML files into a bookmark

Another useful feature to be found in the Bookmarks/View Bookmarks menu option (to be discussed in greater detail below) is the Import Bookmarks function. Netscape can import an HTML file containing hyperlinks and then convert these into bookmark entries. Users of NCSA Mosaic can import their hotlist entries into Netscape using the (unsupported) Mozilize utility, which is located on the Mosaic Communications FTP archive site in the directory at the URL:

```
ftp://ftp.mcom.com/unsupported/windows
```

Viewing and editing bookmarks

Netscape allows you to edit and maintain your bookmark file via the Bookmarks/View Bookmarks menu option. When initially clicking on the View Bookmarks option Netscape presents a list of bookmark entries (Figure 1.44(a)), as stored in the plain text file `bookmark.htm`. At this stage you can add a new bookmark using the Add Bookmark button – once again a document must already be loaded for this purpose. Alternatively, you can double-click on an entry to load that URL into Netscape. Another button, Go To, works in the same way, although it assumes you have selected a bookmark entry. Netscape displays both the resources title and URL in two separate windows as you move through successive items.

The `Up` and `Down` buttons are not navigation buttons, as they may seem at a first glance. In fact these buttons allow you to categorize bookmark entries. For example, you can create a category for a series of bookmark entries and then use the `Up` and `Down` buttons to relocate a particular entry under the heading you require. You can also move header categories in this way. These functions are described in more detail later on in this section. The Find option, as the name suggests, allows you to search bookmark entries for a particular entry. This search covers the URL as well, so this can be a useful option, although you may want to ensure that you are at the top of the bookmark list when searching, since the search starts from the bookmark entry currently selected. Pressing Edit expands the screen, as shown in Figure 1.44(b). Needless to say, the *Close* button closes the bookmark window. It is possible to have the bookmark window and Netscape active at the same time – a useful feature, since you may want to work exclusively on your bookmarks at some stage (you may want to minimize the main Netscape window in this case, leaving the bookmark window open).

▶ TIP

Once you accumulate around 20 bookmark entries, Netscape places an option called 'More bookmarks' at the bottom of the menu, so that you can summon any additional bookmarks that may exist. Earlier versions of Netscape would allow you to accumulate bookmarks until the list wouldn't fit on the screen. Clicking on the 'More bookmarks' option will now load Netscape's main bookmark menu. You may also consider breaking up your bookmarks into hierarchies, as described in this chapter.

Editing an existing bookmark entry

Editing an existing bookmark entry is simplicity itself. To the left of the screen are your resource titles, which identify the Internet resources you have made bookmarks for earlier. Netscape allows you to change any item within a bookmark entry, including its URL, title name, and visit-date/time details. A *description* field allows free-form text of your choice to be added to an entry so that additional details about the resource can be recorded. Useful information you may want to include in the note field provided include details such as usage

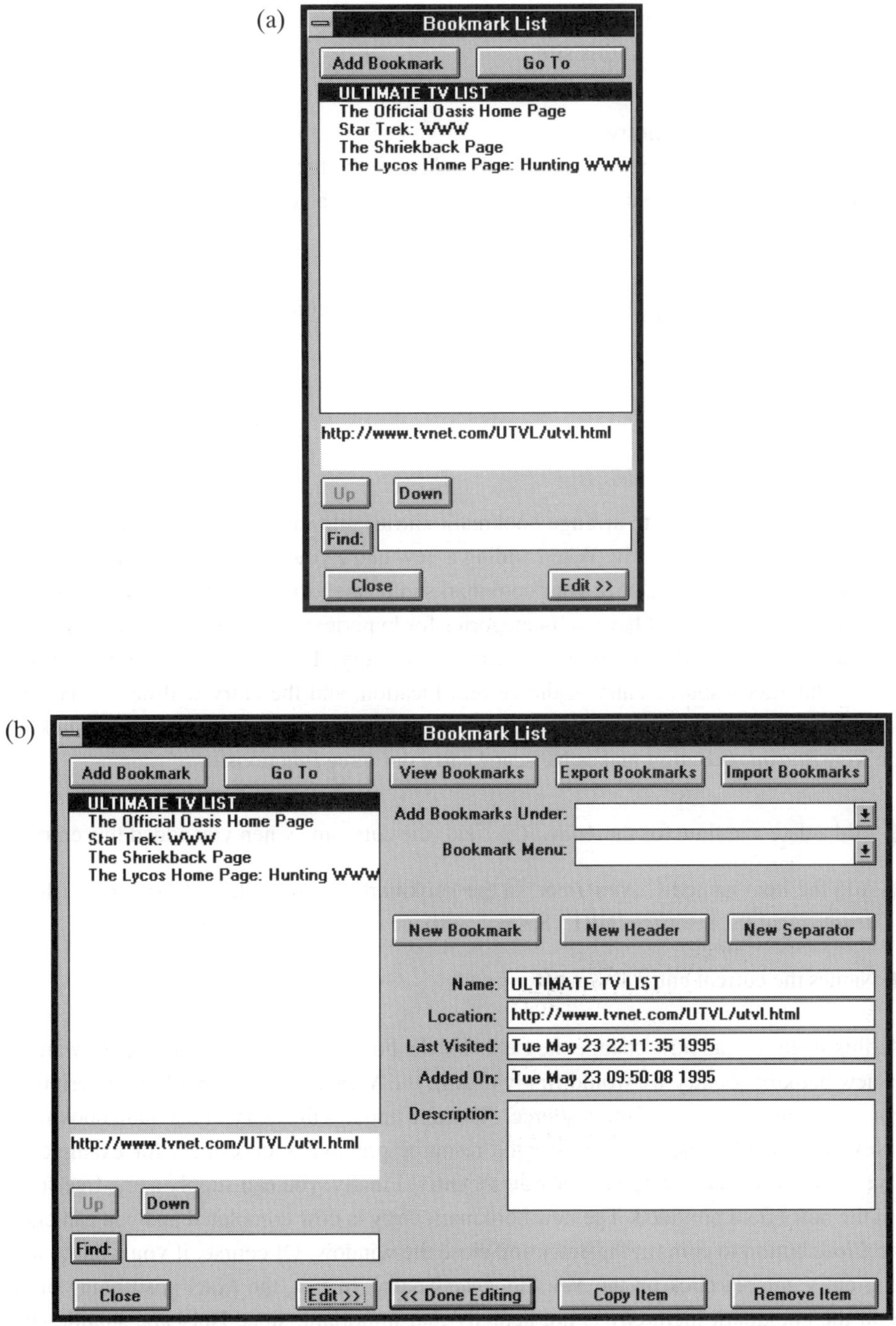

Figure 1.44 The View Bookmarks window. (a) Opening screen; (b) expanded screen.

times when you found the resource to be accessible, as well as content information that reminds you what is located at this site.

Adding a new bookmark entry

This option allows a new bookmark entry to be added to the list at the position required. You must know the URL and resource name so that the entry can be completed. Bookmark entries are categorized into three types by Netscape, namely:

■ Resources: hypertext pages or, indeed, any other Internet resource viewable through the Netscape browser

■ Headers

■ Separators

These items allow Netscape to arrange bookmark entries into different categories in order to arrange them more conveniently. When adding a new entry you should first decide where to place it. It makes sense to organize your bookmarks into categories depending on the resource type; for example, you could have sub-categories for hypertext pages and Gopher servers, or you could place bookmarks in a particular subject category. The *New Bookmark* button will add a new Internet resource entry at the current location, and the entry will be a selectable resource, so that when you click on it the URL of the resource is loaded by Netscape. Clicking on the *New Bookmark* button makes Netscape carry out three functions:

■ Add a date and time for the *Added On* field (the date/time when you added this entry)

■ Add the item named '*? New Item*' in the bookmark list to the left of the screen (the *?* denotes that the resource (URL) has not yet been *visited* via Netscape)

■ Names the current entry as *New Item*

At this stage we can now change the fields for the bookmark entry. Assuming we want to add a new bookmark entry we would firstly change the *Name:* field to something descriptive. As you are typing the name of the resource, Netscape updates the entry in the main bookmark list. Next you should enter the URL of the resource previously described, for example an `http://`, `gopher://`, `ftp://` or `news:` entry. Finally, you can supply some free-form text in the notes field provided. The new bookmark entry is now completed and you can click on the *Close* button to commit the entry and close the window. Of course, if you want to add another entry, simply click on the *New Bookmark* entry. In fact, the exact positioning of an entry in the bookmark hierarchy is not actually that important, since Netscape supplies the *Up/Down* buttons, which can move the current bookmark entry up and down within the main bookmark list at will.

New Bookmark and *Add Bookmark* differ in that the *New Bookmark* button allows you to create a bookmark entry from scratch, whereas the *Add Bookmark* button creates an entry based upon the hypertext page currently loaded into Netscape.

Categorizing and manipulating bookmark entries

As mentioned earlier, you may want to categorize your bookmark entries. This is beneficial, since continuously adding new entries just extends the current list into a rather unstructured state. Eventually the list may become difficult to search and use (even with the *Search* function, bearing in mind that bookmark files can contain many hundreds of entries). To add a new category heading, click on the *New Header* button. Netscape then inserts a new header entry into the main bookmark list – notice the hyphen (–) in the left column of the bookmark list, which means that the entry is *expanded* i.e. visible – see the section below on collapsing and expanding bookmark hierarchies. You can now proceed to change the name of the header to a more suitable description (Netscape will name the new entry 'New Header' as well). As you type a new description for the header Netscape updates the entry in the main bookmark list. Clearly, no other fields can be selected for a header item, since it is not directly selectable.

Once you have created the header item (and have thus created a new *category* for subsequent bookmark entries) you can proceed to add bookmark entries under that header using the *New Bookmark* button (you can also use the *Add Bookmark* button, which places an entry based upon the current hypertext page loaded into Netscape).

Moving entries around

You may want to make use of the *Up* and *Down* buttons as well. These buttons allow bookmark entries to be moved up and down within the current bookmark list. You can create whole hierarchies of entries using these options. A top-level category entry cannot be moved using the *Down* button, although a subordinate URL or header category entry can be moved upwards before the header in question.

Collapsing and expanding hierarchies

All of the bookmark entries that are designated as category headers using the *New Header* option can be collapsed and expanded by double-clicking on the category heading. A *collapsed* heading has a hyphen (–) in the left-hand column, whereas an *expanded* category has a plus sign (+) instead. Bookmark entries can become rather complex to view when fully expanded, so collapsing certain branches of the list reveals only those items that you are interested in.

Viewing your bookmarks as HTML

The *View Bookmarks* button makes Netscape load the current bookmark file (`book-mark.htm`), allowing you to view all of your entries as a hypertext file with all the necessary HTML hyperlinks. When categorizing information Netscape provides two further options entitled *Add Bookmarks Under* and *Bookmark Menu*. Use the former to choose a heading under which to add a new bookmark entry. The latter option is used to select a particular bookmark category to use, rather than displaying the entire list.

Removing bookmark entries

The *Remove Item* button can be used for this purpose, although beware when removing a category, since Netscape will also erase all sub-entries in the process. Netscape will ask you for confirmation in the case that more than one entry will be removed.

Copying bookmark entries

An entry can be copied using the *Copy Item* button. This function makes Netscape duplicate the current entry, be it a category header or a URL entry.

Separators

Finally, a word on separators. These are basically what they say they are – lines of hyphens that allow different bookmark items to be separated from one another.

The Options menu

The Options menu is the most extensive in the Netscape system. Netscape's complete behaviour can be changed using the options provided here, including changing fonts, colours and helper applications, to name but a few. Figure 1.45 illustrates the Options menu as seen through Netscape.

Seven options are selectable in the Options menu. The checked (ticked) options enable and disable certain system functions. Show Toolbar toggles on and off the main Netscape icon toolbar – thus making the main text area slightly larger, whereas Show Location toggles the URL, or *Location:* field from view – again this makes the text area slightly larger in the process. The Show Directory Buttons option simply enables or disables the buttons which load up parts of Netscape's home server (`netscape.com`), for example the *What's New!* and *What's Cool!*

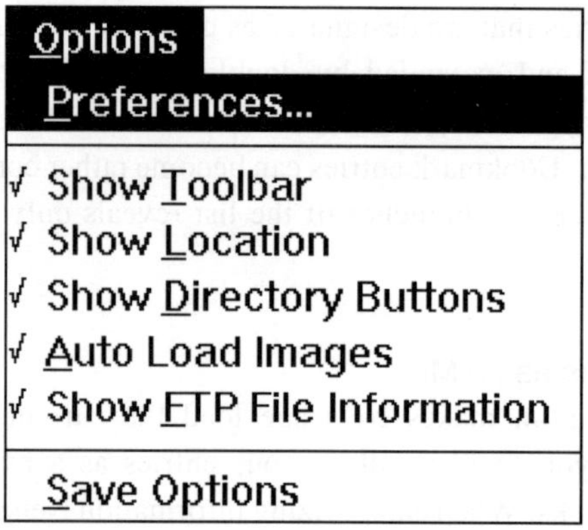

```
┌─────────────────────────────────┐
│ Options                         │
│ ▀▀▀▀▀▀▀▀▀▀▀▀▀▀▀▀▀▀▀▀▀▀▀▀▀▀▀▀▀▀▀ │
│   Preferences...                │
├─────────────────────────────────┤
│ √ Show Toolbar                  │
│ √ Show Location                 │
│ √ Show Directory Buttons        │
│ √ Auto Load Images              │
│ √ Show FTP File Information      │
├─────────────────────────────────┤
│   Save Options                  │
└─────────────────────────────────┘
```

Figure 1.45 The Netscape Options menu.

buttons. The Auto Load Images option toggles on and off the loading of in-line images within the current page. You can use Netscape's main toolbar to achieve this as well. Disabling in-line images speeds up document loading from the Internet quite considerably (a small iconized picture with a question mark is used in place of the original image). Finally, there is Show FTP File Information. When browsing an FTP server's file system (see Chapter 2), Netscape extends the description of each file by placing a small icon representing the *file type* of each file on the screen (e.g. binary file, plain text file) and also places each file's date and time of creation, along with a description of the file (e.g. *Directory, HTML File*). This option simply toggles this feature on and off. The last option, Save Options, saves all of the current settings to disk (to the `netscape.ini` file), thus enabling you to keep your personal Netscape preferences for the next time that you use the package.

The most extensive option is the first item in the Options menu. When clicking on the Preferences option you will see a window resembling that shown in Figure 1.46.

The first field at the very top of the screen controls which options are displayed in the lower portion of the window. When you initially click on the Preferences option, Netscape loads the category chosen when Netscape was last used. Figure 1.47 illustrates the other preference categories, and these are then dealt with in turn in the sections below.

Fonts and Colors

The Fonts and Colors screen, as shown in Figure 1.47, controls the presentation of text within the main hypertext screen area. Netscape 1.1 now supports additional character sets, starting with Japanese in the beta 1.1 release, allowing a wider selection of characters to be used within Netscape. The *For the Encoding* option allows for the selection of an appropriate character set. Both proportional and fixed fonts are supported in Netscape (proportional fonts use different character sizes, as opposed to fixed size, or monospaced, fonts). Monospaced fonts include **courier**, for example, and an example of a proportional font is **Times New Roman**, which is in use here. Hypertext documents make use of proportional and fixed fonts through HTML (HyperText Mark-up Language). You may find that Netscape marks up a page in a font that is not to your preference, so it is possible to make the base font smaller or larger, according to your personal requirements. Text, background and hyperlink colours can all be modified. The *Let Document Override* option informs Netscape to allow the settings in a hypertext document to take precedence over the colour settings already in place (see Chapter 3 on the HTML `<body>` tag to see how to control Netscape's colours). *Always Use Mine*, as the name suggests, informs Netscape to use the colour settings already in place, so that any colour settings implemented within another hypertext document will simply be ignored in this case.

The next three options control the colouring of hyperlinks. Netscape keeps track of all the hyperlinks, i.e. places you visit (URLs), by updating a file called `netscape.hst`. The *Links* option allows you to alter the colour of normal (*inactive*) links, while the *Followed Links* option changes the colour for all hyperlinks already visited – this is mainly used as a reminder mechanism to show you which parts of the Web you have already visited. Text colours can also be changed using the *Text* colour option. To change a particular colour, simply click on

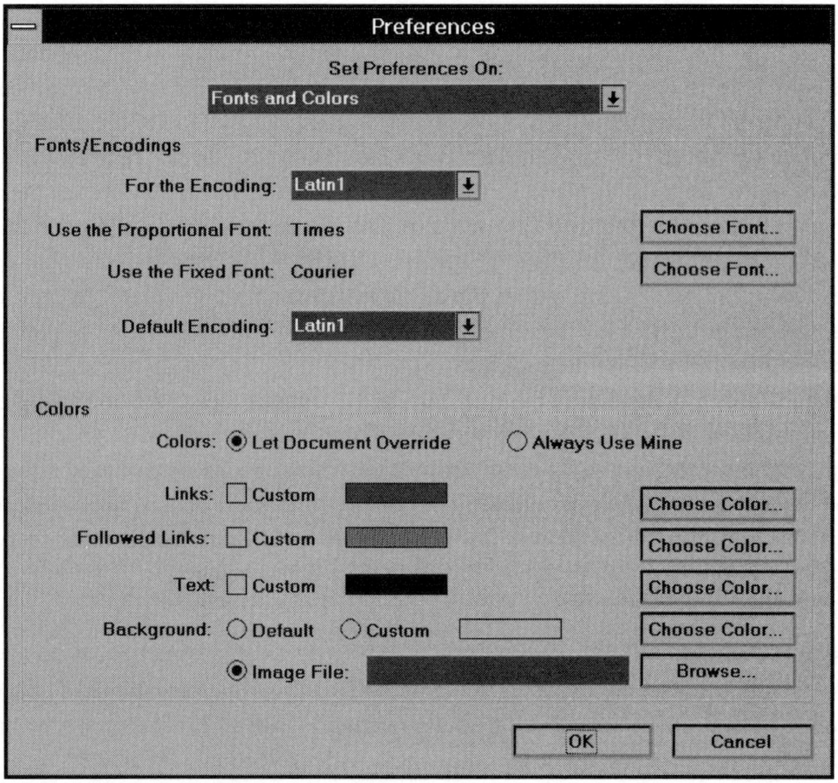

Figure 1.46 The opening Netscape Preferences window (Fonts and Colors).

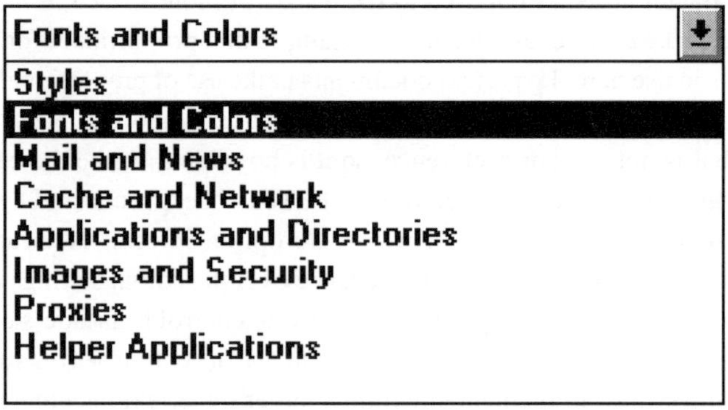

Figure 1.47 The preference categories in Netscape.

the *Choose Color* button and choose accordingly. The check-box to the left of the word *Custom* allows you to enable or disable the current colour setting quickly. You will have to check the box in order to use a new colour scheme, and enable the radio-button *Always Use Mine* to implement any new colour scheme. Solid background colours can also be chosen. By default,

Netscape uses a solid grey background colour. Click on the *Custom* radio-box and then click on the *Choose Color* button to select a colour of your choice.

An alternative to a solid background colour is a tiled bitmap. Netscape allows you to reference such a file, as long as it stored in the GIF or JPEG formats (Netscape also supports X-bitmap files, or XBM files). Any valid URL can be used, so it is possible to reference a remote image using the `http://` prefix – although this is not recommended, since the background cannot be activated when you are using Netscape off-line (Netscape will **not** give an error message if you are off-line, however). Clicking on the *Browse* button will allow you to search your hard disk for an appropriate background image. Finally, Netscape will read in the current document again to effect the new colour changes after you click on the *OK* button.

Styles

The Styles window, as shown in Figure 1.48, controls the appearance of items such as toolbars and other visual screen objects, including hyperlinks and home pages. As can be seen, the *Window Styles* area controls the toolbar style and the initial home page that is loaded by Netscape. Toolbars can be iconized, text-only or combinations of both. If you want to load a default home page (the first hypertext page to be loaded when starting Netscape) this can also be chosen with the options shown. By default, Netscape 1.1 will load the URL `http://home.netscape.com/home/welcome.html`, as shown. In the second half of the screen, Netscape allows you to enable or disable the underlining of hyperlinks within a document, and gives you some hyperlink expiry options. As mentioned earlier, Netscape keeps track of all the hyperlinks visited, and colours these differently by default. A hyperlink can be associated with an *expiry period* (specified in days) – a default of 30 days is specified by Netscape. *Expiry* in this context means that a followed hyperlink, i.e. one already visited, will change colour for the period specified, at which time it will revert to an *unvisited* hyperlink. Netscape stores the date of a hyperlink's access, so it knows when an expiry period has been exceeded. The *Expire Now* button does what it says – it expires all hyperlinks in the Netscape hyperlink history file (`netscape.hst`) so that they are all designated as being '*not yet visited*', thus changing them back to their default colour, or at least to whatever colour you have specified in Netscape's Preferences screen. Netscape will ask you to confirm that you want to do this when the option is selected.

Mail and News

Netscape has both the ability send electronic mail (email) and USENET news. The Mail and News window configures Netscape to handle these features. Without proper configuration, you will find that Netscape does not allow you to post email or news to the Internet without first configuring the appropriate options. When you sign up with an Internet service provider it will most probably be running its own news and email servers, which in turn handle the distribution of messages to and from the Internet. Netscape 1.1N can only handle one-way email, from your computer across to the Internet, although two-way access is possible when using USENET news, where you can both read and post articles (assuming you have access to the necessary servers). As such, it may be possible to use a publicly available email/news

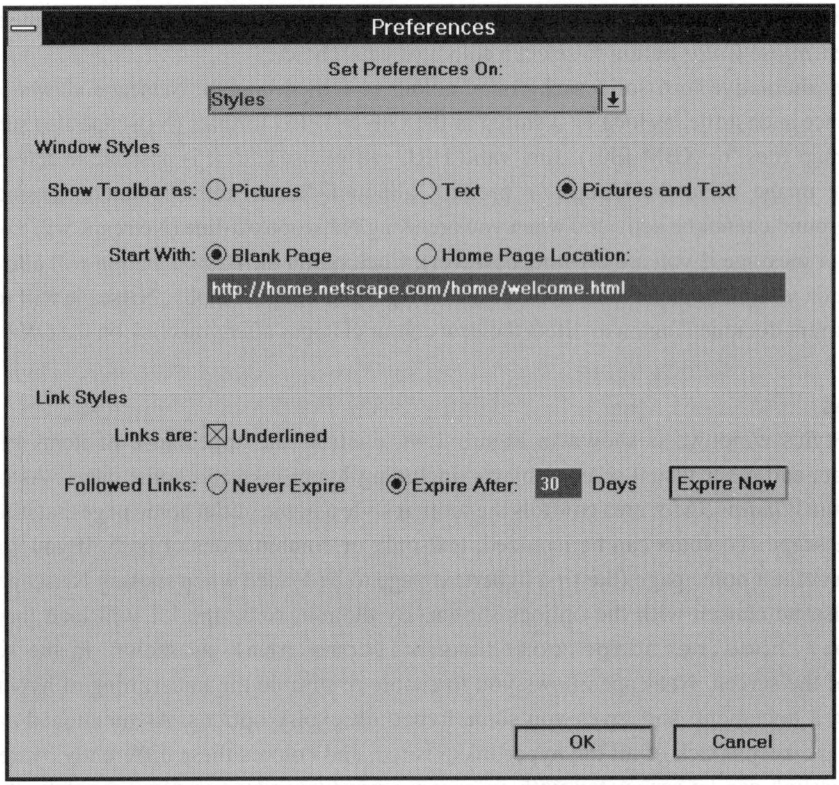

Figure 1.48 The Styles preferences window.

server for such purposes – although these are now somewhat of a rarity on the Internet due to over-use.

Figure 1.49 illustrates the Mail and News screen. In order to user electronic mail, Netscape asks you to provide the name of an *SMTP server*. SMTP (Simple Mail Transfer Protocol) is the principal email protocol used on the Internet, and your service provider will have designated a machine to deal with the processing of email messages accordingly. A typical name is `mailhost.cityscape.co.uk`, for the Internet service provider CityScape UK, although this will clearly change between different providers. If you cannot find the name of your service provider's email server, contact them directly or search your communications software's configuration files for an Internet hostname that starts with *mail* or *smtp* etc. (the exact name of this file will be system-dependent).

In order to send email, Netscape builds up a *header* which precedes the actual content of your message – all email messages have such headers, which specify details such as the sender's and recipient's names, among other things. Fundamental items of information that you should provide include your real name (compulsory), your email address (compulsory, although not

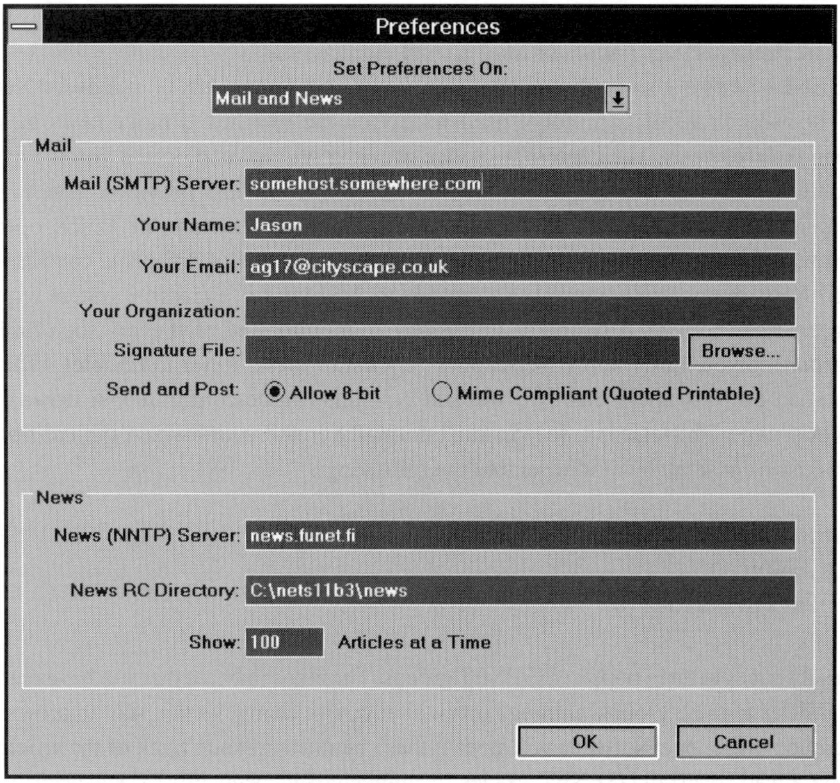

Figure 1.49 The Mail and News preferences option.

validated) in the form `user@host`, an organization name (i.e. company name – an optional value) and the location of a *signature* file. Signature files are appended to an email message. They typically contain the sender's contact details, e.g. telephone/fax/email details, although many now include jokes, sayings and all manner of ASCII art (drawings made up of letters, numbers and punctuation). A signature file must be a plain text file; use the *Browse* button to locate the file once you have created it with a suitable text editor (e.g. the DOS `EDIT` command or Windows Notepad). The *Send and Post* line is new to Netscape 1.1N. It allows you to specify the encoding scheme for binary file attachments, which can now be sent via email. Binary files are basically files that are not simple ASCII text, such as images, programs and other proprietary file formats (e.g. databases and spreadsheets). Netscape supports the *8-Bit* and *MIME compliant* formats. 8-bit files are binary files (simple text-based email is 7-bit data transfer), and if selected the attached file will be *UU-encoded* – a process whereby a binary file is converted into an ASCII representation. MIME encoding is similar, although many email packages will automatically separate and extract such attachments automatically, making it easier for the recipient to deal with any file(s) that you send. The recipient must be able to deal with UU-Encoded/MIME-encoded files to handle any files that you send in these formats, and an abundance of freeware and shareware packages (e.g. Eudora or Mail-It) will facilitate this.

USENET news is also configured through the current screen. NNTP stands for Network News Transfer Protocol, a protocol used widely on the Internet to move news messages between Internet hosts. Your Internet service provider will have allocated you the name of a suitable news server, which you should then specify in the field provided. The *News RC Directory* (RC stands for *Run Command*, an aged term taken from the UNIX operating system which refers to a configuration file) specifies the name of a file that contains all of the USENET groups that you want to subscribe to. USENET is a massive system with over fifteen thousand forums. It would be impossible to monitor and read every such forum, or *newsgroup*, so you must supply Netscape with a list of these. Refer to Chapter 4 for more information on Netscape's `newsrc` file and how this can be configured. A `newsrc` file does not arrive with Netscape, so you must normally create your own. A typical `newsrc` file entered from scratch could resemble the following:

```
alt.books.technical: 0
alt.beer: 0
alt.sex.wizards: 0
```

which subscribes to three popular USENET groups. The zeros indicate that you have read none of the articles in these groups, although this will of course change as you start to browse each newsgroup, whereupon Netscape will update these numbers to keep track of the articles that you have already read (all USENET articles are numbered independently). If you need to obtain a list of newsgroups that exist, launch Netscape and enter the URL `news:news.lists`. The USENET group `news.lists` has a large listing of all the main USENET forums that exist on the Internet. Alternatively, just type the URL `news:*` and every newsgroup on the current news server will be displayed. You may find that a `newsrc`-formatted file is available on your system already with another newsreading package (e.g. WinVn or the Trumpet Newsreader).

Netscape will actually create an example `newsrc` file for you if one doesn't already exist when you select the *Newsgroups* button from the Directory toolbar, or from the Directory/Go To Newsgroups option. The file created will contain a few sample USENET groups, as follows:

■ `news.announce.newusers` (*Announcements for the new USENET user*)

■ `news.newusers.questions` (*Questions that new USENET users ask, and answers*)

■ `news.answers` (*Answers to USENET questions*)

Controlling article quantities

A new option found in Netscape 1.1 allows you to specify the number of USENET articles to download (Netscape 1.0N did not have this option). When you come to browse USENET you will see a hyperlink entitled *Earlier articles* and *Later articles*. These hyperlinks can be clicked on to load the next batch of articles (each *batch* of articles being determined from the number you specify in the field provided – see Chapter 4 for more information on using Netscape as a newsreader).

Cache and Network

As the name suggests, the Cache and Network window controls the way in which Netscape buffers the information it retrieves, as well as controlling the underlying network functionality of the overall program. Figure 1.50 illustrates the *Cache and Network* window.

Netscape uses both memory and disk-based caches (*virtual memory*) for storing hypertext pages. If the disk cache is set to an amount greater than 0, Netscape saves each page you visit to disk. If, at a later stage you call up a URL that is already in the disk cache, and (more importantly) it has not changed compared with the on-line (Internet-situated) version of the file, Netscape will load that page immediately from disk rather than fetching it from the network again. You can control how Netscape verifies such documents by clicking on the appropriate radio-button: *Once Per Session* (a URL is checked against the disk cache once only per Netscape session – the recommended setting); *Every Time* (the URL is checked against the disk cache every time that URL is loaded – thus slowing performance); and *Never* (the URL

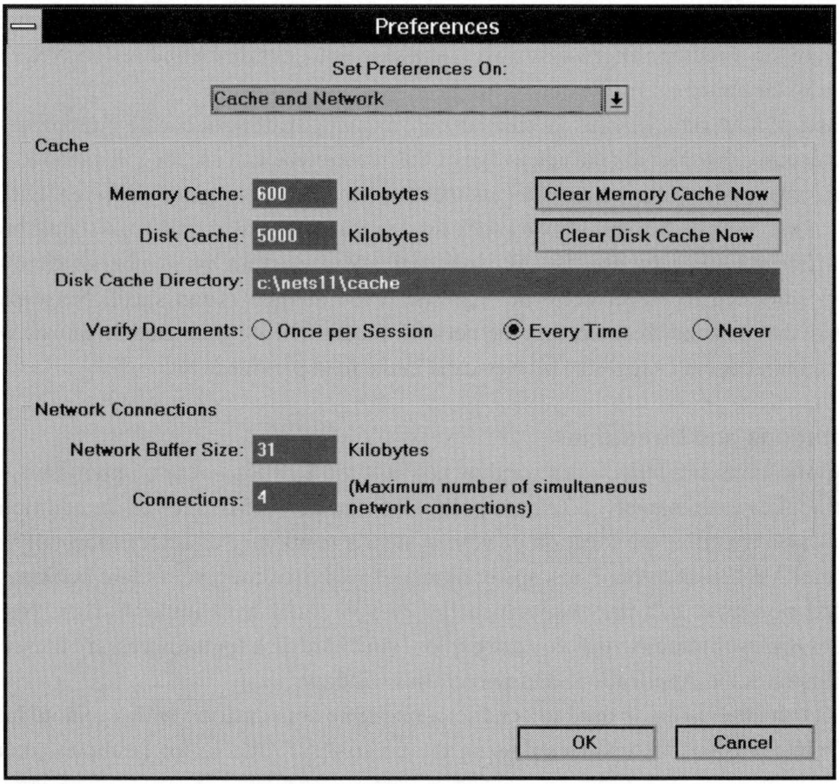

Figure 1.50 The Cache and Network preferences window.

is not checked against the disk cache – this will be quicker to execute, although the page might have been more quickly loaded if the disk cache saved it – something we will never know in this case; and of course if a page is in cache it will always be brought from the cache). The disk cache files themselves can be identified by the `.moz` extension. These files will contain data loaded in the past, perhaps from the current Netscape session (e.g. HTML and GIF files). A separate file named `fat` (the disk cache *File Allocation Table*) contains the names of all the cache files along with their last access dates etc., so that they can be checked against a request for a duplicated URL that may already be in a cache file on disk.

Two buttons, *Clear Memory Cache Now* and *Clear Disk Cache Now*, are also provided. These clear the current cache pools, deleting all the files in the disk cache directory, and clearing any pages already in memory respectively. The memory and disk cache sizes can also be specified. Defaults will be provided, although it will almost certainly be the case that you will have more disk space than physical memory, so the disk cache size will be significantly larger. Both sizes are specified as kilobytes, so the 600 kbyte figure for the memory cache is just over half a megabyte of memory. When installing Netscape, a separate disk cache directory is created – this is made a subdirectory of the directory in which you place the main Netscape program. This setting can be changed by altering the field value shown on the screen, although Netscape will not validate it here – you should ideally ensure that the directory exists by creating it before it is referenced, although you can create the directory afterwards; just make sure you shut down and restart Netscape to allow it to take account of the new settings.

Netscape now *multi-threads* its connections, meaning that it can handle multiple sessions simultaneously. In order to take advantage of this feature you can use the File menu to open a new window, whereupon you can start another session using a completely different URL. The *Connections:* field specifies how many such sessions can be handled, and 3 or 4 should be more than sufficient for general use. The *Network Buffer Size* specifies the number of kilobytes of memory allocated to buffer network requests. If the amount is too small, Netscape may complain that it cannot keep up with the network requests being generated. It may be wise to keep the initial default suggested by Netscape in the field provided.

Applications and Directories

The Applications and Directories window controls the locations of two important types of helper applications, namely a *Telnet* application and an HTML viewer. In addition, this window also specifies the location of your system's temporary directory (normally this is `\TEMP` or `\TMP`), and your Netscape bookmark file. By default, your main bookmark file is called `bookmark.htm`, although in theory you could have multiple files. Netscape provides *Browse* buttons so that you can explore your hard disk for the necessary files. Figure 1.51 illustrates the Applications and Directories window.

A Telnet application is used to conduct a real-time conversation with a remote Internet host. Telnet sessions are conducted using the `telnet://` URL; for example, you could type:

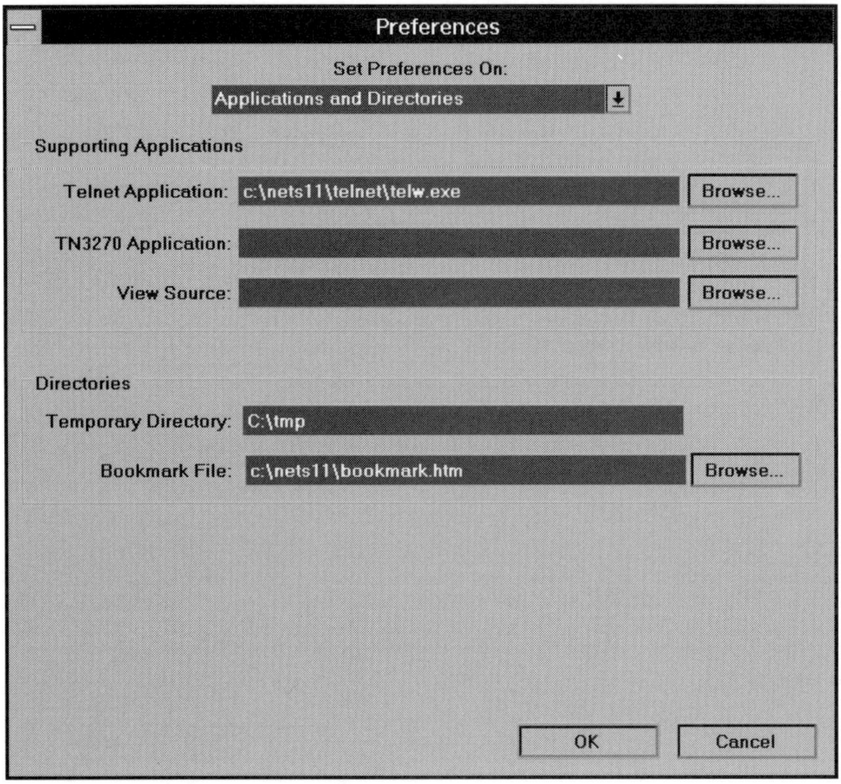

Figure 1.51 The Applications and Directories preferences window.

```
telnet://archie.doc.ic.ac.uk
```

to run the Archie (file location) service based at Imperial College London. All Telnet sessions are conducted externally to Netscape; for example you could log in to a distant UNIX machine and interact with it to check your email etc. Many hundreds of Telnet-based resources exist on the Internet, including on-line libraries, games and a myriad of other commercial and academic resources. Telnet applications themselves are not that abundant, especially for the Microsoft Windows environment – you may want to refer to the appendices for the locations of some popular Telnet applications, for example the TELW (Telnet for Windows) that arrives as part of some other WinSock tools. Netscape also provides a field for a Telnet-3270 application. This is a Telnet program that has an IBM 3270 emulation capability. A lesser known `tn3270://` URL is also available to allow access to this program instead of a standard Telnet tool. Refer to Appendix C for the WinSock tools page.

Images and Security

The Images and Security window of the Preferences option controls Netscape's image-load-

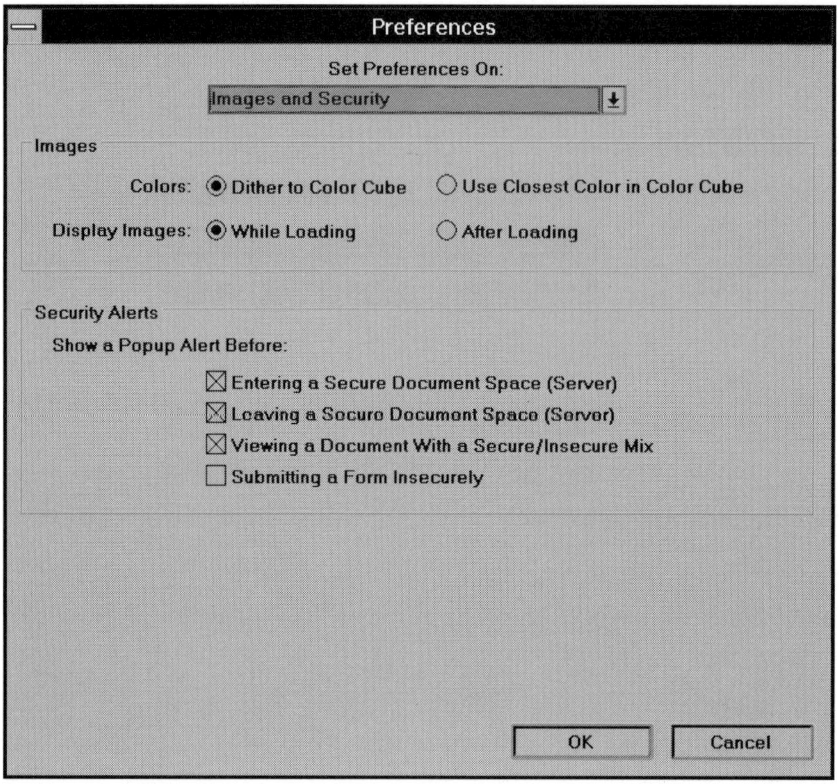

Preferences

Set Preferences On:

Images and Security

Images

Colors: ⦿ Dither to Color Cube   ◯ Use Closest Color in Color Cube

Display Images: ⦿ While Loading   ◯ After Loading

Security Alerts

Show a Popup Alert Before:

☒ Entering a Secure Document Space (Server)

☒ Leaving a Secure Document Space (Server)

☒ Viewing a Document With a Secure/Insecure Mix

☐ Submitting a Form Insecurely

OK   Cancel

Figure 1.52 The Images and Security screen.

ing and internal security facilities. Netscape has brought many new features to bear in these respective areas. As can be seen from Figure 1.52, Netscape 1.1 allows images to be rendered in one of two different ways, depending on the capabilities of your screen display. The *Dither to Color Cube* option, when enabled, specifies that Netscape dithers images (*dithering* is the process whereby the pixels in an image are manipulated so that they more closely resemble the original image). Some images may not be shown correctly within Netscape when you actually come to view them. Images captured in a higher resolution than your own screen are a prime example, and this option attempts to correct the problem by dithering the resulting picture. The *Use Closest Color in Color Cube* option uses a different technique, whereby a *closest colour* match is used. In this instance Netscape replaces the colours within the original image (i.e. the colours that it cannot reproduce because of your own screen's limited display capabilities) with a colour in the current Netscape colour palette in order to obtain as close a match to the original image as possible. As a rule of thumb, the dithering process takes longer to perform than direct colour substitution.

As for image-loading, Netscape can now download an image and a hypertext document in unison, thus making it possible to select a hyperlink before waiting for an image to be fully downloaded. Selecting the *While Loading* option makes this possible. The *After Loading* option, when selected, will make Netscape retrieve an image and render it on the screen before allowing you to continue – a slower alternative, especially if you tend to click away on hyperlinks before retrieving a complete image (you may consider disabling in-line images in this case of course).

Netscape 1.1 has four security-related options that concern the transmission of information from the current hypertext page (e.g. through a form) to a remote Web server located on the Internet. All of the options control the display of a pop-up alert box on the user's screen. Selecting the first option, *Entering a Secure Document Space*, will show a warning message when you enter a secure server environment. When entering a secure environment the `http://` prefix in the main Netscape *Location:* (URL field) changes to `https://` – the 's' standing for *secure*) and the key shown in the bottom left-hand corner of the Netscape window becomes intact, implying that encryption is being used and security is in use. A warning can also be generated when leaving a secure server using the *Leaving a Secure Document Space* option – useful to remind you that you have moved back to a non-encrypted channel, although the key icon in the status bar will also remind you. The *Viewing Document With a Secure/Insecure Mix* option allows a warning to be generated when the server being contacted uses a mixture of secure and insecure pages. Finally, the *Submitting a Form Insecurely* option allows a warning to be generated when the information you are about to send in a fill-out-form is plain text i.e. unencrypted – a useful option to have when you may be sending financial information such as credit card details and the like (at least until *DigiCash* and *CyberBucks* become widely used on the Internet). All of the options described here are check-boxes and can all be enabled, if required.

Helper Applications

Helper applications are external (third-party) programs that allow Netscape to *view* different file formats. The term 'helper application' is new to Netscape. Mosaic users may be more familiar with the terms *viewer* or *filter program*. Netscape can currently deal with the following file types *without* a helper application:

- ASCII (tagged) Hypertext pages (`.HTM`) that conform to HTML versions 1.0 to 3.0. Plain ASCII files can also be read into Netscape.

- Images that are stored in the GIF (Graphics Interchange Format: `.GIF`) and X-bitmap formats.

- Images that are stored in the JPEG (Joint Photographic Experts Group: `.JPG`) format.

- Bitmapped images included as part of the HTML `<embed>` tag (Netscape for Microsoft Windows 1.1b1 onwards only), e.g. Windows `.BMP` bitmaps (a suitable helper application must be available, however).

- Audio files in the `.AU` and `.AIF` formats using the pre-supplied `naplayer.exe` utility.

All of the file formats detailed above can be handled from within the Netscape application, i.e. within its document-viewing area. In order to view files outside of this environment Netscape must be configured to use an appropriate helper application. But why would one want to view images and files externally from Netscape in the first place? Well, in the case of images, the user may wish to load an image into a separate window via an appropriate application, and then continue to use Netscape to browse some text relating to that image. Audio files may of course need to be played more than once – hence the provision of a *buffer* feature in the `naplayer.exe` which allows the file to be stopped and replayed etc.

There are of course many proprietary file formats that Netscape cannot support internally which must be viewed externally using a suitable helper application. It goes without saying that the vast majority of helper applications are Windows-based programs – a fundamental requirement for any helper application is that it must stay in the Windows environment when the file you want to view is actually loaded. An abundance of Windows-based helper applications are available as shareware and freeware tools directly from the Internet (see Appendix D). These include programs to handle text formats such as ASCII, PostScript, HTML and the like, as well as still image formats including GIFs, JPEGs and BMPs (Windows bitmaps), and of course motion video formats e.g. `.AVI` (Microsoft Audio Visual Interleave files) and `.MPG` (MPEG – Motion Picture Experts Group) files. Audio files can also be played from an appropriate helper application, although you should be aware that Netscape arrives with its own such application, called NAPLAYER. You can even obtain applications to de-archive compressed archives (such as PKZIP `.ZIP` files) so that files downloaded from the Internet can be processed immediately.

Figure 1.53 illustrates the Helper Applications screen within the Netscape Options/Preferences screen.

The configuration of Netscape's helper applications is a very simple task. First, you should be aware that every image format has a *name*, *filename extension* and an associated *helper application*. For example, a Windows bitmap file has the type name `image/bmp`, a filename extension of `.BMP`, and can be viewed through the Windows 3.x program `pbrush.exe` (although better alternatives are available which allow more control over image viewing, and after all, you may not want to actually *edit* the image). In order to convey all of this information to Netscape you must enter the appropriate options in the Helper Applications screen, as shown in Figure 1.53.

If you click on the scroll-bar in the Extensions screen Netscape will show all of the current file types and their associated helper applications. You can then scroll through successive entries in this way until you find a file type for which you want to install a helper application. This does of course assume that you have installed the helper application in its own directory on your computer's hard disk. Netscape understands five different types of file, namely:

■ Video (animations, e.g. `video/avi` for a Windows Audio Visual Interleave file)

■ Text (plain text files, e.g. `text/html` for an HTML formatted file – a *tagged* ASCII file)

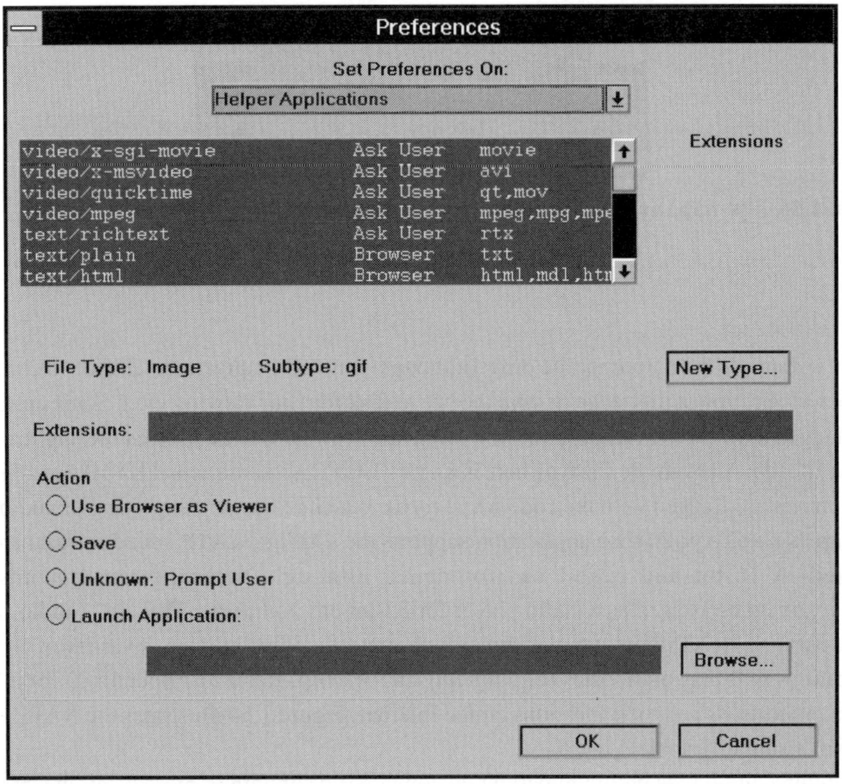

Figure 1.53 The Helper Applications screen.

■ Image (still image files, e.g. `image/gif` for a Graphics Interchange Format file)

■ Audio (sound files, e.g. `audio/au` for an audio file)

■ Application (all other formats, e.g. compressed files and other proprietary formats)

If you are using Netscape for the very first time the package will not be installed with any helper applications, apart from the `naplayer.exe` audio player. No such programs arrive with Netscape since they are separate packages affected by different licensing arrangements etc. Windows can already *associate* various file types with their default Windows applications, and Netscape can handle the most common file formats found within the Windows environment using this mechanism. For example, it will load a `.BMP` image into `pbrush.exe` and a `.wri` (Windows Write file) into `write.exe` (these settings will be overridden by any new helper applications that you install via Netscape at a later stage, of course).

By looking at the *Extensions* list at the top of the window you can see that some entries have the text *Ask User* by them. This means that an associated helper application has not been configured for this file type, and thus an attempt to view an image with the filename extension

Figure 1.54 The `naplayer.exe` program interface.

shown will result in an appropriate error (although you will be given the chance to configure a helper application at this stage or save the file to disk for later viewing etc.). Some entries are also flagged as *Browser*, meaning that the Netscape browser will be used as the application to display the file. An example file type here is `text/html`, i.e. some actual HTML text. Finally, some entries are flagged with the code `naplayer` which relates to the playing of audio files. Netscape's `naplayer.exe` application supports the `.AU` and `.AIF` sound formats and can be used in 16-bit and 32-bit environments, although Netscape recommends that `naplayer.exe` is used as a audio player for 32-bit environments. The `.AU` (**au**dio format for the Sun and NeXT computer platforms) is ubiquitous on the Internet. A variety of different applications will play audio files (e.g. *Wplany* and *Wham*). Refer to Appendix D for a list of helper applications and their locations on the Internet. Figure 1.54 illustrates the NAPLAYER program's simple graphical interface.

Handling audio files within hypertext documents is dealt with in more detail in Chapter 3, which deals with HTML and how audio files can be incorporated into hypertext documents. The `naplayer.exe` application is considered in more detail later on in this chapter.

Adding a new file type and helper application

To add a new helper application for a file type, press on the *New Type* button. Netscape responds with a small window asking you to enter a MIME type and subtype. MIME is an acronym for Multipurpose Internet Media Extensions. Figure 1.55 illustrates this window with an `image/bmp` entry. As you will have seen from the *Extensions* window, an individual entry for a particular file type is made up of two separate parts, for example `image/bmp` for a bitmapped Windows image file. The first part of the entry (in this case `image`) is referred to as a MIME type, while the second part is known as the subtype – the filename extension in this case. The MIME type therefore categorizes the entry, and the subtype identifies the file type. Subtypes are needed because many different formats exist for different media types; for example, images come as GIFs, BMPs and JPGs, among many others.

After entering a new MIME type, Netscape adds an entry for the new type in the *Extensions* screen. It also highlights the entry for you to see. You can now decide which filename extensions identify the file type. For an image type of `image/bmp`, which is a Windows bitmap image, the extension `.BMP` is used. In the case where the MIME subtype is the same

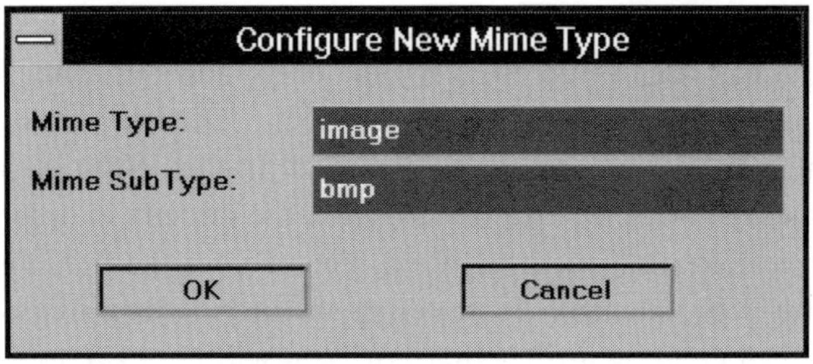

Figure 1.55 The MIME type response window with a new `image/bmp` entry.

Figure 1.56 Specifying two extensions for a JPEG image file (`jpg` and `jpe`).

as the image's filename extension, Netscape sets the extension accordingly. However, some files are named using different schemes. UNIX systems, which are predominant on the Internet, can use longer filename extensions, and of course some file types may have different extensions even though they use the same file format. An example here is `.HTM` for DOS HTML-formatted files and `.HTML` under UNIX. To overcome this problem Netscape provides a field in which you can specify the extension of a given file. When Netscape eventually handles a request to retrieve a file with that extension it can load an appropriate helper application to deal with the format (e.g. to view an image file or play an audio file).

Ensure that multiple extensions are separated by a comma (`,`) as shown in Figure 1.56, which shows some alternate extensions for a JPEG compressed image file, where the extensions `.JPG` and `.JPE` are sometimes used. The extension settings change as you move though the list of MIME types.

▶TIP

The different filename extensions used by Netscape are important, since you will access files stored on other types of computer (e.g. UNIX-based systems). Since these have different naming conventions, Netscape needs to know the filename extension for both environments (e.g. `.html` for UNIX and `.htm` for DOS). It is wise to leave the default extensions supplied by Netscape, or at least copy these when installing a new helper application.

A particularly confusing part of the Netscape helper applications screen is the fact that once an application has been installed, Netscape only shows its name in the *Extensions* screen at the very top of the window; the actual path and filename are not shown anywhere else on the screen and therefore cannot be modified. In fact, Netscape actually uses this screen to update the `netscape.ini` initialization file directly in order to place an entry for the helper application previously installed. You can use the field displayed in Figure 1.53 to update a file type extension by selecting an entry in the *Extensions* list at the top of the screen and then entering a file extension. You will not have to retype the name of the helper application, however; Netscape already has this stored away in its initialization file, as described. There is also no *Delete* button for removing existing MIME type entries, although manual editing of the `netscape.ini` will solve this problem. Expect a later release of Netscape to include such a deletion facility. In order to update an entry's helper application, simply move to the entry you want to change and then re-type the fully qualified pathname name of the file you want to use (e.g. `drive:\directory\filename.ext`).

When creating or modifying a MIME type entry Netscape allows you to control how a file matching a particular extension is actually downloaded. These options are shown as radio-buttons along the bottom of the window, namely: *Use Browser as Viewer*, which makes Netscape the viewer for the file loaded; *Save*, which prompts the user to save the file to disk, rather than viewing it immediately; *Unknown: Prompt User*, which displays a window with a series of options asking the user to either: (i) save the file to disk, (ii) configure a viewer for the file, or (iii) cancel the request; and finally *Launch Application*, which allows a specific helper application to be *launched* (i.e. run) with the file requested. Netscape provides a field to specify the fully qualified pathname to a particular helper application for the current MIME type. The selection for each radio-button changes as you move though the list of MIME types situated in the main list at the top of the window.

A *Browse* button is also supplied which allows you to search your hard disk for a suitable helper application. Figure 1.57 illustrates a series of subdirectories that have been structured

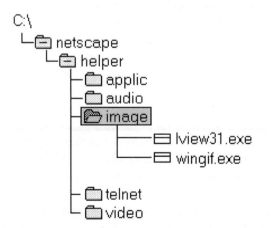

Figure 1.57 A typical helper applications directory structure (image tools shown).

according to each type of helper application – after all, you don't want to spend hours scouring your hard disk for that elusive program.

▶TIP

It makes sense to arrange your helper applications into a hierarchy, so that you can browse them more easily when configuring Netscape. For example, you could have a `\NETSCAPE\HELPER` directory, and then each type of application could have its own subdirectory, such as:

`C:\NETSCAPE\HELPER\IMAGE\`

for still image viewing tools (e.g. *Lview31*, a popular image-viewing helper application – see Appendix D). You can use the Windows File Manager or DOS, to create the directories required (Figure 1.57).

CHAPTER

2

URLs: Uniform resource locators

2.1 **Introduction**

The URL, or *uniform resource locator*, is a most fundamental concept which all Web browsers understand – a mechanism for specifying the *type* and *location* of a particular resource on the Internet. The distinction between the *Web* and the *Internet* becomes clearer through an understanding of URLs. Another term you will hear constantly throughout your travels on the Web is *hyperlink*. To all intents and purposes a hyperlink is a URL that is embedded within a hypertext document. Hyperlinks are activated by clicking on them with your mouse. You can consider URLs as *places* on the Internet (although equally, they can also point to *local* resources, such as a file on your own machine's hard disk). Netscape provides you with a field on the screen (the *Location:* field) which allows a URL to be typed in manually. In addition it also has a *Go* menu, which may contain places (URLs) already visited, and it also has bookmark and history features which allow past URLs to be invoked.

URLs are used to access many different information resources on the Internet, including:

- Local files (multiple formats)

- Web servers (which serve hypertext pages in the HTML format)

- Gopher and veronica servers (tools for indexing documents and retrieving them)

- News servers, or NNTP servers (for access to USENET articles)

- Interactive Telnet-based resources (for access to real-time services such as on-line databases)

- FTP (file transfer protocol) servers – archives of public information, e.g. software

Web servers now make up a large proportion of the Internet, and the growth in the number of Web servers in particular has been enormous over the past two years. The *Web* is a collective term for all of the Web servers that exist on the Internet (along with all the Web clients, such as Netscape). Applications such as Netscape run on *top* of the Internet, that is to say that the Internet is the communications infrastructure and software protocol that facilitates access to various Web servers located on the Internet. The four remaining categories (gophers, news servers, Telnet servers and FTP servers) are also Internet-based tools that can be *accessed* via the World-Wide Web, which is to say that a browser such as Netscape can interface with an appropriate gopher, news or Telnet-based service through use of an appropriate URL.

2.2 **Local file URLs: `file://`**

Local files can be handled easily by Netscape using the `file://` URL prefix. The file type is not implied from the URL, so the `file://` prefix can be used to load hypertext pages, images and just about any file for which an appropriate helper application exists. It is possible for Netscape to be used without an Internet connection using HTML files accessed directly from your local hard disk via the `file://` URL. If you are developing HTML pages that exist in different directories of a hard disk you will have to learn the `file://` URL and syntax. The `file://` URL takes the form:

```
file:///drive|/directory/filename
```

where `drive` is a single letter that represents the name of a DOS disk drive (commonly C for a hard disk, D for a CD-ROM and A for the first floppy disk etc.) on a personal computer. Notice that no colon (:) is used after the drive letter, as is the normal DOS convention. The `directory` and `filename` parts represent the *fully qualified* pathname of the file to be loaded. If a leading directory is not specified, Netscape assumes the file exists in the current working directory. Note that the / slashes used to the right of the | character (as directory separators) can also be changed to \ characters if required (which DOS normally uses).

`file://` examples

    file:///c|/index.htm

Loads a hypertext (HTML) file (`index.htm`) from the root directory (`C:\`) of the C drive.

    file:///c|\index.htm

Same as the above, using alternative separator character '\'.

    file:///c|/htmlfile/root.htm

Loads a hypertext (HTML) file called `root.htm` that exists in the directory `C:\HTMLFILE`.

    file:///c|/image_directory/people/man.gif

This URL seems to be UNIX-based – notice the name of the first directory, which would be invalid under DOS. The file being loaded is an image (GIF format) which Netscape will load accordingly (either via a helper application, such as *Lview*, or directly into the current Netscape window, depending on Netscape's configuration).

    file:///

Makes Netscape load a list of available disk drives on your system, including virtual drives (e.g. RAM disk software). Figure 2.1 illustrates a typical screen when typing this URL into Netscape (notice that because disk drives do not have creation/modification dates associated with them Netscape uses the standard IBM PC creation date!).

    file:///C|

Makes Netscape load a graphical hierarchy of the C: drive (*root* directory), as shown in Figure 2.2. Note that `file:///C|` and `file:///C|/` are equivalent. Netscape will also insert an

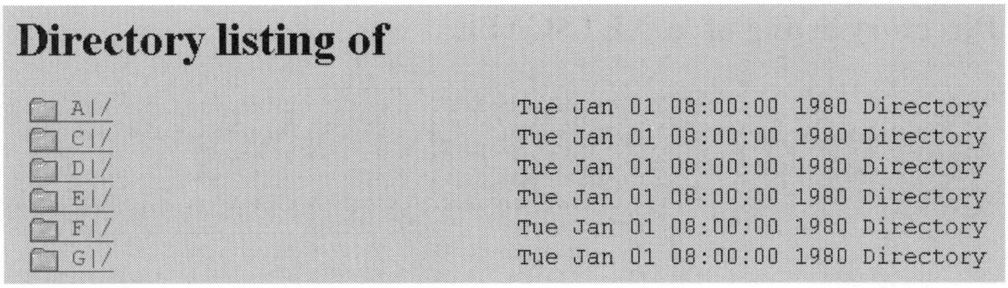

Directory listing of

📁 A|/	Tue Jan 01 08:00:00 1980 Directory
📁 C|/	Tue Jan 01 08:00:00 1980 Directory
📁 D|/	Tue Jan 01 08:00:00 1980 Directory
📁 E|/	Tue Jan 01 08:00:00 1980 Directory
📁 F|/	Tue Jan 01 08:00:00 1980 Directory
📁 G|/	Tue Jan 01 08:00:00 1980 Directory

Figure 2.1 The `file:///` URL in action.

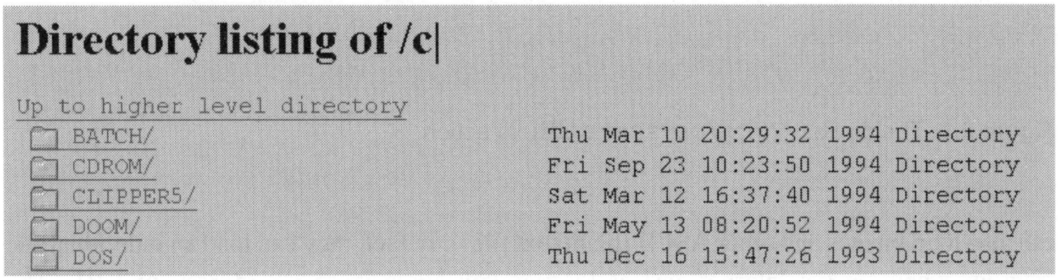

Directory listing of /c|

Up to higher level directory

📁 BATCH/	Thu Mar 10 20:29:32 1994 Directory
📁 CDROM/	Fri Sep 23 10:23:50 1994 Directory
📁 CLIPPER5/	Sat Mar 12 16:37:40 1994 Directory
📁 DOOM/	Fri May 13 08:20:52 1994 Directory
📁 DOS/	Thu Dec 16 15:47:26 1993 Directory

Figure 2.2 The `file:///C|` URL in action.

Up to Higher Level Directory hyperlink into the page – this simply takes you to a disk drive listing, as shown in the previous listing.

    file:///C|/NETSCAPE

Returns the contents of the `C:\NETSCAPE` directory (Figure 2.3). Netscape provides a default set of icons for different file types – these can be disabled by un-checking the Show FTP File Information option found in the Options directory.

The `file://` URL can be used for more than just local files. It can also be used in the same way as the `ftp://` URL (to be discussed) to download files from Internet FTP (File Transfer Protocol) sites.

2.3 **Hypertext URLs: `http://`**

Hypertext pages are the most commonly accessed resources on the World-Wide Web. They are essentially ASCII files with embedded *tags* that adhere to a language known as HTML (HyperText Mark-up Language). HTML is itself covered in depth within Chapter 3. A hypertext URL is prefixed with the characters `http://`, an acronym for HyperText Transfer Protocol (HTTP). In fact, `http://` URLs can load more than just hypertext documents: they

Directory listing of /c|/NETSCAPE

```
Up to higher level directory
 BMP/                           Mon Jan 30 21:03:04 1995  Directory
 BOOKMARK.HTM       715 bytes   Wed Mar 15 16:56:30 1995  Hypertext Markup Language
 CACHE/                         Mon Jan 16 20:21:56 1995  Directory
 COOKIES.TXT         95 bytes   Tue Mar 07 10:39:08 1995  Plain text
 HTM/                           Mon Jan 30 21:03:14 1995  Directory
 LICENSE              8 Kb      Thu Dec 15 20:29:12 1994
 NETSCA.TXT          17 Kb      Tue Jan 31 19:00:54 1995  Plain text
 NETSCAPE.EXE       827 Kb      Fri Dec 16 15:01:12 1994  Binary executable
 NETSCAPE.HST        27 Kb      Thu Mar 09 17:02:08 1995
 NETSCAPE.INI         2 Kb      Thu Mar 02 20:00:26 1995
 NEWS/                          Fri Mar 31 11:04:24 1995  Directory
 NEWSRC             436 bytes   Sun Mar 26 14:08:20 1995
 README.TXT           2 Kb      Wed Jan 04 17:02:30 1995  Plain text
 SETUP.EXE          267 Kb      Sat Oct 29 11:16:04 1994  Binary executable
 SETUP.INS           16 Kb      Tue Jan 03 15:04:38 1995
 SETUP.PKG           89 bytes   Tue Jan 03 15:04:40 1995
```

Figure 2.3 The `file:///C|/NETSCAPE` URL in action.

can also load images and other ASCII (plain text files). In fact, they can load an individual file from anywhere on the Internet, just as long as you know its exact *address*, or URL. The `http://` URL therefore takes the complete syntax:

```
http://hostname:port/filename
```

where `hostname` is an Internet hostname, the name of a physical computer that is connected to the Internet network, of which many thousands exist, and `filename` is the name of a file that you want to retrieve (and/or directory name). The `port` element is a numeric value identifying the port number at which a Web server responds. In the majority of cases you can omit this, since a default port (commonly 80) will be used. Port numbers are found as a consequence of the Internet Protocol (IP), which allows a single host computer to deal with more than one type of protocol. Some servers may allocate a different port number, and where applicable this must be quoted literally. Not all Internet hosts are Web servers (the Web is not the whole Internet remember), so if you try to connect to a machine that is not running the HTTP protocol you will simply be refused access. So, how do you know which sites run the HTTP protocol? In order to advertise this fact network administrators dedicate a single machine to the task of serving Web documents to the Internet public, and the name of this machine is then prefixed to their main Internet hostname. For example, `www.microsoft.com` is a Web server attached to a network on the Internet host `microsoft.com` – the commercial (`.com`) software giant. Another mechanism – the URL – also identifies a Web site by prefixing the hostname with the letters `http://`, the latter method being the easiest way of identifying a Web server. Refer to Appendix B for a list of many hundreds of Web servers that you can visit. Chapter 5 examines a number of tools that can help you find the many millions of documents that exist on the many thousands of Web servers that are now in existence on the Internet.

Web servers with numeric addresses

Introducing yet another caveat, you should be aware that not all Web servers may actually advertise the fact that they are actually running HTTP. The vast majority of Web servers' hostnames start with the letters `www` to indicate that they are indeed Web servers. Thus, a machine called `spock.trekker.com` could be a Web server without giving the game away via its name. Many hosts use a technique known as *aliasing*, whereby the name of one server can be substituted for another, and vice versa. To confuse matters a bit further, Internet host names can also be numeric IP (Internet Protocol) addresses. Luckily, not many of these URLs are in use, although they are directly equivalent to a character-formatted hostname. All Internet hosts have a unique numeric IP address (for example `155.181.16.12`) which is their *identity* on the Internet, rather like a phone number. The host is also allocated a textual name, e.g. `www.host.co.uk`, which is more readable to the end user, although both can be used interchangeably.

The `filename` part of the `http://` URL is also optional. If omitted, the Web server should serve a default hypertext page, referred to as a default *home page* in Web-speak. A home page is rather like a glorified contents page with hyperlinks to other resources. The popular filename for many home pages is `index.html`, although a Web server could be configured to use a different name, and many are. The structure of a filename is dependent on the pathname that leads to it. Most operating systems (DOS and UNIX alike – two popular operating systems on the Internet) use a hierarchical storage system to keep their files. This hierarchical structure is known as a *file system*, made out of directories and subdirectories – structures that categorize files into different areas on a disk. Each hierarchy (or directory *level*) is represented in Netscape by a / character (thus the more '/'s, the lower into the hierarchy that you are moving). All file systems have a *root* directory, or top level – also referred to as the main *parent directory*.

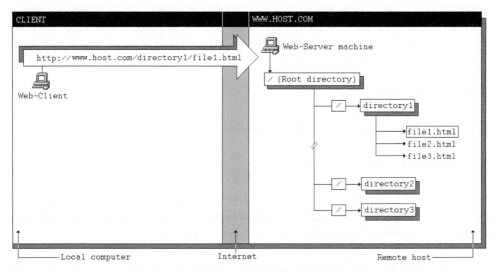

Figure 2.4 Diagrammatic view of a URL and target file system.

Figure 2.4 illustrates how a URL relates to a file system hierarchy. In the diagram, the client (a person using Netscape) has issued a request for the URL `http://www.host.com/directory1/file1.html`.

The right-hand side of the diagram illustrates how the URL is matched against the target host's file system in order to serve the file required (in this case an HTML-formatted file). Notice how each / character relates to a new hierarchy level in the file system (as with the `file://` URL which was explained earlier).

Accessing Macintosh hierarchies

A rather strange URL you may see from time-to-time is one structured for an Apple Macintosh-based computer. The Macintosh's native operating system allows spaces in filenames (DOS and UNIX do not), and thus a special code must be inserted into the URL for each respective space when you quote it within Netscape or from within an HTML file. This code is `%20`, which is a hexadecimal code that translates to a decimal of value of 32 – 32 being the ASCII code for a space.

`http://` examples

`http://www.somewhere.com/index.html`

Loads the page `index.html` from the Internet host named `somewhere.com`. The file `index.html` resides in the root directory of the site shown – notice the initial / character after the host name, which indicates that the file resides in the top-level directory of this computer's hard disk. You can also tell that this machine is not a DOS-based personal computer, since the `.html` extension is illegal under DOS. This is most probably a UNIX-based machine. The name `index.html` is most commonly known as a default home page, although many Web servers use different naming conventions.

`http://www.somewhere.com/`

Loads a default home page from the Web server `www.somewhere.com`.

`http://www.somewhere.com`

Same again. The final / character is implied (i.e. you want to be served a home page from the top-level (*root*) directory – an index or contents page for that site. The final / character can thus be omitted, although many like to include it for completeness.

`http://158.152.12.24/index.html`

Loads the page named `index.html` from the site with the numeric IP address `158.152.12.24`.

> `http://www.somewhere.com:8001/`

Loads a default home page from the site `www.somewhere.com` whose Web server answers on port `8001`. It looks like a dedicated Web server computer is not yet available and they are running their Web interface from an existing network machine. A default home page will be loaded, perhaps `index.html`.

> `www.somewhere.com`

Omitting the initial `http://` prefix in Netscape is allowed. Netscape assumes that you are contacting a Web server for a hypertext (HTML) page. A default home page will be served automatically.

> `http://www.somewhere.com/images/gifs/cat.gif`

This URL loads an image file (`cat.gif` – a Graphics Interchange File) from the host `www.some-where.com` that resides in the `/images/gifs` directory of that machine's file system.

> `http://http1.host.com/html/cat.htm`

Loads a hypertext page (`cat.htm`) that resides in the `/html` directory of the host shown. The filename indicates that the machine may be DOS-based, although this name is also valid under UNIX of course.

> `http://http1.host.com/people`

Specifies that a default page be loaded for the directory `/people`. This is an unusual URL in that no exact filename is given. Unless a default hypertext page has been allocated for loading when specifying this directory this URL will fail and Netscape will issue a suitable error message. Otherwise, a suitable page will be served.

> `http://webhost.apple.com/HTML%20Applications/contents%20page.html`

This is a Macintosh-based Web page, since the `%20`s in the URL specify that spaces are allowed within filenames. This URL therefore loads a hypertext file named exactly as: `/HTML Applications/contents page.html`

> `http://http1.myhost.com/~fred/contents.html`

Another interesting example that crops up again and again. The host is UNIX-based, since the tilde character (~) is a UNIX-based feature that loads a user's home directory. For example, `~fred` may translate to a directory `/usr/users/fred`. The full directory name could be used, although it seems many users do not know the whereabouts of their files, hence the shorthand notation. UNIX *expands* the tilde as soon as it is encountered.

```
http://http1.myhost.com/~jim
```

Same concept as above. A default home page will be served.

```
http://www.somewhere.com/dir1/index.html/
```

This URL looks incorrect, and will probably cause an error. A hypertext file has been requested, so it seems, from the name `index.html`, although it is quite possible for the file `index.html` to be a directory file (under UNIX, that is). So, if this file is a directory, a default page should be loaded. If it is a non-directory file, an error should occur, since the final character in the URL is a /, indicating that a directory is to be referenced.

▶TIP

There is also an `https://` URL in Netscape, which establishes a connection to a *secure* Web server (known as a Netscape *NetSite*). Some Web servers, if running the HTTPS protocol (*secure HTTP*), may actually change your URL to `https://` automatically, although many require that you specifically enter a `https://hostname` style URL.

If you are contemplating sending sensitive details (such as credit card numbers) to a remote Web server, try re-connecting to the server using the URL `https://` to ensure that encryption is enabled. If it is, the small key in the lower left-hand corner of the screen will be blue and intact. Many servers now support secure HTTP (HTTPS) - Netscape Corporation's own home page details many such sites.

2.4 **Gopher URLs:** `gopher://`

Gopher is an information retrieval tool that indexes the titles of many thousands of files on the Internet, particularly those stored on anonymous FTP (file transfer protocol) sites and other Gopher servers. A variety of graphical (e.g. *Wgopher*) and textual (e.g. via Telnet) Gopher clients are widely available, although Netscape can interface to a Gopher server directly through use of the `gopher://` URL, thus doing away with the need for a separate Gopher tool. A

Gopher menu is, by default, hierarchical in nature, rather like a file system. Netscape represents this hierarchy using its standard hyperlinks, and individual files are displayed using a combination of hyperlinks and icons. As with normal hypertext pages you can view the contents of any file for which a suitable helper application is available. The syntax of the `gopher://` URL is:

```
gopher://hostname:port/filename
```

where `hostname` is the name of a Gopher server machine and `port` is an optional port number that the Gopher server answers on. By default this is 70, and you will rarely have to supply this number unless a host specifically requires it. The filename part of the URL allows you to load a particular file from the server, although these are normally very long and tedious names to type, so it is best to navigate through to the entries you require using the hyperlinks supplied. As mentioned, Gopher (derived from the phrase 'Go For Information' – a gopher is also the mascot of the University of Minnesota, where Gopher was originally developed) is primarily a document-searching tool, and a very good one at that. Many graphical Gopher clients exist, and there are thousands of text-based Gopher servers that can be accessed via the Internet. A graphical Gopher environment is better, however, since Netscape will supply the necessary hyperlinks and will also annotate any file(s) recovered during a search using small descriptive icons.

Searches are performed using a keyword entered by the user when required (the HTML `<isindex>` tag is used for this purpose – see Chapter 3) and all searches are substring-based. For example, a search term of *net* would match *Internet* and of course *net* by itself. One small problem with Gopher is that the actual searching itself is carried out on the document title, rather than on the document's file contents. This means that if a title is structured badly or misspelt you may never find the resulting document. Gopher is still a premier searching tool nevertheless, and you will find yourself constantly returning to Gopher as a general-purpose document searching tool. Figure 2.5 illustrates a typical Gopher page, as marked up by Netscape. Notice the small icons to the left of each hyperlink, which indicate the type of file that will be loaded by the hyperlink for that entry.

As mentioned, Gopher menus are hierarchical, so wherever you see a ▢ icon you know that clicking on the appropriate hyperlink for this entry will take you to further (related) subentries. Many other icons are used by Netscape to illustrate different types of hyperlinks within Gopher menus, as Figure 2.6 illustrates.

As you browse Gopher menus, Netscape will expand the current URL to reflect the directory area that you are currently in (Gophers are arranged hierarchically into directories). It therefore follows that if you know the exact URL of a particular file on a Gopher server, you can get directly to it using the URL that refers to that file (this will be displayed on the Netscape screen in the *Location:* field at the top of the screen).

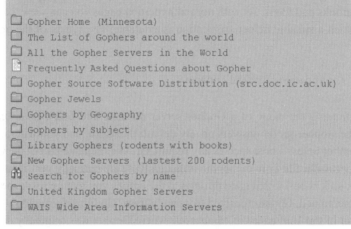

Figure 2.5 A typical Gopher menu as seen through Netscape.

Figure 2.6 A selection of Gopher icons used by Netscape.

Conducting a Gopherspace search

You can browse a Gopher menu for the information you require by simply clicking on the appropriate hyperlinks, although Gopher's real power is as a document-searching tool.

In order to conduct a Gopher search look for the ▓ icon. Netscape will then present a field so that you can enter a search term. Any results (i.e. files) will then be shown to you on the screen accordingly using hyperlinks, and you can click on the appropriate link that interests you in order to retrieve the information required. It is unlikely that a single Gopher server will have all the information you require. Gophers tend to specialize in certain information, perhaps local to a particular college or university etc. Some Gophers may just offer links to better-known servers.

A tool known as *veronica* has therefore been developed that allows much more powerful Gopher searches to be conducted. You will find a veronica search option in many Gopher menus – normally they are kept in a section such as *Other Information Services*, although the actual name may vary and the option may be embedded within a lower directory. The veronica program searches all of the known Gopher servers on the Internet based on a search term that you supply. The collective name for all of these Gopher servers is *Gopherspace* – a term you will come to see on many Gopher servers scattered around the Internet, and one you should choose when conducting a search of any kind if you are to have any chance of locating the information you require. Remember that Gopher itself has nothing to with the Netscape package. Netscape is merely interacting with the Gopher server in order to convert its information into a graphical representation (you may want to try using Netscape's File/View Source) feature with a Gopher menu in order to see the resulting HTML tags for that particular page.

`gopher://` **examples**

    gopher://gopher.brad.ac.uk

Loads the Gopher menu at Bradford University, UK.

    gopher://info.mcc.ac.uk:2347/7

Loads a veronica server (at port `2347`) from Manchester University, UK. The interface to this service is via a default hypertext page served from the directory `/7`. One of the tags in the resulting document is an `<isindex>` tag, which allows a search term to be entered and submitted to the veronica server. Invoke the File/View Source option to see the tags for the page. Chapter 3 discusses such HTML tags in more detail.

▶TIP

Another searching tool is WAIS (Wide Area Information Server). This service makes use of the `wais://` URL, although you will need a proxy server to make use of this service. It is therefore easier to use the Web WAIS gateway at WAIS Inc. directly, which is `http://www.wais.com`

2.5 **Telnet-based URLs:** `telnet://`

Telnet is a very old tool which was first developed as part of the UNIX operating system. It is a program that allows you to establish a real-time connection to another computer on the

Figure 2.7 Netscape's *Unable to find application* warning.

Internet, and then interact with it just as if you were using that computer locally. Thus, you could use Telnet to log in to a UNIX computer to check your email, or perhaps browse one of the Internet's many thousands of on-line databases and bulletin boards, not to mention existing Internet tools such as text-based Gophers and Archie servers. Netscape provides the `telnet://` and `tn3270://` URLs for Telnet access – the latter allows access to an IBM 3270 emulation Telnet program (as specified in `netscape.ini`) in order to interface specifically to IBM mainframe computers.

In order to use the `telnet://` or `tn3270://` URLs you must quote the name of the machine you wish to contact immediately after the `//` characters. For example, you could type:

```
telnet://launchpad.unc.edu
```

whereupon Netscape would load a Telnet client, as set up in the Options/Preferences screen. If you do not have a Telnet client installed on your system (examples are the WinSock Telnet clients *Ewan* and *WinTel*), Netscape will issue a warning, as shown in Figure 2.7.

If a Telnet helper application is installed, Netscape loads it and then passes the name of the host in the URL directly to the program (if a suitable Telnet helper application is not configured it will not let you proceed any further). All interaction with the host then takes place via the Telnet program and you can move between Netscape and the Telnet program at will. The name of the host you supply will be validated by your service provider's name server, and if it cannot be located the Telnet application should issue a warning message. Remember that Netscape has no control over the Telnet program.

▶TIP

Telnet can be used to contact a UNIX host directly, in which case you will reach a UNIX program called `login` whose task is to log in an *authorized* user to that system for access to its files etc. It is *not* wise to try repeatedly to attempt to gain access to a system to which you do not have an authorized username and password. Most Telnet calls to a site are logged, and the administrator of the host in question will probably complain to your Internet service provider (especially if you are a student with Internet access and are randomly typing in addresses!).

`telnet://` and `tn3270://` examples

```
telnet://info.brad.ac.uk
```

The host `info.brad.ac.uk` answers with a Gopher interface (text display, of course), so this demonstrates another way of accessing Gopher, although the Web interface using the `gopher://` interface is much better. This example serves another point, namely that it is not possible to access every Gopher using a `gopher://` URL. Only Gophers running the necessary Web-compliant software will respond correctly.

```
tn3270://ibm1.somehost.com
```

Contacts an IBM mainframe (assuming host `ibm1.somehost.com` is an IBM mainframe). A suitable 3270-emulation Telnet program must be configured before this can be used.

A number of Telnet client programs that can be used with Netscape are documented in Appendix D.

2.6 USENET (NetNews) URLs

USENET is the Internet's discussion forum, where well over 15 000 separate topics are discussed. Each newsgroup has a unique name, arranged in a dotted notation; for example, `comp.infosystems.www.misc` is a newsgroup that deals with miscellaneous Web topics, which is itself part of a computing (`comp`) hierarchy. USENET hierarchies are identified by the first part of the newsgroup name. Netscape is a fully fledged newsreader that can now read and post USENET messages when linked to an appropriate news server machine. A default news server is configured in the Options/Preferences/Mail and News option. Your Internet service provider will normally provide you with such a facility, although it is now possible to link into other news servers on the Internet through use of an appropriate Netscape URL. Many of the URLs described in this section are unique to the Netscape browser (the `news://` URL is the more commonly accepted URL understood by the vast majority of Web browsers). The main newsreading URLs understood by Netscape are:

- `news:`

- `news://server-name/group`

- ■ news:*group*

- ■ newsrc://*server-name*

- ■ newspost:*group*

The first form of URL allows an alternative news server (*server-name*) to be specified when accessing a USENET newsgroup (as specified by *group*). The news: URL is mainly used to load up a particular newsgroup using either the default news server installed under Netscape or using an alternative server of your choice. The newsrc: URL is used to make Netscape load a main list of newsgroups that you have subscribed to, as stored in a file called newsrc, hence the URL name. The newsrc file contains a list of newsgroups that you want Netscape to track – also known as *subscribed* newsgroups. As mentioned, Netscape can be configured to use a default news server through the Options/Preferences/Mail and News menu, and this will be the server contacted when you use the news:group, news: and newsrc: URLs.

News servers can suffer from a variety of problems, most commonly overloading (leading to slow response times) and down-time (complete unavailability due to breakdown or maintenance etc.), so the ability to reference an alternative server is an extremely useful feature to say the least. In saying this, however, the ability to access an alternative news server can also be a problem. When you initially subscribe to an Internet service provider they should provide you with the address of a news server that you can access – normally this will be their own server. If this becomes unavailable the task of finding a replacement can be very difficult: public news servers are a very rare breed indeed, although the tips below should get you started.

▶TIP

You can see a list of public news servers by looking at the URL below, which calls up the *Free Internet News Sources* document:

http://www.helsinki.fi/~lsaarine/news.html

If you are using Netscape with a network connection, it is likely that you will have access to a news server provided by your Internet provider. See Chapter 4 on using USENET news and Netscape for other servers.

In addition, not all news servers carry every USENET newsgroup. For a start, there are just too many newsgroups for a single news server to deal with. For this reason many Internet service providers carry only the mainstream groups and hierarchies. If a particular newsgroup cannot be located via your news server, contact your administrator to request that it be carried. A problem with using multiple news servers can be that your news configuration file (newsrc) may be updated with article numbers that simply don't exist on other servers. When switching between news servers this may become a problem, as some article numbers may overlap, or may simply not exist at all. This may lead to the possibility that you may miss some articles completely. For this reason you may want to load every article from the news server when switching news servers in this way.

Using the `newsrc:` URL you can also subscribe to different newsgroups, rather than using Netscape's screen icons (see the later examples). `newspost:` is similar to `mailto:` (the *compose a mail-message* URL), although this allows you to compose a USENET article and post it to the news server instead of the mail server. You should use this URL along with the name of the group that you want to post to. If you omit the group name it will not be placed in the *Group:* field of the posting screen.

`news://` **examples**

    news:alt.books.technical

Loads the articles from the USENET newsgroup `alt.books.technical`. A default news server, as specified in the `netscape.ini` file, will be used.

    newsrc:

Loads a list of news servers that have been visited in the past, upon which Netscape will then load your `newsrc` file to allow selection of an appropriate newsgroup. If no such servers exist, i.e. you have only ever used one server (your default news server perhaps), your newsgroups selection screen is directly loaded – showing each newsgroup that you have subscribed to.

    newsrc://news.somehost.com

Same as the above, except a different news server is used (this may contain different articles since different news servers are configured differently).

    news://news.somewhere.com/alt.books.technical

Loads the articles from the USENET newsgroup `alt.books.technical` from the hypothetical news server `news.somewhere.com`.

    newsrc://news.somewhere.com/*

This simply makes Netscape show you all of the groups you have subscribed to. You can use `newsrc:` by itself if you require, although this syntax includes the name of your chosen news server.

  `news:*`

This URL loads every group from the current news server. The asterisk (`*`) is a wildcard that matches every group name, a feature first introduced in Netscape v1.0N.

  `news:`

Same as the above. All groups will be loaded that are currently in your `newsrc` file using the default news server specified in Netscape's configuration.

  `news:alt.*`

Another wildcarded newsgroup name, this time specifying that all groups in the `alt` (*alternative lifestyle*) hierarchy should be loaded (e.g. `alt.abortion` through to `alt.zen` – this will be a *long* list). The default news server stored in `netscape.ini` will be used.

  `newsrc://news.somewhere.com/?SUBSCRIBE=alt.books.technical`

A useful URL that subscribes to the USENET group `alt.books.technical`, i.e. adds the newsgroup to your designated `newsrc` file. Your main newsgroups list will be updated immediately and then shown to you on the screen.

  `news:alt.books.technical?ALL`

Loads every article from the newsgroup specified (using the default news server that you have specified in Netscape's Options/Preferences/Mail and News menu.

  `newspost:alt.books.technical`

Makes Netscape enter *message-compose* mode so that you can type in a new article and then post it to the USENET group specified (in this case the newsgroup `alt.books.technical`).

  `newspost:`

Same as the above, although you will have to type in the name of the USENET group that you want to post the article in once the message window appears.

2.7 **FTP URLs:** `ftp://`

FTP (file transfer protocol) is both an application and a communications protocol. In a nutshell, it is the primary tool for transferring files over the Internet. Many thousands of FTP servers (or *sites*) exist, and a large proportion of these allow public access. Such sites are referred to as *anonymous* FTP servers, since a registered username and password to gain access to the server are not required (the word *anonymous* is used as a username, and your email address as a password, e.g. `yourname@yourhost.com`). The information you can retrieve via FTP is diverse. Software is abundant, in the form of freeware and shareware; indeed many of the world's largest software conglomerates have a presence, for example Microsoft Corporation (`ftp.microsoft.com`), IBM (`ftp.ibm.com`) and Novell (`ftp.novell.com`). Aside from software, FTP is a great way of accessing general information in the form of computer documentation and the complete text of books and other publications. The `ftp://` URL accepts two syntaxes:

- `ftp://hostname`

- `ftp://hostname/directory/filename`

where `hostname` is the name of an FTP site that you wish to contact and `directory` and `filename` specify the pathname to a particular file that you want to download. A useful feature of Netscape is that you can *browse* a remote computer's file system for the file(s) that you require. Netscape will create a graphical representation of the file system (i.e. the hard disk, or indeed CD-ROM) that you are navigating, where all directories and files will be hyperlinks that you can select in order to examine. The distinction between the two `ftp://` syntax descriptions depends on whether or not you know the exact name of a file to download (i.e. the hostname, directory (if applicable) and filename). If you specify a path to a file (rather than to a directory), Netscape attempts to download the file. If a directory is specified Netscape shows you the file(s) in that directory and you can then choose a file to download (assuming such a file exists), or you can move to another area of the file system using the hyperlinks provided.

Only individual files can be downloaded using `ftp://` (no wildcards are allowed, as with conventional FTP client programs), and you cannot (yet) upload information to a server – only file downloading is catered for. However, Netscape does understands the difference between *binary* files (executable files, images, compressed files etc.) and *plain text* files (e.g. ASCII documents) – so there is no need to specify which type of file you want to download, as with some dedicated FTP client programs. The process of *logging in* to an FTP server is also automated by Netscape. Netscape feeds the FTP server the name *anonymous* and sends an email address as a password. Even though your email address may be configured through the Options/Preferences/Mail and News menu, Netscape will still be able to gain access if this has not yet been set up (just about any random string will normally facilitate access to an anonymous FTP server, just as long as the *at* sign – @ – is mentioned somewhere, e.g. `anonymous@`). Figure 2.8 illustrates the feedback obtained from

Current directory is /

```
|
| Welcome to ftp.microsoft.com!
|
| Please enter your "full e-mail name" as your password.
|    Report any problems to ftp@microsoft.com
|
| Refer to the index.txt file for further information
|
```

KBHelp/		Wed Apr 05 10:16:00 1995	Directory
LS-LR.ZIP	548 Kb	Sun Apr 09 03:52:00 1995	zip compressed file
MSNBRO.DOC	27 Kb	Mon Nov 28 00:00:00 1994	
MSNBRO.TXT	22 Kb	Tue Feb 08 00:00:00 1994	Plain text
Services/		Wed Nov 02 00:00:00 1994	Directory
Softlib/		Thu Mar 30 10:36:00 1995	Directory
WhatHappened.txt	802 bytes	Thu Aug 25 00:00:00 1994	Plain text
bussys/		Thu Mar 30 18:03:00 1995	Directory
deskapps/		Fri Oct 07 00:00:00 1994	Directory
developr/		Wed Dec 21 00:00:00 1994	Directory
dirmap.htm	7 Kb	Fri Mar 31 15:29:00 1995	Hypertext Markup Language
dirmap.txt	4 Kb	Fri Mar 31 09:32:00 1995	Plain text
disclaimer.txt	712 bytes	Thu Aug 25 00:00:00 1994	Plain text
index.txt	860 bytes	Wed Oct 05 00:00:00 1994	Plain text
ls-1R.Z	715 Kb	Sun Apr 09 03:52:00 1995	compressed file
ls-1R.txt	5650 Kb	Sun Apr 09 03:51:00 1995	Plain text
peropsys/		Fri Oct 07 00:00:00 1994	Directory
support-phones.txt	4 Kb	Wed Oct 20 00:00:00 1993	Plain text

Figure 2.8 Netscape browsing the root directory of `ftp://ftp.microsoft.com`.

the address `ftp://ftp.microsoft.com`. Notice how Netscape annotates each file with a small icon. These annotations can be disabled by un-checking the Show FTP File Information option found in the Options directory. Only hyperlinks are shown if this option is unchecked, which results in slightly faster operation.

Unlike conventional FTP client programs, Netscape does not keep a continuous channel open to the FTP server you eventually contact. The logging-in process is thus reinvoked whenever you change directory etc. With a busy server (such as Netscape's own FTP server `ftp.netscape.com`) this may result in a failed login due to user-load. In such cases you will simply just have to try again. Do this by clicking on the URL field using the mouse and then pressing the RETURN key to re-send the same `ftp://` URL. Alternatively, you can press the *Reload* button, since the URL should still be in the main URL *Location:* field towards the top of the screen.

Notice how directories (or *folders*) have a ▭ icon. These entries facilitate navigation through the file system of the computer that you have contacted. If you have such annotations disabled you can still identify which files are directories, since Netscape appends a / character to the filename (for example, the entry `Services/` shown in Figure 2.8). Figure 2.9 illustrates a typical file entry as seen through the Netscape browser.

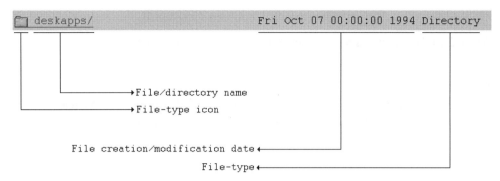
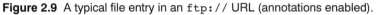

Figure 2.9 A typical file entry in an `ftp://` URL (annotations enabled).

Downloading a file

Depending on the type of file you download, Netscape can behave quite differently. Text files (ASCII text) and HTML-formatted ASCII files will, by default, be loaded into Netscape when you download them – although you can specify that such files be loaded into an alternative helper application using Netscape's Options/Preferences/Helper Applications option (see Chapter 1 for more information on configuring helper applications). Once you click on an actual file's hyperlink (as opposed to a directory file), Netscape examines whether or not it has a helper application installed for that file format according to the filename extension allocated (e.g. `.ZIP` for a PKZIP archive or `.TXT` for a plain text file).

If you click on a file for which a helper application is not installed, Netscape warns you that such a helper program is not configured and gives you the options of: (i) saving the file to disk; (ii) configuring a viewer for the file; or (iii) cancelling the download. In the vast majority of cases you will just want to download the file directly to your hard disk and then process the file later, although some files can be processed further immediately after they are downloaded. For example, a compressed file could be decompressed, or an image file or audio clip could be loaded directly into a suitable viewer, thus saving you the task of doing this outside Netscape when the file is fully transferred to your machine. Look at the Netscape status bar at the bottom of the screen for the words *Document: Done*, which indicate that the file has been retrieved successfully. The progress of the transfer will also be shown up to this point, and the red file-transfer indicator bar in the lower right-hand corner of the screen will also indicate the progress of the file transfer.

▶TIP

While downloading a file using `ftp://` make sure that you do not change screens using the *Back/Forward* buttons etc. If you change the URL while the file is being transferred Netscape 1.1 will ask you if you want to abort the transfer. If you need to enter a new URL, use the File/New Window option to open a new Netscape window, and then type in the URL you need there. The download

Document: Received 7552 bytes

Figure 2.10 Typical status bar message during an `ftp://` file transfer.

should then continue safely in the other window. Earlier versions of Netscape would abort file transfers without asking your permission first.

Shift-clicking to save files

A good tip to remember if you simply want to download a file and bypass anything to do with helper applications is to *shift-click* on the hyperlink for the file that you want to download; that is, press the SHIFT key and then click on the hyperlink for the file that you want to download. Netscape will then ask you for a name under which to save the file (although a default will be provided, and possibly truncated if the filename is too long, so change this accordingly) and the file saved to your hard disk. You can also specify the local directory in which to save the file – something you cannot do otherwise. By default, Netscape saves all such files to the same directory as the main Netscape program. be sure to watch the status bar to see the progress of the file transfer. Netscape will start the transfer with the message *Saving drive:\filename* (where *drive:\filename* is the file and directory that you have chosen), followed by the continuously updated message *Received n bytes* while the file is transferred, as shown in Figure 2.10, where *n* is the amount of data, in bytes, received. Be sure to watch the red progress bar in the bottom right-hand corner of the screen as well, since this will quickly tell you how much of the transfer is left to go (the red bar extends completely to the right when the transfer is completed).

`ftp://` examples

```
ftp://ftp.microsoft.com
```

Tells Netscape to contact the FTP server at host `ftp.microsoft.com` and navigate its file system. Netscape will load the *root* (top-level) directory by default.

```
ftp://ftp.microsoft.com/
```

Same as the above. The final / is normally used just to specify the root directory (/), which is the default in any event and which can therefore be omitted.

```
ftp://ftp.netscape.com/windows/n16e11n.exe
```

Informs Netscape to download the file n16e11n.exe, which resides in the directory named /windows (the file in this case is version 1.1 of the Netscape program) from the Netscape FTP server at the host ftp.netscape.com. If the file n16e11n.exe was a directory file, Netscape would show you the contents of that directory instead. This is why many URLs include the final / character, so as to avoid any confusion between *files* (or *ordinary files*, as they are sometimes known) and *directory* files – although Netscape can tell the difference.

▶ TIP

You can use the file:// URL in the same way as the ftp:// URL to download files from remote FTP servers. The file:// URL is mainly used to load *local* files.

```
ftp://ftp.somehost.org/doc/misc/misc1.txt
```

Downloads the file misc1.txt to your computer. The file will be loaded into Netscape by default (the same happens with HTML and other ASCII-formatted files as well – see the tip below). If you want to save the file use the File menu and the Save As option.

▶ TIP

Netscape will load HTML and ASCII files (.TXT and .HTM files) automatically, rather than using a helper application. You can overcome this by *shift-clicking* on the filename, which will bypass the use of a helper application (instead, Netscape will immediately ask you for a filename and will then download the file accordingly under that name).

2.8 Email URLs

The only electronic mail URL in Netscape is mailto:, which opens a window to allow you to compose a message and then submit this to an email (SMTP) server, as configured in the netscape.ini file through the Options/Preferences/Mail and News option. Netscape 1.1N cannot specify an alternative mail server through the mailto: URL (as with news:).

It is also possible to specify the name of the recipient in the mailto: URL, for example:

```
mailto:fred@somewhere.com
```

in which case Netscape will enter the recipient's name (fred@somewhere.com) into the appropriate field – a shortcut technique to save you entering the person's email address again at the next stage. Once you have entered the URL, Netscape provides a window where you can send a simple text message, attach a MIME-compliant attachment (e.g. a binary file such as an image). When you click on the *Send* button to post your email you will know that it has been sent successfully when the email window disappears. If your mail server is not functional Netscape doesn't normally provide an error message. Instead it simply closes the message composing window very abruptly! If your mail server is incorrectly named, a name server (DNS) failure should occur, however. Watching the status bar at the very bottom of the screen for the '*Contacting host*' message is the best advice to take in order to ensure that your email is actually getting through to the mail server that you have specified.

C H A P T E R

3

Creating your own Web pages using HTML

3.1 **Introduction**

Netscape, and for that matter any of the graphical Web browsers in existence, understands a language known as HTML, or *HyperText Mark-up Language*. Everything seen through Netscape is HTML-formatted. Every image, hyperlink, bullet and paragraph break is provided courtesy of HTML. HTML itself is best described as a *tag language*, that is to say that small markers (known as *tags*) are embedded within the text of a document in order to tell Netscape how a hypertext page should look when it is viewed on the screen. More recently, new HTML tags have been added that can also control the colouring of pages and hyperlinks, background patterns, and the layout of complex table structures.

HTML was itself born out of a much larger language known as SGML, the Standard Generalized Mark-up Language – an ISO standard in its own right. HTML currently falls into three categories, namely HTML versions 1.0, 2.0 and 3.0. Version 1.0 HTML is mandatory for all Web browsers and contains all of the most basic text-formatting facilities. Version 2.0 is slightly more advanced, and has support for in-line images (images that appear *within* a hypertext document) and fill-out-forms (FOFs) which allow user input to be obtained within a hypertext document. HTML 2.0 is being finalized as this book is being written. Netscape version 1.0N is to all intents and purposes an HTML versions 1.0 and 2.0 browser, since it has advanced features such as image support and forms as standard. HTML 3.0, or *developer's* HTML, is a slightly different matter. At the time of writing, HTML 3.0 is still very much a draft standard and as such is constantly *evolving*. Netscape 1.1N has added some of its own HTML tags for use within hypertext documents, and are proposing that these will be included in any final HTML 3.0 standard that is eventually ratified. Two very important additions which fall within Netscape HTML 3.0 are *table structures*, *background/foreground patterns/colours*, and *dynamic documents*. Netscape 1.1N also supports table structures and background/foreground patterns (these are also part of the draft HTML 3.0 specification). Netscape 1.1 also handles different character sets (e.g. Japanese). Beyond HTML 3.0 is VRML, a virtual reality HTML dialect, but that is beyond the scope of this book.

▶TIP

HTML is much too large a language to explain completely within a single chapter. The reader is directed to the hypertext pages at the URLs:

```
http://www.w3.org/hypertext/WWW/MarkUp/MarkUp.html
http://www.hpl.hp.co.uk/people/dsr/html/html3.dtd
```

for in-depth discussions of the HTML language (including the HTML 2.0 and 3.0 SGML DTDs – *Document Type Definitions*).

HTML itself consists of a series of *tags* that encapsulate parts of your document text in order to tell Netscape how that text should appear on screen, e.g. whether or not a sentence is displayed in *italics* or as **bold** text. Tags are *parsed*, or interpreted by the Netscape program – they do not appear on the screen when the document containing them is loaded into Netscape (although there are ways of embedding literal HTML tags within documents – this is dealt with later). The more complicated tags allow images, hyperlinks (clickable addresses that load Internet resources), check/radio-boxes and fill-out-forms (for controlled user input) to be inserted into hypertext documents. Further enhancements in Netscape that adhere to level 3.0 HTML, such as tables, are also available and are covered in more detail later within this chapter. Much of the core HTML language will be discussed and demonstrated within the remainder of this chapter. Eventually, all Web browsers should support the same universal HTML language constructs. Alas, this is not the case at the moment. It is possible that a person using NCSA Mosaic who is viewing a Web page made up of Netscape HTML tags may not receive the same results – although none of Netscape's HTML constructs will actually *crash* your Web browser (or at least they shouldn't). Instead they will simply be ignored, or at worst will be displayed incorrectly on the screen. This chapter examines the core of the HTML language, and moves on to examine HTML 3.0 and the Netscape enhancements and how these differ with respect to each other. If you want to publish your own work on the Internet via the World-Wide Web, then learning HTML is an essential prerequisite.

All HTML files contain text, that is the actual *content* of a document. If you like, you can edit a plain text file (it must be plain text though, i.e. ASCII) and then save this under a name of your choice – not forgetting the important `.htm` extension – and then load this directly into Netscape using its *Open File* (CTRL+O) option from within the File menu. You may also want to browse some existing HTML files from other sources, such as from the Internet itself.

3.2 Creating a hypertext document – some fundamentals

Before examining HTML in more detail, let us quickly browse through some concepts to get you started with the design of a simple hypertext document. In fact, you only need to learn a few basic HTML tags to create a reasonably attractive hypertext page, so if you are an HTML novice start here. This is a whistle-stop guide to getting you started; a more detailed treatment of Netscape's HTML constructs follow later.

Text layout tags

To start with, be aware that HTML does not understand the concept of multiple spaces, tabs and other indentations within a document that you would introduce in order to make a document more readable to the human eye. Every literal tab and paragraph break that is required must be inserted using an appropriate tag, otherwise Netscape will render (mark-up) the text in one large continuous chunk. Single spaces will be interpreted properly – literal text is rendered to the screen verbatim.

▶TIP

When designing your HTML pages, start Netscape and a suitable ASCII editor, such as *Notepad* (`notepad.exe`), so that you can work on a sample file locally. You can then switch between Netscape and your editor using the Netscape *Reload* button (or CTRL+R) to see the tags as they appear in the Netscape program. Be sure to use an ASCII (plain text) editor.

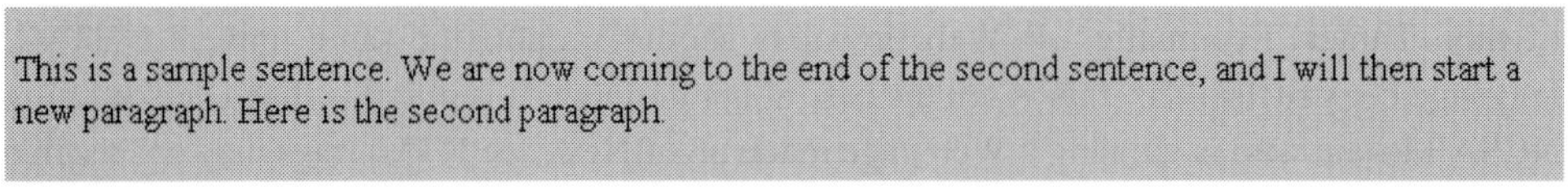

This is a sample sentence. We are now coming to the end of the second sentence, and I will then start a new paragraph. Here is the second paragraph.

Figure 3.1 The text in Example 1 as seen through Netscape.

Assume that you have typed in the following text with a suitable editor, saved it and then loaded it into Netscape (using the File menu and the Open File option):

Example 1: Some sample text (non-HTML formatted).

```
This is a sample sentence. We are now coming to the end of the
second sentence, and I will then start a new paragraph.
Here is the second paragraph.
```

In Netscape this text would look like that shown in Figure 3.1. As can be seen, the paragraph break has been ignored, and the second paragraph has simply been appended to the first. Only *single* spaces in-between words are interpreted as spaces by Netscape's HTML parser. In order to format paragraphs two tags called <br> and <p> must be used.

In order to obtain a paragraph break in HTML, the <p> tag is used. This tag allows a new paragraph to be started by physically inserting a blank line immediately after the position of the tag. Here is a slightly modified version of Example 1 with the new tag in place.

Example 2: Text with paragraph break.
```
This is a sample sentence. We are now coming to the end of the
second sentence, and I will then start a new paragraph.<p>

Here is the second paragraph.
```

The HTML in Example 2 would be rendered in Netscape as shown in Figure 3.2.

As can be seen from Example 2, the second paragraph now starts at the correct point, effectively giving us two visible paragraphs of text. Of course, since Netscape is really ignoring the blank line before the second paragraph (which has been inserted purely for HTML-readability), this could be omitted. In fact we would achieve exactly the same results

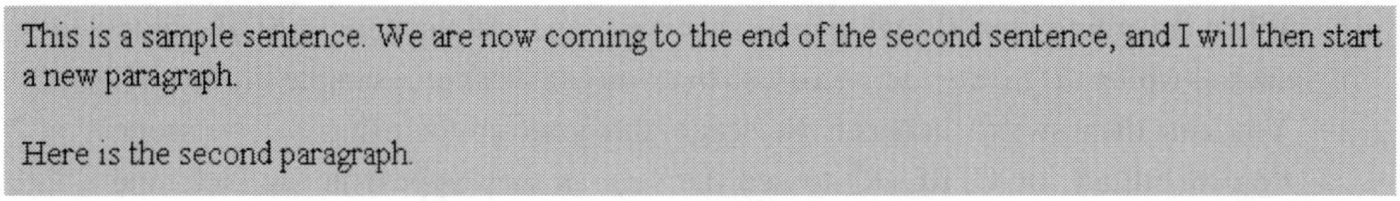

This is a sample sentence. We are now coming to the end of the second sentence, and I will then start a new paragraph.

Here is the second paragraph.

Figure 3.2 The text in Example 2 as seen through Netscape.

by structuring our HTML as shown in Example 3 below.

Example 3: Another way of structuring Example 2.

```
This is a sample sentence. We are now coming to the end of the
second sentence, and I will then start a new paragraph.<p> Here
is the second paragraph.
```

As a rule of thumb, format your HTML text as you would normally within a word-processed document. In this way, your text will be more readable in its *raw* mode, and it will resemble roughly the same structure when viewed through Netscape. Bear in mind that the size of Netscape's window will make the text wrap differently. Netscape automatically word-wraps all sentences by default, so there is no need to use a hard return (line break) at the end of each line (unless you want to do so on purpose, of course). Example 3 is slightly difficult to read, since the paragraph break is embedded within the sentence – a bad habit to say the least, although valid HTML.

The `<br>` (line break) tag is similar to `<p>` in that it breaks the line at the point the tag is specified, although it does not create a new paragraph, i.e. it does not insert a blank line afterwards. Use the `<br>` tag when you want a line to break but not start a new paragraph, for example:

Example 4: Two sentences in one paragraph.

```
Here is one line.<br>
Here is another line.<br>
```

Figure 3.3 illustrates the text shown in Example 4, as rendered through Netscape. Since the `<br>` tags have been used at the end of each sentence, Netscape will break the lines at the points specified rather than joining both sentences together.

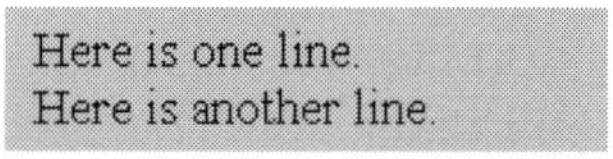

```
Here is one line.
Here is another line.
```

Figure 3.3 The text in Example 4 as seen through Netscape.

▶TIP

If you need to include special characters within your text (e.g. foreign characters or copyright signs), you need to use an HTML *entity code*. These special codes will provide the characters you require. See Appendix G for details of common entity codes that Netscape understands.

Titles and headings

Two other features that you will need to learn concern screen titles and headings. All hypertext documents should have a title which identifies the content of the current document, whatever this may be. The HTML tag-pair `<title>...</title>` is used for this – your title text being inserted in-between the two tags, as shown in Example 5.

Example 5: An example document title.
```
<title>The Tortoise Home Page</title>
```

In Netscape, the tags in Example 5 make the title bar display the text *The Tortoise Home Page*, as shown in Figure 3.4. Be sure to place your `<title>` tags at the very top of your document. If no `<title>` tag is specified in your document, Netscape provides a default, which is simply '*Netscape*' by itself.

Netscape - [The Tortoise Home Page]

Figure 3.4 The Netscape title bar after loading Example 5.

▶TIP

You can spruce up your HTML pages by using an 'animated title'. To do this simply place a series of `<title>` tags in your document, and make each successive tag slightly different, for example:

```
<title>W_____</title>
<title>Wo_____</title>
<title>Wor_____</title>
<title>Worl_____</title>
<title>World_____</title>
<title>WorldW_____</title>
<title>WorldWi_____</title>
<title>WorldWid____</title>
<title>WorldWide___</title>
<title>WorldWideW__</title>
<title>WorldWideWe_</title>
<title>WorldWideWeb</title>
```

Loading these tags from a local file on your hard disk will result in a very quick animation that you may not notice. However, when the file is loaded over an

HTTP connection (i.e. via a modem, by someone visiting the page) the animation should slow down significantly. It is not generally recommended to use multiple `<title>` tags in a document, although it can look good!

Headings are another easy facility to make use of. Netscape controls the size of the text on the screen using a variety of tags (you will learn about the `<font>` tag later), although to get started try using the HTML tags `<h1>...<h6>`, which allow a portion of text to be displayed in a larger font size. Netscape has six levels of heading, numbered 1 to 6. A pair of tags must be used to encapsulate the text you want to make larger, or smaller, as shown in Example 6. The `<h1>` tag produces the largest heading, whereas `<h6>` produces the smallest heading.

Example 6 – Heading example
```
<h1>This is a level 1 heading</h1>
<h3>This is a level 3 heading</h3>
<h6>This is a level 6 heading</h6>
```

You can use heading tags for titles, section headings and many other purposes besides. Figure 3.5 illustrates the effect of Example 6 as viewed through Netscape.

Notice also how each heading tag creates an automatic paragraph break as well. You may want to read the later section on the `<font>` tag to achieve similar, more powerful, effects.

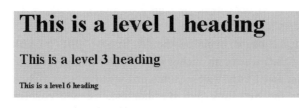

Figure 3.5 Example 6 as rendered by Netscape.

Handling in-line images

Many Web pages have images embedded within them (these are also known as *in-line* images, since they appear within the current hypertext document). The basic tag for including an image within a document is the `<img src="URL">` tag, where `URL` is the location of an image stored in the GIF or JPEG formats. The image you specify can be called from anywhere on the Internet if you specify a URL using the `http://` prefix. A filename mentioned by itself is assumed to exist in the current working directory of the disk where the current hypertext page is located. Example 7 illustrates the `<img src>` tag in action.

Example 7: Simple image example
```
Here is an image: <img src="http://www.host.com/images/file.gif">
```

In the case of Example 7, an image is retrieved from the Internet host `www.host.com` in the directory `/images` named `file.gif` (a GIF image file in this case). If you are working locally with Netscape, i.e. without an Internet connection, or if you are accessing files from just one directory from within a single directory of a Web server, you can call an image from the current directory just by using the more compact version: `<img src="file.gif">`. Netscape understands the concept of *relative* URLs, so that if you call up a URL such as `http://www.gold.net/users/ag17/index.htm`, a reference in `index.htm` structured as `<img src="file.gif">` assumes that `file.gif` resides at `http://www.gold.net/users/ag17/file.gif`.

Moving around with hyperlinks and anchors

A hyperlink (hypertext link) is a key concept in both Netscape and the Web generally. The World-Wide Web could be considered as a series of links to different parts of the Internet. A hyperlink is a clickable region of the screen that invokes a uniform resource locator (URL). URLs are the addresses of Internet resources, if you may remember. Once a valid URL has been invoked, Netscape will attempt to locate the resource referenced and then display it accordingly. The word *display* is used loosely, since Netscape can deal with many different types of media, including text, sound and video. As we are dealing solely with text in this small section, the concept of an *anchor* must be learned. An anchor is a label that a hyperlink points to. Thus clicking on a hyperlink with the address of an anchor results in immediate movement to that anchor. Anchors are useful to provide a mechanism whereby the user can move around a hypertext document, perhaps to different sections. Contents pages and indexes are prime candidates for anchors.

In order to create a clickable hyperlink the `<a href="URL">LinkText</a>` tag is used, where URL is the name of an anchor or any other Internet resource, such as another hypertext document, and `LinkText` is some text that becomes a clickable region of the screen that invokes the hyperlink. For the moment, we will concentrate on hypertext documents. For example, we could create a hyperlink that loads a document from another host on the Internet, as shown in Example 8.

Example 8: Hyperlink example
```
<a href="http://www.host.com/htmldocs/file.html">Click here</a>
```

In this example, the text *Click Here* becomes a clickable hyperlink on the user's screen. By default, Netscape underlines all hyperlinks and colours them blue (both defaults can be changed, however). As you move over the hyperlink with the mouse cursor, Netscape shows you the URL associated with the hyperlink at the bottom of the screen on the status bar. The mouse cursor also changes from an arrow to a small hand. Thus, clicking on the hyperlink in Example 8 would load the file named `file.html` (an HTML-formatted file), and this would be loaded into Netscape accordingly. However, if we wanted to move to a *specific* point within another file we would have to use an anchor. Anchors are created using the HTML `<a name="label">...</a>` tag, where `label` is the name of the anchor. You will of course also need a hyperlink to point to the anchor. The format for a hyperlink that points to an anchor in another file is:

```
<a href="filename#anchorlabel>Text To Click On</a>
```

where `filename` is the hypertext document to load, e.g. `file2.html`, and `anchorlabel` is the label that you want to jump to within the document, as specified with the `<a name...>` tag. So in file #1 (assume this is called `index.html`) we could have the hypothetical example:

```
<a href="http://host.com/file.html#section1>Click Here!</a>
```

which would make the text *Click Here!* into a hyperlink that loads a hypertext page from the Internet host (Web server) `host.com`, and file #2 (`file.html`) would have the HTML tag:

```
<a name="section1">Section 1: Introduction</a>
```

Figure 3.6 illustrates the concept diagrammatically. You can have as many anchors as you like in this way, thus building up an index or contents page to point to relevant documents located at other Internet sites.

You can of course use anchors in local hypertext document as well, simply by omitting the filename in the HTML `<a href>` tag, as shown in Example 9.

Example 9: A local anchor.
```
<a href="#mylabel">Click here</a>
```

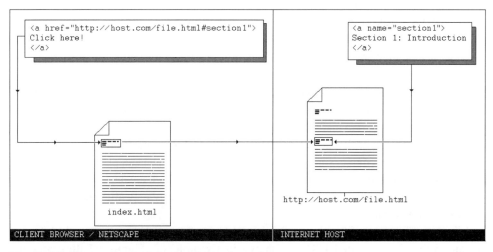

Figure 3.6 Diagrammatical view of a remote anchor.

In the above example the anchor labelled #mylabel is assumed to exist within the current hypertext document for an anchor called mylabel. In order to jump to this label you would need to place an appropriate <a name="mylabel"> tag in the current file at the point required.

▶TIP

If you intend to publish your own information on the Internet and you are uploading files to an Internet Web server, the http:// prefix can be omitted for <a href> hyperlinks when they refer to a file or anchor that exists in another file situated on the current Web server in the same directory. The http:// prefix is only required when pulling a file from another Internet host. In theory, any locally designed pages can be used when loaded onto a Web server where all files exist in a single directory. This feature is known as a *relative* URL, i.e. the file is relative to the main URL of the first file (home page) that is loaded.

Don't forget also that any URL prefix can be used within a hyperlink, so that access to other Internet resources such as Gophers (gopher://) and USENET news servers (news:) is also possible.

Incorporating sound into your documents

In order to incorporate an audio element into your document you will need a suitably configured helper application. Netscape 1.1N arrives with an audio player called naplayer.exe which will play .AU and .AIF formatted audio files. You must reference the audio file using a hyperlink, as shown in Example 10.

Example 10: A hyperlink to a local audio file
```
<a href="cuckoo.au">Listen to the Cuckoo!</a>
```

Other helper applications are also available from the Internet such as *Wplany* (Windows Play Any File) and *Wham*. If you want to play Windows .WAV files, you can use the Windows soundrec.exe (Sound Recorder) to play such files. Ideally, your audio-playing application should play the file as soon as it has been downloaded. The Windows soundrec.exe program loads the file first, after which you must click on the play button to hear the file's contents, but the Netscape NAPLAYER application will play the file immediately. And of course, since the file is kept in a buffer, you can play it over and over again. Some applications play the file and then terminate, which means that you must keep reloading the file from scratch (Netscape's disk caching facility may alleviate this problem if enabled, however).

Likewise, if the audio file exists on another Web server located elsewhere on the Internet, use an http:// formatted URL, as shown in Example 11. Figure 3.7 illustrates the Netscape NAPLAYER program's main interface.

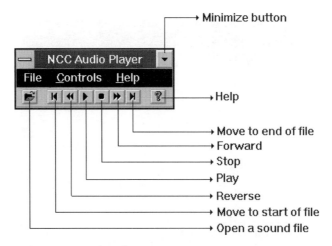

Figure 3.7 The `naplayer.exe` interface.

Example 11: A hypothetical hyperlink to a remote audio file.
`<a href="http://host.com/sounds/cuckoo.au">Listen to the Cuckoo!</a>`

Incorporating video into your documents

Netscape must have a suitably configured helper application in order to play video (animation) files. Such files arrive in a variety of formats, although MPEG (Motion Picture Experts Group), and AVI (Microsoft Audio Visual Interleave) files seem to be the most popular on the Internet at present. A variety of helper applications for video animations exist, including *Mpeg32*, which will play MPEG (`.MPG`) files, and the Windows 3.x application `mplayer.exe`, which will play AVI-formatted files with the appropriate configuration (e.g. sound card). MPEG animations are by far the most common on the Internet. Example 12 illustrates an HTML hyperlink to a video clip.

Example 12: A hypothetical hyperlink to a remote video file.
`<a href="http://host.com/video/earth.mpg">The Planet Earth</a>`

Please refer to the appendices for a list of helper applications and their locations on the Internet.

You should now have a basic understanding about the HTML language and how it deals with text, images and hyperlinks. The next section covers the core of the HTML language, including some of the latest features of the proposed HTML 3.0 standard. If you have access to a Web server and a scripting (programming) language, you can develop *dynamic documents* that allow in-line images to be animated – a new feature that arrived with Netscape. Refer to end of this chapter for more details and program examples.

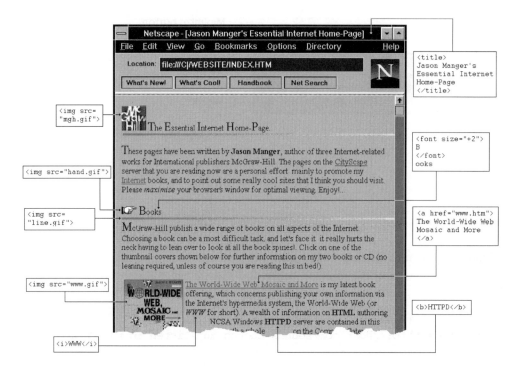

Figure 3.8 Home page with tag annotations.

▶TIP

HTML 3.0 should have a new tag, known as `<meta>`, which allows documents to be automatically reloaded after a certain period. Documents can also be chained together, so that it is possible to give the effect of an animation, e.g. by using an `<img src..>` tag. Netscape 1.1 also facilitates server *push/pull* features that allow dynamic images to be sent by a Web server in order to facilitate real-time (i.e. regular) updating. The `<meta>` tag is already part of the Netscape 1.1N program.

Figure 3.8 illustrates a typical home page (main hypertext page), and is annotated with the HTML tags that make up various parts of the page.

3.3 **Fundamental HTML tags to learn**

This section presents the most fundamental tags that are common to all HTML browsers. The tag-language constructs presented in this section can be used with Mosaic, Cello,

WinWeb, GWHIS and a variety of others besides. The eventual results that you will see are very much dependent on the client browser that you use. You may also find that many tags carry out the same operations. The tags in this section span HTML versions 1.0, 2.0 and more recently, HTML 3.0.

Whenever you see the Netscape icon expect to find information on HTML tags that have been enhanced by Netscape, i.e. they are proposals for inclusion in the evolving HTML 3.0 standard, or are Netscape tag *extensions*. You will also find information on Netscape's HTML enhancements that fall within and without of the HTML 3.0 draft specification in these sections.

Comment tags

Syntax: `<! CommentText>`

Comments allow annotations and notes to be inserted into an HTML document. They will be ignored by the Netscape parser. Comments may be carried over onto multiple lines, and Netscape-HTML allows whole portions of HTML to be encapsulated within comments to allow HTML developers to remove portions of their HTML in order to temporarily remove such sections etc.

Main use: To insert comments into a text file, and to remove existing HTML code for testing purposes.

Example 1: Simple comment

```
<! This is my home page (c) A.N.Other 1995>
<title>Here is a page title</title>
```

Example 2: Comments on multiple lines

```
<!
Here is a comment on multiple lines. Simply
carry over the comment text and end this with
the required end tag
>
```

Example 3: Commenting out some existing HTML code

```
<! *** the following HTML has been commented out ***
<title>Here is a page title</title>
<a href="#anchor1">Here is a hyperlink</a>
>
```

Example 4: Long comment on one line

```
<!--------------This is commonly used---------------->
```

N Netscape supports nested comments more reliably now, and also handles the commenting of literal HTML, so that portions of a Web page can be omitted with ease. There are no actual tag alterations as such. The older HTML browsers required < ! – to start a comment; this is no longer the case.

Address tags

Syntax: `<address>`**`AddressText`**`</address>`

The address tag provides the user with a way of including details of a document's author, and perhaps address on the Internet. Netscape will italicize the address text by default. The text (**`AddressText`**) placed between the address tags does not take any special format, and can be free-form (typically fewer than 80 characters).

Main use: To provide details of HTML author and their addresses (email/Internet hostname etc.).

Example 1: Basic address text

```
<address>
The Netscape Navigator / Author: Jason Manger /
wombat%spuddy@uunet.uu.net
</address>
```

N No major differences occur between Netscape-HTML and earlier versions of the `<address>` tag.

Hyperlinks and anchors

Syntax: `<a href="`**`URL`**`">`**`LinkText`**`</a>`

Inserts a hyper-reference (or *hyperlink*) to another Internet resource. **`LinkText`** will be made into a clickable hyperlink (an *event region*) on the screen, and will be coloured blue and underlined by default so that the link is highlighted. Hyperlinks allow the user to move around documents and to access distant Internet resources.

Main use: To allow the user to move around the Web (as well as moving to local documents).

The `href=` part of the tag can be (i) a link to another part of the current document (an *internal anchor*); (ii) a link to part of an external document (*external anchor*); or (iii) a link to any other Web resource with a valid URL, for example a Gopher server (`gopher://`), News group (`news:`) or any valid hypertext HTML page (`http://`). In the case of *internal anchors* you must supply an additional tag called `<a name>` which marks the spot where you will be transported to after clicking on the appropriate `<a href>` tag. The `<a name>` tag is detailed below. External HTML documents can be loaded using a `<a href>` tag using the prefix `http://` followed by the Internet host name and then a pathname to the HTML file in question. It is also possible to jump to a specified region of a document by appending a hash (#) and then the name of the anchor, which itself corresponds to an `<a name>` tag in that document, so that the user is taken to a specific part of the text rather than to the start of the document (the default location when a document is loaded without such an anchor). Remember to use the `</a>` tag to mark the end of the text for the hyperlink. You can also break a hyperlink using the `<br>` tag in-between the `<a href..>` tag and the closing `</a>` tag (useful for a hyperlink on more than one line).

Example 1: A simple hyperlink to load the file `index.htm` *at host* `www.somewhere.com`, *which itself resides in the directory* `/html`.

```
<a href="http://www.somewhere.com/html/file2.htm">
Click here to load the file file2.htm
</a>
```

Example 2: A hyperlink to a local file (`html.htm`*) that resides on the current machine's local hard disk (*`C:` *drive in DOS parlance) in the directory:* `c:\windows\mosaic\htm`.

```
<a href="file:///C|/windows/mosaic/htm/html.htm">Click here</a>
```

Example 3: A hyperlink to load a default home page (normally `index.html`*).*

```
<a href="http://www.microsoft.com">Click here</a>
```

Example 4: A hyperlink calling a Gopher server at host `gopher.brad.ac.uk`.

```
<a href="gopher://gopher.brad.ac.uk">Click here for a Gopher</a>
```

Example 5: A hyperlink to load the USENET group `uk.jobs.offered`. *A default NNTP news server will be used, as configured in* `netscape.ini`.

```
<a href="news:uk.jobs.offered">Read UK Jobs!</a>
```

Example 6: A local hyperlink to load a file from another directory.

```
<a href="../file.htm">Click on Me!</a>
```

No major differences occur between Netscape-HTML and earlier versions of the `<a href>` tag.

▶ TIP

Try to avoid using multiple font sizes with an `<a href>` hyperlink, since by default, all hyperlinks are underlined in Netscape (unless disabled using the Options/Preferences menu). This results in a horrible visual effect whereby the underlining is staggered at different levels, i.e. the hyperlink line is not straight. To overcome this problem ensure that all characters are the same size (at least until a fix arrives).

Inserting an anchor hyperlink

An anchor can immediately be identified in a URL, since a hash (#) is used. Only hypertext pages can have anchors inserted into them. So, for example, if we had a hyperlink such as:

```
<a href="http://www.somewhere.com/files/myfile.htm#welcome">
Click here!
</a>
```

the file `myfile.htm` would need to have an `<a name>` tag to identify the anchor called 'welcome', as specified after the # in the `<a href>` tag of the *calling* file (the calling file is the file with the hyper-reference). If Netscape cannot find an anchor, an error message will be displayed and you will be left at the top of the file most recently referenced. So, in the context of our example above, the file `myfile.htm` would also require the following tag to provide a point (an anchor address) to jump to:

```
<a name="welcome"><h1>Welcome to this section</h1></a>
```

You do not have to encapsulate the `<a name>` tag around some text. Instead you can just keep the anchor reference on a single line by itself, for example:

```
<a name="welcome"></a>
<h1>Welcome to this section</h1>
```

and the user will still be moved to the correct section of text. When Netscape finds the anchor, it aligns the first portion of text with the top of the main window so that the user can see the position. It is best to make anchors point to chapter or section headings so that the user can see that they have reached the correct area immediately (the <h1> tag in the above example simply makes some text into a level 1 heading (using a larger font), as described below in more detail).

Inserting bold text

Syntax: <b>**BoldText**</b>

Marks up a portion of text in a **bold** typeface. This mark-up effect is useful for emphasizing certain items of text in a document. The older <emp> (emphasize text) tag can also be used in most browsers, such as Mosaic, although not Netscape.

Main use: To emphasize words or sentences in an HTML document.

Example 1: Simple emboldened text string

    <b>Here is some bold text.</b> Here is some normal text.

Figure 3.9 illustrates the emboldening effect shown in Example 1 as viewed through Netscape.

N: No major differences occur between Netscape-HTML and earlier versions of the <b> tag, although <strong> is starting to be used more within many Web documents on the Internet instead of <b>.

Here is some bold text. Here is some normal text.

Figure 3.9 Example of bold text using the <b> tag.

Inserting block quotes

Syntax: <blockquote>**QuoteText**</blockquote>

This tag is used to enter a text quote (e.g. from a person, or an extract from a book). Netscape will indent all text quoted, although apart from this the tag is not very useful in any other capacity. The quoted text can run on to more than one line. No quotation marks (") are inserted by Netscape.

Main use: To insert a quote from another source. See also `<cite>`.

Example 1: Simple block quote text.

```
<blockquote>
Such stuff as dreams are made on.
</blockquote>
```

[N] No major differences occur between Netscape-HTML and earlier versions of the `<blockquote>` tag.

Body text tags

Syntax: `<body>HTML-body-text</body>`

The `<body>` tag is used to encapsulate the main *body* of text that makes up an HTML document. It is not a compulsory tag, although it will be required by Netscape users who need to change screen patterns and text colours etc. (see the Netscape notes below).

Main use: To denote the main body of an HTML file (optional). See also: `<head>`.

Example 1: Denoting some body text.

```
<head>
<title>This is a title</title>
</head>
<body>
This is the main text of the <b>body</b> of my HTML file.
</body>
```

[N] Netscape uses an enhanced version of the `<body>` tag which allows the foreground and background colours to be changed (mostly as in the HTML 3.0 draft specification). Refer to the later section on the `<body>` tag for more information and examples.

Line break tags

Syntax: `<br clear=left|right|all>`

Inserts a line break at the current position (like a carriage return). The <br> tag is not like a paragraph break tag (<p>) since it does not insert a blank line immediately afterwards.

Main use: To enforce a line break in a sentence. See also <p>.

Example 1: Simple line break (two sentences, each on successive lines).

```
Here is one sentence.<br>Here is another.
```

Netscape handles line breaks in a more reliable fashion than previously. Lines can now only be broken where actual *empty space* occurs in the document. A new <nobr> and </nobr> set of tags has also been introduced. These tags stop line breaks in those parts of the text encapsulated by them. The <br> tag has also been extended because Netscape has introduced the concept of *floating images* within HTML documents. By itself, <br> acts like the pressing of the carriage return key.

The CLEAR=left, CLEAR=right and CLEAR=all options have been introduced. So, for example, <br clear=left> would break the current line at the position specified, and would then move vertically until the left margin was clear of images. Likewise, the right option does the same for the right margin, while the all option moves down vertically until both margins are clear of any images. *Floating images* are explained in greater detail within the section on the <img src> tag, where examples are also given.

Citation text

Syntax: <cite>**CitationText**</cite>

This tag is slightly redundant, although still carried over into Netscape. It allows a citation to be included, such as a quote from another source. Netscape will *italicize* the citation text specified, although you could achieve the same effect by using the <i> tag by itself.

Main use: To insert a citation, such as a quote from another person. See also <i>.

Example 1: Simple citation.

```
For more essential information on the Internet see my book:
<cite>The Essential Internet Information Guide, McGraw-Hill
1994</cite>
```

No major differences occur between Netscape-HTML and earlier versions of the <cite> tag.

Pre-formatted tags (monospaced fonts)

Syntax:

```
<code>PrefText</code>
<pre>PrefText</pre>
<tt>PrefText</tt>
```

These tags act differently, note. The `<code>` tag will insert text in a monospaced font, such as `courier`, although it will not place a line-feed after the closing tag, i.e. it will not issue a `<br>` after the `</code>` tag. This tag is therefore of use for embedding monospaced fonts within an existing (non-monospaced) sentence – perhaps to quote a computer command etc. The `<pre>` tag will also change the encapsulated text into monospaced text, but will insert a line-feed, rather like a `<br>` tag. The teletype text `<tt>` tag is analogous to the `<code>` tag.

These tags are important since they also make HTML interpret *white space* (e.g. tabs and spaces) (by default, remember, HTML ignores any white space within a document).

Main use: Inserts monospaced computerese text (`courier` font) into a sentence.

Example 1: Monospaced font embedded in a normal sentence (Figure 3.10).

```
The DOS <code>dir</code> command displays a listing of the files
in the current directory.<p>
```

The DOS `dir` command displays a listing of the files in the current directory.

Figure 3.10 Example 1 as seen through Netscape.

Example 2: Complete monospaced example for command output (DOS DIR command).

```
Here is a typical <code>DOS</code> directory listing:<p>
<pre>
c:\httpd> dir
 Volume in drive C is PC-486DX        Serial number is 2C51:16F6
 Directory of  c:\httpd\*.*
              <DIR>        7-31-94   1:16p
 ..           <DIR>        7-31-94   1:16p
CGI-DOS       <DIR>        7-31-94   1:17p
CONF          <DIR>        7-31-94   1:17p
LOGS          <DIR>        7-31-94   1:17p
SUPPORT       <DIR>        7-31-94   1:17p
```

```
hosts                 56    9-15-94 12:25p
httpd.exe        210448    6-12-94  6:24p
210,504 bytes in 2 file(s)           210,504 bytes allocated
                                  15,328,896 bytes free
</pre>
```

Netscape also supports `<code>` and `<tt>`. The default fixed pitch font you eventually use can be changed through Netscape's Options/Preferences menu.

Descriptive lists

Syntax:

```
<dl>
<dt>header-item
<dd>text-item
</dl>
```

Inserts a series of tabbed items, known as a *descriptive list*, where `<dt>` marks the heading and `<dd>` the subheading (tabbed in from the left margin accordingly). These tags are useful for lists of items, where each item has a header and a description, hence the name *descriptive list*. It is possible to include multiple `<dd>`s to include more than one line of descriptive text. The formatting is not very fancy; each description is simply tabbed to the right.

Main use: To insert a list of item descriptions.

Example 1: Simple descriptive list of Internet-related acronyms (Figure 3.11).

```
<dl>
<dt>WWW
<dd>World-Wide Web
<dt>HTTP
<dd>HyperText Transfer Protocol
<dt>HTML
<dd>HyperText Mark-up Language
</dl>
```

Example 2: Simple descriptive list with bullets.

Many descriptive lists have bullets added to them in order to enhance their appearance, as

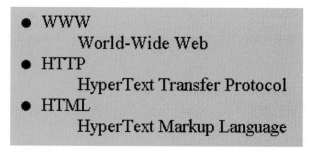

Figure 3.11 The list in Example 1 seen through Netscape.

shown in the HTML extract below using the HTML `<ul>...<li>...</ul>` (*unordered list*) tags. Figure 3.12 illustrates the final effect as seen through Netscape.

```
<ul>
 <dl>
  <dt><li>WWW
  <dd>World-Wide Web
  <dt><li>HTTP
  <dd>HyperText Transfer Protocol
  <dt><li>HTML
  <dd>HyperText Mark-up Language
 </dl>
</ul>
```

Figure 3.12 The bulleted descriptive list in Example 2 seen through Netscape.

 No major differences occur between Netscape-HTML and earlier versions of the `<dl>` tag.

Fill-out-forms

Syntax:

```
<form method="Method" action="Script">
<input type="Type" size=Size name="cName">
<input type="submit" value="ButtonText">
</form>
```

Forms (or *fill-out-forms* – FOFs) can be the most complicated area of HTML. Creating a form is simplicity in itself; the actual process handling the form data sent to it can be significantly complex. The METHOD= part of the <form> construct specifies a *posting method*. Currently, the methods POST and GET are valid. POST sends the form data as one continuous stream of data and the process (Web server script) receiving the data must do so on the standard input stream (*stdin*). The GET method simply creates an environment variable called QUERY_STRING, which holds the data instead (probably the simpler posting method), and which the server process can examine to extract the necessary form fields that the user has populated.

All forms must have an <input type> tag embedded within them that defines the type of field and its size etc. Normal text can be embedded within the form as well to include field labels to show the user what the expected input should be (see examples). In addition, an <input type> tag with a "submit" value provides a button on which the user must press in order to send the form data to the server script named in the ACTION= part of the form (without this no data can be submitted). You can include any other tags within the form in order to format the form text accordingly.

A myriad of languages can be used for form scripts (which are specified in the ACTION= part of the <form> construct), such as C (DOS/UNIX), Perl (DOS/UNIX), Icon (DOS/UNIX), DOS batch files, UNIX shell scripts and Xbase languages. Just as long as the host language can read environment variables (GET method) and/or the *standard input* stream (POST method) they can be used as form scripts. Forms are exchanged using a standard known as the Common Gateway Interface (or *CGI*). For more information on FOFs refer to my earlier book *The World-Wide Web, Mosaic and More*, which has a whole chapter devoted to this very subject, including many examples of CGI form scripts.

Main use: To allow user input via a screen form, e.g. for a credit card transaction.

▶TIP

You do not have to have an Internet connection in order to use HTML forms, since you can run a suitable Web server locally on the same computer as Netscape and then link into this to serve requests. A good Web server to start with is NCSA's *HTTPD Server*, which is itself covered in great detail within *The World-Wide Web, Mosaic and More*.

Example 1: Simple form to submit a person's name and email address.

```
<form method="GET" action="/cgi-bin/myscript.exe">
Full Name: <input type="text" name="fullname" size="40"><p>
Email Name: <input type="text" name="Emailname" size="40"><p>
<input type="submit" value="Submit data">
</form>
```

The HTML above supplies two text fields for user input. They are both named using the NAME= construct of the `<input type>` tag. Fields must have unique names so that the server script handling the form can identify each field properly (perhaps to store them in a database). Forms are also sent in an *encoded* format. Forms with a GET method are sent in the format `field1~value&field2~value`, whereas POST method forms are sent in the format `field1=value&field2=value` (note the equals signs instead of tildes). It is up to the script (here an executable DOS `.EXE` program) to parse these details in order to extract the field values. The executable program could be a program written in a scripting language such as C, Icon or Perl, or any other language that can compile a source program to a standalone executable file. In the context of our example, the form could submit an encoded string to the server as:

```
fullname~Jason+Manger&Emailname~ag17@cityscape.co.uk
```

assuming the values `Jason Manger` and `ag17@cityscape.co.uk` were entered into the two fields provided. Notice also that a plus sign (+) will replace all spaces submitted in a field; hence a name value entered into a field, such as `Jason Manger`, will get submitted to a server as `Jason+Manger`. Figure 3.13 shows how the HTML in Example 1 is marked up by Netscape (with some trial text entered into the fields).

 No major differences occur between Netscape-HTML and earlier versions of the `<form>` tag. A small difference concerns the `type="SUBMIT"` button: the text is

Figure 3.13 The resulting form area from Example 1 as viewed through Netscape.

allocated more space around the inside of the button, so it is no longer necessary to have literal spaces in the button text (i.e. a `value=" Submit "` – noting the additional leading and trailing spaces – is not required, unless you require an unusually large button).

▶TIP

A useful feature in HTML is to provide just a button to invoke an action, i.e. a form without any input fields, as with a normal form. To do this, simply create a form without any field definitions; for example:

```
<form action="http://home.netscape.com">
<input type="submit" value="Contact Netscape's Server">
</form>
```

Note that there is also no `METHOD=` entry, and that the `ACTION=` value now invokes the URL you require, here a hypertext home page.

Heading and chapter titles

Syntax:

```
<h1>Level 1 Heading</h1>
<h2>Level 2 Heading</h2>
<h3>Level 3 Heading</h3>
<h4>Level 4 Heading</h4>
<h5>Level 5 Heading</h5>
<h6>Level 6 Heading</h6>
```

Denotes a heading. Headings are numbered 1 to 6 in HTML (decreasing in size as the header number gets larger). Use headers for chapter and section headings or for titles etc. See also `<font>`.

Main use: To denote chapter and section headings (titles, section headings etc.) within an HTML document.

Example 1: Simple heading

```
<h1>Chapter 1 - Introduction to Netscape</h1>
```

Example 2: Headings embedded within a descriptive list (Figure 3.14).

```
<dl>
<dt><h2>WWW</h2>
<dd><h4>World-Wide Web</h4>
<dt><h2>HTTP</h2>
<dd><h4>HyperText Transfer Protocol</h4>
</dl>
```

No major differences occur between Netscape-HTML and earlier versions of the heading tags.

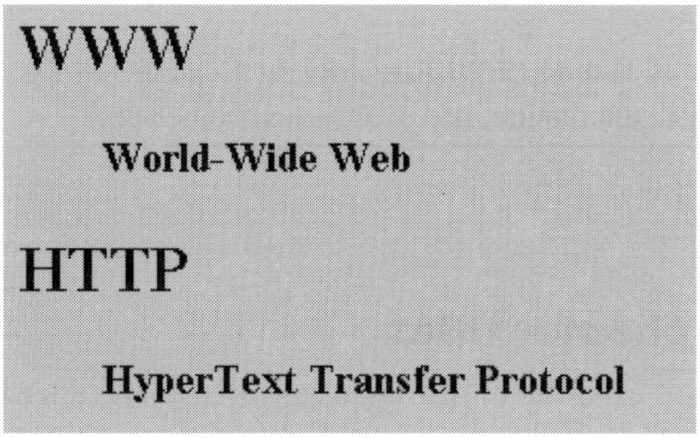

WWW

World-Wide Web

HTTP

HyperText Transfer Protocol

Figure 3.14 Example 2 as seen through Netscape.

HTML header elements

Syntax:

<head>**HeaderText**</head>

Denotes the header part of a document, where tags such as `<title>` and `<isindex>` should ideally be placed within a document. See also `<html>`, `<title>`, `<body>` and `<isindex>`.

Main use: An optional tag that makes documents conform more strictly to the HTML standard. Denotes the *header* part of an HTML document.

Example 1: Simple use of the <head> tag within an HTML document (NB: this is the advised layout).

```
<html>
  <head>
   <title>This is a screen title</title>
  </head>
 <body>
  This will be the body of the HTML file...
 </body>
</html>
```

 No major differences occur between Netscape-HTML and earlier versions of the <head> tag.

Horizontal rules

Syntax:

```
<hr>
```

Inserts a *horizontal rule* (and implied <p> paragraph break afterwards). A useful tag for breaking up text into sections and to underline headings etc.

Main use: Separating sections; dividing up parts of a document; underlining titles/headings; fancy effects.

Example 1: Simplest use of the HTML 1.0 <hr> tag.

```
<b><h1>Section 1</h1></b><hr>
```

 Netscape-HTML redefines the <hr> tag and adds some new options that can alter the appearance of horizontal rules, relating specifically to their thickness and height. The new tag keyword extensions are:

- **SIZE=n**
  Alters the vertical thickness of the horizontal rule. Valid numbers (for n) range from 1 to 100 (this is not a percentage figure, strictly speaking, since larger values will result in the same thickness of rule).

- **WIDTH=number|percentage%**

Alters the width of the rule. Figures can be expressed in a pixel size, or as a percentage relative to the document's width. A literal width value of around "970" will occupy the complete width of the screen. If too large a number is used, Netscape will carry the rule off the right-hand side of the screen. Percentages are much easier to use, since they relate to the current window size automatically. Be sure to quote the "%" sign at the end of such numbers.

■ `ALIGN=left|right|center`
This tag has been included since rules are not, by default, the width of the current Netscape screen. These new options therefore allow the rule to be pushed to the left, right or centre of the screen accordingly (UK users should note the spelling of the final option). Please note that when the `WIDTH=` option is specified and the size given is less than the screen's width, Netscape will centre the rule on the screen by default (use the `ALIGN=` option to correct this if you wish).

■ `NOSHADE`
This, when specified, simply omits the default shadow effect on horizontal rules.

Example 2: A half-screen horizontal rule aligned to the right of the Netscape screen with a vertical width of 5 units; shading enabled.

```
<h2>Introduction to Netscape
<hr align=right size=5 width=50%></h2>
```

Figure 3.15 illustrates Example 2 as rendered within Netscape.

Introduction to NetScape

Figure 3.15 Example 2 as seen in Netscape.

Example 3: Example of shaded and unshaded rules.

```
<hr width=45% size=5>
<hr width=45% size=5 noshade>
```

Figure 3.16 illustrates both the rules in Example 3 as rendered within Netscape. By default all horizontal rules are shaded, thus giving a three-dimensional impression when marked up on the screen. Horizontal rules placed using the `<hr>` tag also insert an implied carriage return (although the effect is more like an HTML `<p>` paragraph break, so if you want to underline a title using HTML's header tags, such as `<h2>` in Example 2, you may want to

Figure 3.16 Example 3 as viewed through Netscape (top: *shaded*; bottom: *unshaded*).

place the closing header tag after the horizontal rule tag to decrease the vertical space after the title and the rule.

See the section on dynamic documents for more information on the use of animated `<hr>` tags.

HTML encapsulation tags

Syntax:

`<html>`**HTML document**`</html>`

Top-level document element. Denotes that the document that follows is in the HTML format. Used to encapsulate the entire HTML document, and should ideally be the first tag used. Make use of this tag in your documents. Some Web servers have been known to serve your HTML text as plain text (i.e. displaying the literal tags) rather than HTML marked up text.

Main use: Ensuring that your text is served in the HTML format by a Web server. See also `<head>`, `<body>`.

Example 1: Simple use of the `<html>` tag

```
<html>
<head>
<title>Here is a title</title>
</head>
<body>
Here is some <i>italic</i> text. Here is some <b>bold</b> text.
</body>
</html>
```

No major differences occur between Netscape-HTML and earlier versions of the `<html>` tag.

Italic text

Syntax:

```
<i>Italic Text</i>
```

Italicizes the text **Italic Text**.

Main use: To render text into *italics*. A good effect for quotations, and to emphasize certain words.

Example 1: Simplest use of the <i> tag.

```
<i>Here is some italic text</i>
```

No major differences occur between Netscape-HTML and earlier versions of the <i> tag.

In-line images

Syntax:

```
<img
align=left|right|top|texttop|middle|absmiddle|baseline|bottom|absbottom
src="URL-Imagename"
width=w-pixel height=h-pixel
border=value
vspace=value hspace=value
alt="Text">
```

Inserts an in-line image into the current HTML document, where the name of the image is URL-Imagename, and can point to an image anywhere on the Internet (or on a local disk). The alignment is optional. Image support is an essential requirement in Netscape, to allow visual imagery to be supported within a hypertext document.

Main use: To insert an image into a hypertext document at the point specified.

The <img..> tag is probably the most heavily modified tag within Netscape. New tag elements to control the positioning of images to a much greater degree have now been implemented in HTML 2.0 and 3.0, and are detailed below. Netscape now supports both the GIF (Graphics Interchange Format) and JPEG (Joint Photographic Experts Group) image formats. The new HTML keywords LEFT and RIGHT refer to an entirely new image type known as a *floating image*. An `ALIGN=left` image will *float* downwards and over to the left margin of the screen, and any subsequent text will then wrap around to the right-hand side of the image. Similarly, an `ALIGN=right` image will also align with the right-hand margin, and any text will wrap around to the left of the image. As in previous versions of HTML, `ALIGN=top` aligns an image with the top of the (tallest) item of text within the current line. The new tag element `texttop` performs the same operation, albeit more reliably. `ALIGN=middle` aligns the top of an image to the highest element in a sentence, while the `absmiddle` centres the image to the middle of the sentence, rather than to the top of the highest element (i.e. letter) of the current sentence.

Two other new tags, `WIDTH` and `HEIGHT`, control the physical dimensions of an image. Both of these tags were introduced to speed up the loading of images over a network connection (when these tags are in use, a person viewing a document does not have to wait for an image's size to be calculated; it is simply downloaded and shown according to the `WIDTH/HEIGHT` settings specified in the tag). Note that an in-line image is measured in terms of pixel size, rather than percentages. Then we have the `BORDER=`**width** setting, which makes Netscape draw a border of width **width** pixels around the image in question. Note that an image that is also a hyperlink, i.e. an `<img src>` with an `<a href>` around it, will need a border to indicate that it is a hyperlink, so a `BORDER=0` (no visible border) would allow you to make an image into a hyperlink without the default blue hyperlink border around it, which many sites are now doing.

Then we have the keywords `VSPACE` and `HSPACE`. With floating images using the `ALIGN=left` and `ALIGN=right` tags, text flows around an image. In such cases the text will be pressed very closely to the image in question, so these options control the widths (in pixels) that separate the vertical and horizontal distances between the text and image. Finally, the `ALT=` keyword allows some *alternative* text to be used in place of an image when Netscape's *Image Loading* feature is disabled. Netscape 1.1N also introduced the ability to click on such an image in order to display it, even though image-loading is actually disabled.

If Netscape cannot read an image because it has been corrupted or damaged, a small icon resembling a torn picture is shown instead, as reproduced in Figure 3.17.

In the case that an in-line image cannot be located, the icon in Figure 3.18 is shown in place of the image (this image is also used in later illustrations as a sample in-line image).

Figure 3.17 Image corrupted/damaged icon.

Figure 3.18 Image not found icon.

Figure 3.19 Icon shown for an image when image loading is disabled.

If in-line images have been disabled, Netscape displays the icon in Figure 3.19.

Example 1: An `<img src>` tag with no alignment (embedded within a sentence).

```
Here is some <img src="picture.gif"> sample text.
```

As can be seen from Figure 3.20, an image inserted into a sentence without any alignment is simply positioned at the point specified, and the text is aligned with the bottom of the image (or the *baseline* of the image as it is often phrased in HTMLspeak – not to be confused with the lowest part of the sentence, i.e. the letter 'p', which is obtained using the `absbottom` keyword – see the later example). Note also that Example 1 also illustrates the default alignment used by Netscape when no `ALIGN=` keyword is mentioned. This is the same as the `ALIGN=baseline` setting.

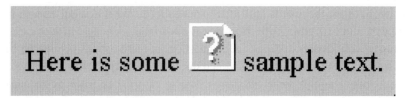

Figure 3.20 An image inserted into the middle of a sentence (Example 1).

Example 2a: An image aligned to the right.

```
Here is some <img align=right src="picture.gif"> sample text.
```

Figure 3.21 illustrates a right-aligned image. In this case the `<img src>` tag is still embedded within the sentence, although in this case Netscape *floats* the image over to the right-hand side of the screen relative to the width of the current Netscape window, and the text is kept together. Images such as these are known as *floating images*, and relate directly to the use of the `ALIGN=left` and `ALIGN=right` tag keywords. The `ALIGN=left` keyword works in the opposite way to this, aligning the image to the left of the screen.

When using floating images, be aware of the direction in which text flows around the image. `ALIGN=left` will make any resulting text flow around it to the right of the image, as

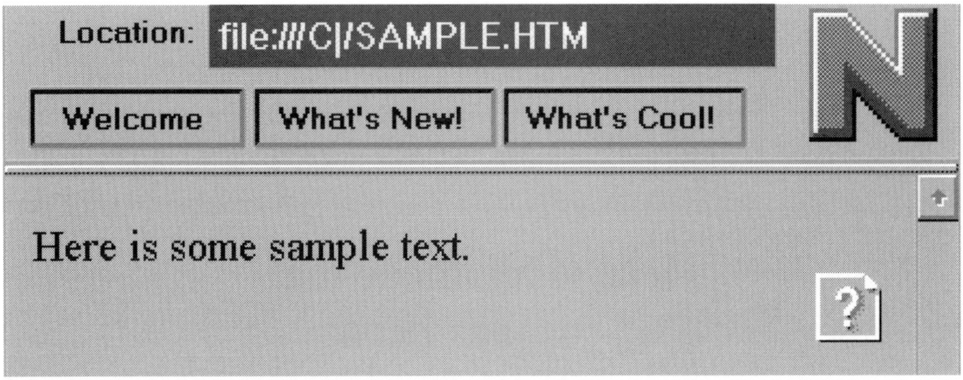

Figure 3.21 A floating image aligned to the right of the Netscape window (Example 2a).

illustrated in Example 2b and Figure 3.22. Note that the size of the sentence and the width of the Netscape window will have an effect on the text flow. In the figures shown the Netscape window has been made deliberately narrow in order to illustrate the required effect.

Example 2b: An image aligned to the left.

```
...
Here is an image <img align=left src="picture.gif"> that
has been aligned to the left of the current window.
```

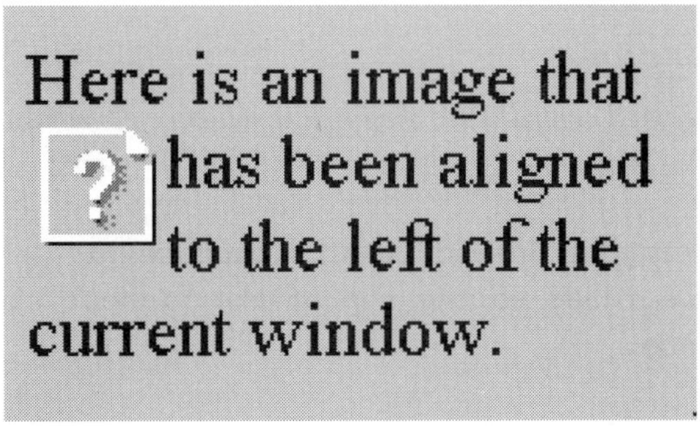

Figure 3.22 Text flowing right around a left-aligned image (Example 2b).

Likewise, text will flow to the left around a right-aligned image (the inverse of Figure 3.22). Remember to use the VSPACE and HSPACE to control the vertical and horizontal space between an image and the text that flows around it, as shown in Example 2c, which uses horizontal spacing to place a gap around the embedded image.

Example 2c: An image aligned to the left with vertical/horizontal spacing (Figure 3.23).

```
...
Here is an image <img align=left hspace=20 src="picture.gif"> that has
been aligned to the left of the current window.
```

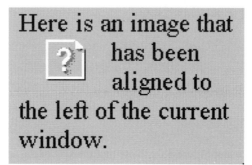

Figure 3.23 Example 2c: extended version of Example 2b (horizontal spacing of 20).

You will also have noticed that horizontal spacing works on both the left and right-hand sides of the image, so you also get a gap between the border of the left-hand side of the Netscape window, as well on the right-hand side between the first piece of text. By its very nature horizontal spacing will lessen the amount of space for the rest of the text on the same line, so some words may actually get *wrapped* (i.e. pushed over automatically) onto the next line.

Example 3a: Image aligned centrally (to the highest sentence element).

```
...
Here is some <img align=middle src="picture.gif"> sample text
that has been aligned to the top of the highest element in the
current sentence.
```

As can be seen from Figure 3.24, an ALIGN=middle keyword is slightly deceptive, in that it aligns the top of an image with the highest letter (or *element*) in the current sentence. Notice how subsequent lines after the sentence with the image embedded within it are pushed down slightly. To get over this, and in order to align an image so that it truly appears centred (i.e. the centre of the image is aligned exactly with the centre of the sentence) the ALIGN=absmiddle keyword needs to be specified, as shown in Example 3b. Note that the middle keyword aligns any resulting text in the same way as the texttop and top tags.

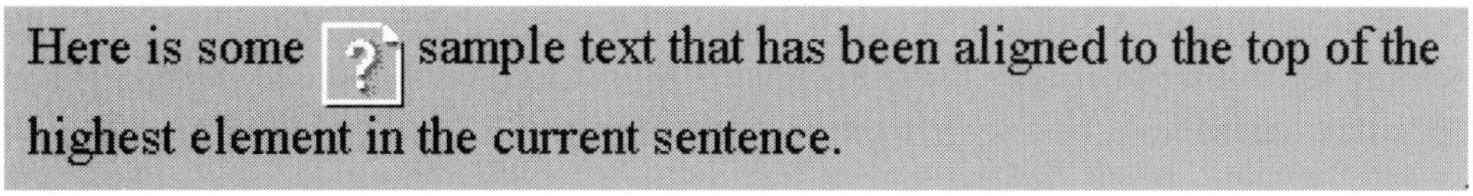

Here is some [?] sample text that has been aligned to the top of the highest element in the current sentence.

Figure 3.24 An image aligned to the top of the highest element in the sentence (Example 3a).

Example 3b: Image aligned centrally (to the exact middle of a sentence) (Figure 3.25).

```
. . .
Here is some <img align=absmiddle src="picture.gif"> sample text
that has been aligned in the middle of the current sentence.
```

Here is some [?] sample text that has been aligned to the middle of the current sentence.

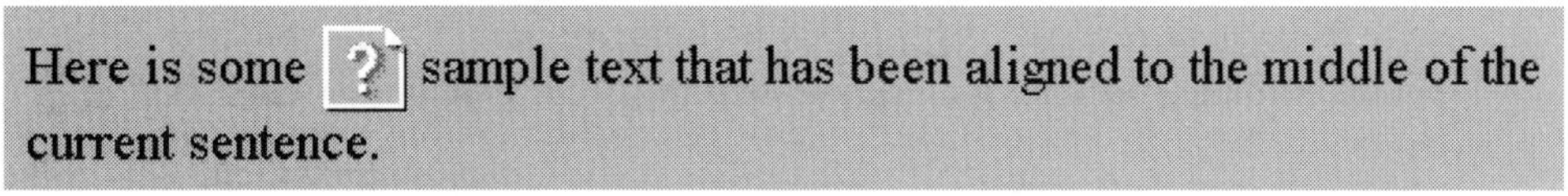

Figure 3.25 An image aligned to the exact centre of the current sentence (Example 3b).

Example 4: Image aligned to the lowest element part within a sentence (Figure 3.26).

```
. . .
Here is some <img align=absbottom src="picture.gif"> sample text
that has been aligned to the lowest element of the current
sentence.
```

Here is some [?] sample text that has been aligned to the lowest element of the current sentence.

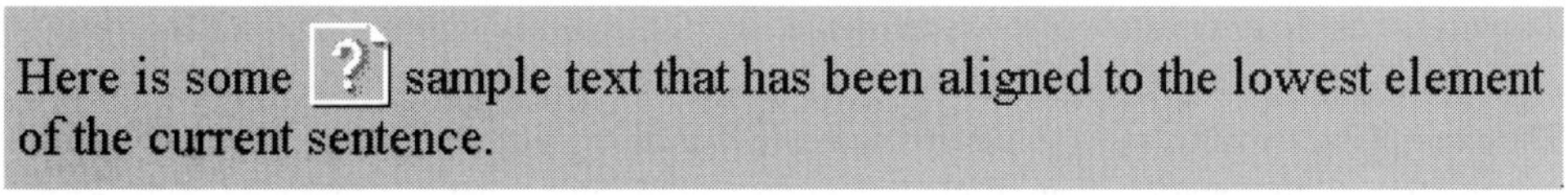

Figure 3.26 An image aligned to the lowest element of the current sentence (Example 4).

▶TIP

Netscape 1.1 introduces a new feature whereby an image can be loaded when image-loading is disabled. Simply double-click on the icon that replaces the image and the resulting image will be loaded automatically.

Although Figures 3.25 and 3.26 look very similar, they *are* different. If you look carefully you can see that the image lies lower in Figure 3.26 (in fact, even beyond the letters 'p' and 'g', which are the lowest elements in the line shown).

▶ TIP

Images are said to be the *scourge* of the Web. A site that uses large graphics in its hypertext documents is going to considerably slow down the operation of Netscape, even with all of its new image-loading capabilities. Try to keep images on the small side, and if you need a large image, try placing a *thumbnail* (a reduced version of the image) as a hyperlink, thus allowing users to call up the complete version of the picture if they require it. See Appendix D for lists of image viewing and editing software.

Small images are very effective in HTML documents when mixed with text, since they can be rendered very quickly by Netscape, and of course the user is not left waiting around for long periods of time for the page to download in its entirety.

▶ TIP

While browsing the Web, you are bound to see some icons and/or imagery that you like. In Netscape 1.1 you can use the right mouse key to bring up a menu while the mouse cursor is located over an image. In this way you can save images to your local disk, and then incorporate these in with your own Web documents. Of course, make sure first that you are not infringing copyright in the process. You will find that most images and icons remain in the *public domain*, luckily.

Example 5: Some alternative text for an image.

The example below illustrates some alternative text used in place of an image. Netscape allows you to click on the image's icon to view the underlying image that is referenced in the `<img src>` tag (Figure 3.27).

```
<img alt="Figure 1: Planet Earth" src="earth.gif">
```

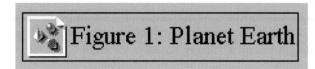

Figure 3.27 Example 5 as rendered through Netscape.

Example 6: Image alignment and line-break usage.

A problem with floating images is that line breaks can often be hard to insert. In such cases, the <br> tag (line break) should be used, along with the CLEAR= keyword. The HTML below illustrates three in-line images with left-alignment, and with text appearing to the right of the image (see Figure 3.28):

```
<! Image #1>
<a href="wwwm&m.htm"><img align="left" src="swwwm&m.gif">
The World-Wide Web, Mosaic and More</a> is my latest book offering,
which concerns publishing your own information via the Internet's
hypermedia system, the World-Wide Web (or <i>WWW</i> for
short). A wealth of information on <b>HTML</b> authoring and the
NCSA Windows <b>HTTPD</b> server are contained in this book,
along with a whole chapter on the Common Gateway Interface
(<b>CGI</b>), a standard way of interfacing HTML forms with
<i>back-end</i> programs such as third-party databases etc.<p>
<! Image #2>
<a href="eiig.htm"><img align="left" src="seiig.gif">
The Essential Internet Information Guide</a> was my first book
for McGraw-Hill Europe, and is now a best-seller (so they tell
me). The EIIG is an in-depth guide to the core Internet services
such as <b>USENET</b>, <b>FTP</b>, <b>Gopher</b> and
<b>WAIS</b>, with added chapters on two previously unpublished
Internet topics: file compression and image processing.<p>
<! Image #3>
<a href="eisk.htm"><img align="left" src="seisk.gif">
The Essential Internet Starter Kit</a> is a new Internet CD-ROM
which contains the complete text and imagery from my earlier two
Internet books, <i>The Essential Internet Information Guide</i>,
and <i>The World-Wide Web, Mosaic and More.</i> This arrives
with no less than <b>10</b> Internet tools, including a copy of
Enhanced Mosaic, the Trumpet WinSock stack, plus a selection of
viewers and HTML editors.
<! Make the line break clear past all the images>
<br clear="left">
<! This starts in the left-margin>
<h3>How to Contact McGraw-Hill<br>
<img src="line.gif"></h3>
```

The salient tag to notice is the <br clear="left"> tag, which breaks the line, making subsequent sentences start at the left margin, thus moving past the three floating images already inserted.

Figure 3.28 The hypertext page in Example 6 as rendered by Netscape.

Without the `<br clear="left">` tag, the very next line ('How to Contact McGraw-Hill...') would appear on the same line as the last sentence that is related to the final image. A `<br>` tag by itself would also yield the same effect, as would a `<p>` (paragraph break) tag.

Transparent and interlaced images

GIF (Graphics Interchange Format) image files can also arrive as *transparent* and *interlaced* images. Transparent images are those whose background colour blends in exactly with that of the browser being used to view the image. In a nutshell, transparent images look better than those images whose background does not properly blend in with the colour used by the browser. Transparent images look as if they are *floating* on the page, and they are used extensively on the Internet. In order to create a transparent image you must have access to a paint program (such as the Windows Paintbrush program, although something that saves to a native GIF would be much better), and a utility to save the image in a transparent format.

GIF images, by default, are stored in the Gif87a format, although images that have transparent backgrounds use the newer Gif89a format. A number of third-party shareware and freeware programs can save images in the Gif89a format, including *Lview Pro* and *GifTrans*. First you must create an image, or import one from another source, perhaps from an existing image file. Next you must choose a unique background colour, and alter your image accordingly. The best candidates for transparent images include those with unusual shapes, such as a text-title set in a different font, or some text with a shadow that has no apparent rectangular boundaries. Rectangular images do not really need to be made transparent, since they can be trimmed exactly to their boundaries. It is also important to ensure that the colour you use as a background is not already used elsewhere in the image, otherwise this will also appear transparent, that is to say that the background colour of the browser window will show through (of course, you may want to do this on purpose in order to achieve this very effect). It may be the case that your image already has a unique background colour (probably grey, as in most icons and thumbnail images), so there will be no need to alter the colouring. Once you have the image ready you can invoke a program such as *Lview Pro*, import the image into it (perhaps even from another format e.g. `.BMP`) and then set the background colour option to the colour you have decided to use for this purpose. *Lview Pro* will present a palette of colours that are used in the image, so be careful to pick the correct one, otherwise the image will not appear transparent. For this purpose, choose a colour that is easily identifiable, e.g. red or yellow. Saving the file in the Gif89a format completes the process, and when you come to view the image in Netscape the background will always blend in with the image, giving the appearance that it is floating on the page. You can tell a non-transparent image since its background tends to be hazy, i.e. the background colour is not solid; rather, it is hatched.

If you are using an existing image file to convert into a transparent version of the same image you may find that the background colour is not actually solid. In such cases it will not be possible to use a paint program to simply refill the background, and you will have to carefully cut around the image to remove the background colour, or cut the image out and paste it into a new document and then allocate a new background colour.

Interlaced images are also used widely on the Internet. A GIF image that is interlaced does not load immediately, but instead loads in stages, a layer at a time. Interlaced images are useful, since they can be loaded alongside document text, remembering that Netscape can load text and images in unison. An image that is not interlaced can only be loaded a portion at a time, so you will see small parts of the image rendered onto the screen as data is transmitted from the network to your computer. Interlaced images do not appear at their full resolution immediately (unlike non-interlaced images). Each layer increases the image-resolution until the complete image is downloaded. *Lview Pro* and *WinGif* are examples of tools that can interlace GIF images (see Appendix D for the exact Internet locations).

▶ TIP

The Yahoo URL database has some useful links to image-related information, especially to transparent images. Refer to the appendices for the URL of Yahoo. The Netscape home page also has some useful links to documents regarding transparent images (see the helper application hyperlinks).

Index tags

Syntax:

```
<isindex prompt="PromptText">
```

Signifies to Netscape that the current HTML document is an index document.

Main use: This tag makes an HTML file into a *search document*, providing a field within the Netscape window for a search string allowing user input. This input is encoded (as with a `<form>` tag – see earlier) and is sent to a server script. `<isindex>` documents are common where an HTML document interfaces to a search program, e.g. a veronica server or Gopher. It is mainly an alternative to a form interface, where just a single field is required. Many of the search-engines in Chapter 5 use `<isindex>` tags to interface to a database back-end. See also `<form>`.

Example 1: Basic use of the `<isindex>` tag (complete HTML file example) (Figure 3.29).

```
<html>
<head>
   <isindex>
   <title>This is a title</title>
</head>
<body>
This is an index document that provides the user with an input field.
Please enter your text into the field and press Enter when ready.
</body>
</html>
```

This is a searchable index. Enter search keywords:

This is an index document that provides the user with an input field. Please enter your text into the field and press Enter when ready.

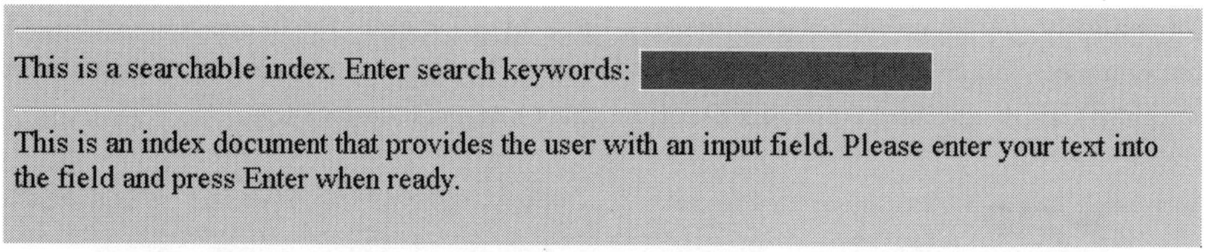

Figure 3.29 Example 1 as rendered by Netscape.

The `<isindex>` tag has changed for Netscape users. The `PROMPT=value` element has now been added allowing the user to specify some alternative text with which to prompt the user prior to the entry of a value. If a `PROMPT` keyword is not used the default text 'This is a searchable index. Enter search keywords:' will be displayed instead. Even though it is recommended that `<isindex>` is used with the `<head>...</head>` tags that denote the header part of an HTML document, the `<isindex>` tag can be placed just about anywhere to control whereabouts the field appears on the hypertext page.

Example 2: Use of the PROMPT keyword with Netscape (extract).

```
<html>
<head>
    <!---Set up header tags--->
    <isindex prompt="Please enter a book title when asked">
    <title>This is a title</title>
</head>
</html>
```

>Ordered lists

Syntax:

```
<ol type=A|a|1|I start=number>
<li type=ol|ul>Item-name
</ol>
```

Inserts an *ordered list* into a hypertext document. Ordered means numbered, to all intents and purposes.

Nested lists can also be used by embedding the appropriate tags within one another. Use as many `<li>` lines as you need for each item in your list. See also `<ul>` for unordered lists, e.g. bulleted lists.

Main use: To list sequences of items, such as indexed items (contents lists etc).

Netscape now has a `TYPE=` keyword to allow different types of list to be generated. The types are `TYPE=A` for upper-case alphabetic lists (A., B., C. ...); `TYPE=a` for lower-case alphabetic lists (a., b., c. ...) and `TYPE=1` (the default) for numbered lists (1., 2., 3. ...). Another useful list types is `TYPE=I`, which uses large Roman numerals as numbers. The new `START=` keyword allows a list to start at a specific number, for example `START=3` would start a numeric list as 3., 4., 5. etc. Of course, alphabetic lists will start at their appropriate *number* also, e.g. `START=5` in a `TYPE=A` list would start as E., F., G. etc.

Netscape has also changed the `<li>` (*list element*) tag so that it uses a `TYPE=` keyword with either the value `ol` (*ordered*) or `ul` (*unordered*). This doesn't seem to make much sense, since the effect still results in an ordered list – the only change being that a number is used instead of a letter, and vice versa. If you want to mix bullets and ordered lists, use a combination of `<ul>` and `<ol>` together.

Example 1: A simple ordered list using numbers (Figure 3.30).

```
<ol>
<li>Item 1
<li>Item 2
<li>Item 3
</ol>
```

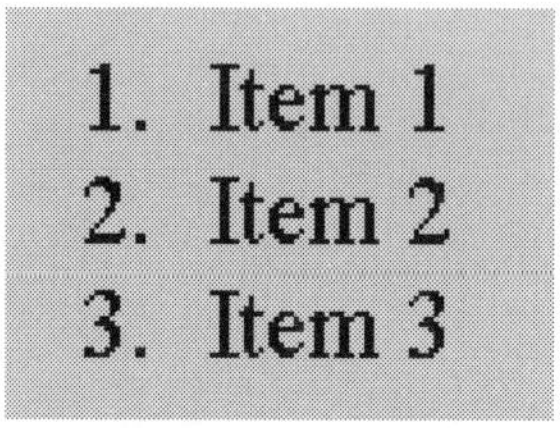

Figure 3.30 The list in Example 1 as seen through Netscape.

Example 2: An ordered list with Netscape's new `TYPE=` keyword (alphabetic list) (Figure 3.31).

```
<ol type=A>
<li>Item 1
<li>Item 2
<li>Item 3
</ol>
```

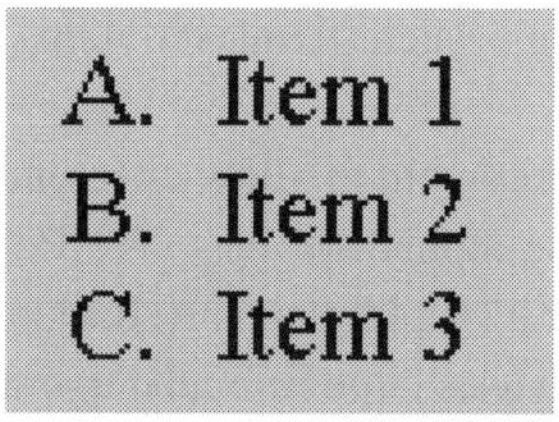

Figure 3.31 The list in Example 2 as seen through Netscape.

Paragraph breaks

Syntax 1:

```
<p align=center>ParagraphText</p>
```

Syntax 2:

ParagraphText<p>

Inserts a paragraph break at the point specified, leaving a blank line after the break before starting any new text. The first syntax description applies to the later HTML versions, as supported by Netscape, and uses two sets of tags to encapsulate a paragraph. Both syntax descriptions are valid in the Netscape browser, although to centre a complete area of text the opening and closing tag sequence will be required. Many people place the <p> tag at the start of a new paragraph, rather than at the end of the previous, which results in the same effect, but just indicates that the new paragraph starts *here*, which is a logical alternative (see examples).

Main use: To break up portions of text to make them more readable, i.e. to start a new paragraph or topic.

Example 1: A paragraph of text with centred alignment.

The example below illustrates the centring of some text on the screen. The
 (line break) tags are required, since otherwise Netscape will join all of the words together on a single line (Figure 3.32).

```
<p align=center>
This is a<br>
sample paragraph<br>
which has been centred<br>
</p>
```

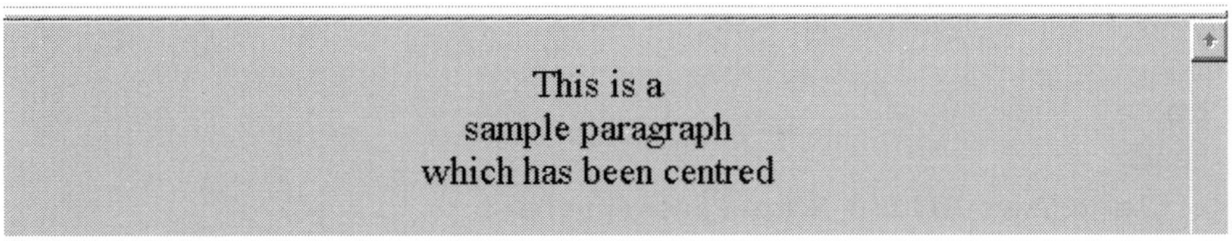

Figure 3.32 Example 1 as rendered through Netscape.

Example 2: Examples of paragraph breaks #1.

```
<p>Here is a new paragraph.
<p>Here is another.
```

Example 3: Examples of paragraph breaks #2.

```
Here is a new paragraph.<p>
Here is the start of another paragraph.
```

As described above, Netscape has introduced the ALIGN=center keyword, which makes the next piece of text after the <p align=center> centred on the line when viewed by Netscape. In addition, HTML now supports <p>...</p> pairs, which should ideally encapsulate a complete paragraph, although a <p> by itself will still suffice.

Document titles

Syntax:

```
<title>TitleText</title>
```

Inserts a title for the current hypertext document loaded into Netscape.

Main use: This is a fundamental tag, normally placed within the <head> section of an HTML document, that places a title for the current document in the title bar of the Netscape window. The title should ideally convey, as accurately as possible, the content of the current document. Every HTML document should have one <title> tag. Without a <title> tag, Netscape provides a default document title, which is simply *Netscape* by itself.

Netscape has not altered or enhanced the <title> tag from earlier HTML versions.

Example 1: A simple header in an HTML document.

```
<html>
<head>
<title>McGraw-Hill's Home Page</title>
</head>
</html>
```

Unordered lists

Syntax:

```
<ul type=disc|circle|square>
```

```
<li type=disc|circle|square>Item-name
</ul>
```

Displays an unordered list of items at the point specified.

Main use: To present an unordered list of items in bullet point fashion. See also `<ol>`.

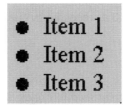 Netscape has enhanced the `<ul>` and `<li>` tags so that it is possible to specify the type of bullet through use of the new `TYPE=` keyword. Circles (black), discs (unfilled circles) and squares can now be specified using the appropriate keyword. By default, a filled circle is used as a bullet. You can mix bullet types by using the `TYPE` keyword within the main `<ul>` and `<li>` tags (see examples). Nested bullets are also possible by simply embedding further layers of `<ul>...<li>...</ul>` tags within others.

Example 1: A simple unordered list using default (round filled circle) bullets (Figure 3.33).

```
<ul>
<li>Item 1
<li>Item 2
<li>Item 3
</ul>
```

Figure 3.33 The bullets in Example 1 as rendered by Netscape.

Example 2: An unordered list using square bullets.

```
<ul>
<li type=square>Item 1
<li>Item 2
</ul>
```

Notice in Example 2 how the `TYPE=square` keyword has been used in the `<li>` tag. This alters the current bullet shape *and* all subsequent bullets, as shown in Figure 3.34.

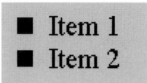

Figure 3.34 The bullets in Example 2 as rendered by Netscape.

Example 3: An unordered list using square and then circle-shaped bullets (Figure 3.35).

```
<ul type=square>
<li>Item 1
<li type=circle>Item 2
</ul>
```

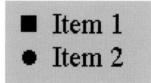

Figure 3.35 The bullets in Example 3 as rendered by Netscape.

Example 4: Nested bullets with different shapes (Figure 3.36).

```
<html>
<ul type=square>
<li>Item 1
 <ul>
   <li type=circle>Item 1.1
   <li>Item 1.2
   <li>Item 1.3
 </ul>
<li>Item 2
<li>Item 3
</ul>
</html>
```

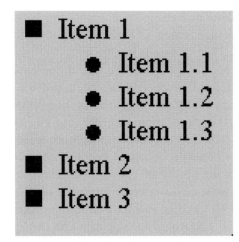

Figure 3.36 The bullets in Example 4 as rendered by Netscape.

In the example above, notice how the nested bullets (with circles) have their bullet-shape mentioned as an extension of the `<li>` tag. If you were to alter the `<ul>` tag to change the bullet shape, the first nested-bullet would be rendered without a bullet at all – a small quirk that can be overcome if you use the bullet format shown.

Table tags

Tables are a major new addition to Netscape 1.1N and are included in the draft HTML 3.0 specification.

Syntax:

```
<table cellpadding=n cellspacing=n border=n>
<tr>
 <th> Header </th>
 <td align=left|center|right rowspan=n colspan=n> Table-Item
 </td>
</tr>
<caption>CaptionText</caption>
</table>
```

The `<table>` tag looks complicated, although it is in fact very simple to use. Firstly, ensure all table tags are inserted within a `<table>` and `</table>` tag, otherwise they will be ignored. The `<tr>` tag informs Netscape that a *table row* is required; thus whenever a `<tr>...</tr>` combination is seen, all table entries within this will appear as one row (horizontally) in the table. The `<td>` and `</td>` *table definition* tags specify an item of text that will appear in one *column* of a table. So, if you have more than one pair of `<td>...</td>` tags, this will be directly equivalent to the number of columns in the table. The number of `<tr>...</tr>` tags dictates the number of rows in a table. The `<td>` tag can also align its contents using the `left`, `center` and `right` keywords.

A row can span across more than one column through use of the `ROWSPAN` keyword, thus making a larger *cell* appear within the table (see examples). A column can also be made into a larger cell through use of the `COLSPAN` keyword (see example). The optional `BORDER` keyword (by itself) makes Netscape draw a border around the table. The thickness of the border lines is determined by the `=n` specified after the `BORDER` keyword, where n is the thickness in pixels. A column can also have a heading using the `<th>` (*table heading*) tag.

A cell can have *padding*, i.e. space made around it by using the `CELLPADDING` and `CELLSPACING` keywords, both of which take values representing the number of pixels to use as spacing. The `CELLPADDING` keyword specifies the spacing around the actual items within cells, i.e. the data within the `<td>...</td>` definitions, while the `CELLSPACING` keyword specifies the amount of space required between a cell structure itself and the table's border. Refer to the example illustrations for comparisons. The `<caption>`**CaptionText**`</caption>` tags allow some text to describe the table to be included.

Main use: To insert a table structure into a hypertext document. It is possible to have images, forms and backgrounds within a table cell – see the various examples.

Example 1: A simple 3×2 (3 col × 2 row) table with a default border.

```
<table border>
<tr>
 <td>Item 1</td> <td>Item 2</td> <td>Item 3</td>
</tr>
        <tr>
 <td>Item 4</td> <td>Item 5</td> <td>Item 6</td>
</tr>
</table>
```

In this table example, we can see that there are two sets of `<tr>...</tr>` tags, and thus the table has two rows. There are six items in the table, identifiable by the fact that there are six sets of `<td>...</td>` tags. The table has three columns because there are three sets of `<td>...</td>` tags within a `<tr>...</tr>` pair. The table will also have a border drawn around it (all such borders separate the internal cells as well) (Figure 3.37).

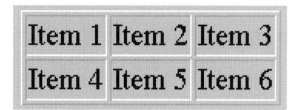

Figure 3.37 The table in Example 1.

Example 2: A table using a ROWSPAN to make one larger cell that spans two rows (Figure 3.38).

```
<table border>
<tr>
  <td>Item 1</td>
 <td rowspan=2>Item 2</td>
 <td>Item 3</td>
</tr>
<tr>
 <td>Item 4</td> <td>Item 5</td>
</tr>
</table>
```

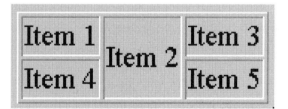

Figure 3.38 The table in Example 2.

Example 3: A table using a COLSPAN to make one larger cell that spans two columns (Figure 3.39).

```
<table border>
<tr>
 <td>Item 1</td>
 <td colspan=2>Item 2</td>
```

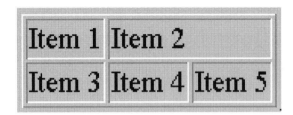

Figure 3.39 The table in Example 3.

```
        </tr>
        <tr>
                <td>Item 3</td> <td>Item 4</td> <td>Item 5</td>
        </tr>
        </table>
```

Example 4: A simple table with normal column headings (Figure 3.40).

```
        <table border>
        <tr>
                <th>Head1</th> <th>Head2</th> <th>Head3</th>
                </tr>
                <tr>
                 <td>A</td> <td>B</td> <td>C</td>
                </tr>
                <tr>
                 <td>D</td> <td>E</td> <td>F</td>
        </tr>
        </table>
```

Head1	Head2	Head3
A	B	C
D	E	F

Figure 3.40 The table in Example 4.

Example 5: A table with two COLSPAN headings in a four column table (Figure 3.41).

```
<table border>
<tr>
 <th colspan=2>Head1</th>
 <th colspan=2>Head2</th>
</tr>
<tr>
 <td>A</td> <td>B</td> <td>C</td> <td>D</td>
</tr>
<tr>
 <td>E</td> <td>F</td> <td>G</td> <td>H</td>
</tr>
</table>
```

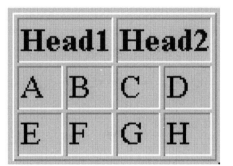

Figure 3.41 The table in Example 5.

Example 6: A table with just row headings (Figure 3.42).

```
<table border>
 <tr><th>Head1</th>
  <td>Item 1</td> <td>Item 2</td> <td>Item 3</td>
 </tr>
<tr><th>Head2</th>
 <td>Item 4</td> <td>Item 5</td> <td>Item 6</td>
</tr>
<tr><th>Head3</th>
 <td>Item 7</td> <td>Item 8</td> <td>Item 9</td>
</tr>
</table>
```

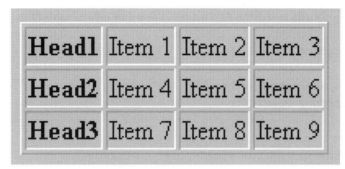

Figure 3.42 The table in Example 6.

Example 7: A table with an image embedded within a cell (Figure 3.43).

```
<table border>
<tr>
 <td>Cell 1</td> <td>Cell 2</td> <td><img src="n.gif"></td>
</tr>
<tr>
 <td>Cell 4</td> <td>Cell 5</td> <td>Cell 6</td>
</tr>
</table>
```

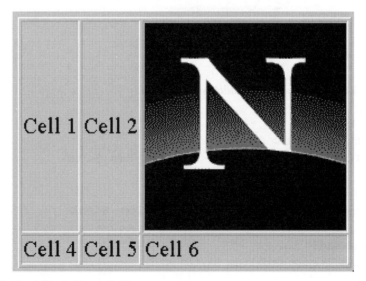

Figure 3.43 The table in Example 7.

In Example 7 an `<img src>` tag has been used to place an image within a table cell. Notice how the image tag is placed within the `<td>...</td>` pair, rather than outside it. The image is a GIF file named `n.gif`, which in this example is a copy of the Netscape logo.

Images are automatically fitted within a cell's dimensions by Netscape, so no special alignment is required in a table such as this. The size of a column can be dictated by a header tag, as in *Example 4* shown earlier, so if the text in a heading makes a cell's width larger than an image, simply use the `ALIGN=` keyword of the `<td>` tag (and not the `<img src>` tag). Figure 3.43 illustrates an image aligned to the centre of a cell. By default Netscape will align the image to the left and will make the depth of the cell equal to the depth of the image. Netscape will also honour spaces in-between `<td>` definitions – a good habit to adopt is to place a leading and trailing space after your cell contents and headings to move them slightly away from the border, making them more readable. Alternatively, use the `CELLPADDING/CELL-SPACING` keywords (discussed below).

The line of HTML that has been altered in the previous example to centre the image in Figure 3.44 is now:

```
<td>A</td> <td>B</td> <td align=center><img src="newn.gif"></td>
```

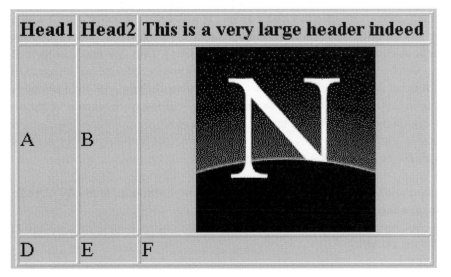

Figure 3.44 An image centred within a cell wider than the image itself.

Example 8: A table with a hyperlink entry within it.

A hyperlink using the `<a href>` tag could also be embedded within a table entry. So, for example, we could have the following single HTML table definition defined as:

```
<td><a href="myfile.htm">Load my file</a></td>
```

The `<a href>` tag in the above line makes the text *Load my file* into a hyperlink, i.e. a clickable region, which in this case loads another hypertext file (the `http://` prefix can be omitted for local hypertext files, since the HTTP protocol is not required to fetch a remote document on the Internet). Note also that the hypertext file referenced here is assumed by Netscape to exist in the current directory, i.e. the same directory from within which Netscape was run in this case (since no initial directory has been mentioned). If you need to load local files in another directory, use the URL syntax: `file:///C|/directory/filename.htm`, which uses the `file://` prefix – a notation used to specify local files.

Example 9: A table with a hyperlinked image within it.

In order to make a complete cell into a hot-spot you must first fill the cell contents with an in-line image using the HTML `<img src>` tag, for example:

```
<td><a href="myfile.htm"><img src="n.gif"></a></td>
```

When Netscape parses the above line it will place a clickable image inside the cell specified. An `<img src>` with an `<a href>` around it will make the image appear with a blue border (by default), which is the standard colour for a hyperlink (unless the hyperlink colour is changed using the `<body..>` tag (see later). Thus, the inside of the cell wall appears to have a blue border, and the entire cell becomes a clickable *hot-region* in its own right. It is not (yet) possible to make a cell wall into a clickable region in any other way apart from this method, since the `<a href>` tag will not work when it encapsulates a `<td>` tag (in Netscape 1.1b1, at least).

Example 10: An example of a nested table.

Tables can also be *nested* within one another, simply by inserting the necessary `<table>` tag definition within another `<td>` entry, for example:

```
<table border>
 <tr>
   <td>Cell 1</td>
   <td>Cell 2</td>
   <! Here is the nested table entry within Cell-3>
   <td>Cell 3
    <table border>
     <tr>
       <td>Cell 3a</td>
```

```
      <td>Cell 3b</td>
     </tr>
     <tr>
      <td>Cell 3c</td>
      <td>Cell 3d</td>
     </tr>
    </table>
   <! End of nested table>
   </td>
  </tr>
 </table>
```

The table above looks complicated at first, although it has only one main row, signified by the single `<tr>` entry that encapsulates all of the other (nested) table tags. Three columns are contained in the table – notice the three main `<td>` entries at the *highest* level. Only the last cell (Cell 3) is structured differently in that it has an additional `<table..>` tag. This additional table definition sets up a nested table within Cell 3 that has a further four cells in a 2 × 2 structure (Cells 3a, 3b, 3c and 3d respectively). Figure 3.45 shows this table as rendered by Netscape.

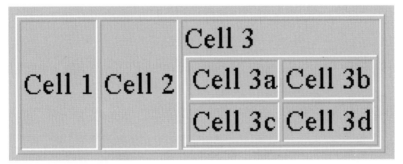

Figure 3.45 The table in Example 10 as rendered by Netscape.

Example 11: Examples of cell spacing within tables.

Cell spacing is controlled using the CELLPADDING and CELLSPACING keywords. Figure 3.46 illustrates a simple nested table with a CELLPADDING setting of 10, while the right-hand table has a CELLSPACING value of 10 (the affected table is shown in white). As can be seen, cell padding controls the space around the items within `<td>` tags, while cell spacing controls the space around individual cells relative to the main table border.

For completeness, here is the HTML for both of the tables in Figure 3.46.

Table 1:

```
<table border>
<tr>
 <td>Cell 1</td>
 <td>Cell 2</td>
 <td>Cell 3
   <table border cellpadding=10>
    <tr>
     <td>Cell 3a</td>
     <td>Cell 3b</td>
     </tr>
    <tr>
     <td>Cell 3c</td>
     <td>Cell 3d</td>
    </tr>
   </table>
 </td>
</tr>
</table>
```

Table 2:

```
<table border>
<tr>
 <td>Cell 1</td>
 <td>Cell 2</td>
 <td>Cell 3
   <table border cellspacing=10>
    <tr>
     <td>Cell 3a</td>
     <td>Cell 3b</td>
     </tr>
    <tr>
     <td>Cell 3c</td>
     <td>Cell 3d</td>
    </tr>
   </table>
 </td>
</tr>
</table>
```

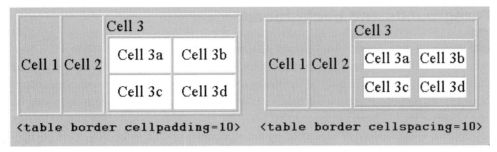

Figure 3.46 Cell padding and cell spacing demonstrated (nested tables in white).

Example 12: Table with a caption.

Captions are small annotations that accompany a table, e.g. a small textual description. The caption will appear at the top of the table and will be centred relative to the width of the table. You can include other HTML tags within the `<caption>...</caption>` tags, e.g. bold and italic effects – in fact, just about anything. The caption tags themselves can appear anywhere within the `<table>...</table>` definition, although it makes sense to place them at the very top or bottom to aid readability. The example below illustrates a table with a caption (Figure 3.47).

```
<table border>
<tr>
<td>Item 1</td> <td>Item 2</td> <td>Item 3</td>
</tr>
<tr>
<td>Item 4</td> <td>Item 5</td> <td>Item 6</td>
</tr>
<caption><i>Example Table 12</i></caption>
</table>
```

Example Table 12

| Item 1 | Item 2 | Item 3 |
| Item 4 | Item 5 | Item 6 |

Figure 3.47 The table in Example 12.

Foregrounds and backgrounds

Netscape also supports background patterns and foreground colour schemes for Web documents, and both of these features have been included in Netscape 1.1. These work in the same way as Windows when it *tiles* a bitmap file (or *wallpaper*) on your screen's desktop. Netscape can also alter foreground colours so that these show up over the background properly. The <body> tag has been enhanced in HTML 3.0 to include these new capabilities. Images are dithered when loaded, so depending on the capabilities of your video driver images may not appear exactly as viewed in other image-viewing packages. The <body> tag's extended syntax in Netscape is now:

Syntax:

```
<body background="ImageFile"
bgcolor="#rrggbb"
text="#rrggbb"
link="#rrggbb"
vlink="#rrggbb"
alink=#rrggbb">
```

The BACKGROUND= tag specifies a name for an image that will be used to tile the Netscape document area. An image can be stored in the GIF or JPEG formats (JPEG take slightly longer to import since they are, by default, compressed). The BGCOLOR= is a Netscape specific feature (not yet in HTML 3.0) and is used to control the screen's background colour without the need to fetch a file, i.e. the colour is solid, rather than a patterned bitmap. All colour codes are specified using the form #rrggbb, where rr is the proportion of colour used (rr – Red, gg – Green, and bb – Blue. Values range from 0 to 255, and are specified as hexadecimal – the lowest value being 0 and highest FF (hex), or 255 decimal. For example, black is #000000, blue is #0000FF and yellow is #FFFF00 – see Table 3.1 for a list of further examples.

Use the TEXT keyword to refer to the colour of the normal body text within a hypertext document. LINK specifies a normal hyperlink (unselected), VLINK a visited link, i.e. one already clicked on and saved in your netscape.hst (URL history file), and ALINK is an active link, i.e. a link colour as it is being processed by Netscape. Background patterns only last while you remain in the *same* document with the <body> tag that originally set the background. As soon as you move to a new document (by clicking on a hyperlink for example), the background will alter accordingly, and vice versa.

Main use: To control screen colours and patterns and make the document more attractive to the end user.

Example 1: A solid background: blue BGCOLOR (solid) with yellow TEXT (100% red and green).

```
<body bgcolor="#0000FF" text="#FFFF00">
```

Example 2: Example of a background pattern in Netscape (extract) with yellow text.

```
<body background="embossed.gif" text="#FFFF00">
```

Example 3: Example of a background loaded from Netscape's Web server.

Once your own Web documents are on the Internet at a suitable server, you may refer to any valid background image file that resides on the Internet. Netscape's Web server has a *background sampler* directory with many dozens of patterns for use as backgrounds. Here is an example of one that loads a grey fabric background (Figure 3.48):

```
<body background="http://home.netscape.com/home/bg/fabric/gray_fabric.gif">
```

▶TIP

A background image loaded in a document using the `<body back-ground...>` tag will not be shown if you disable image loading within Netscape. This helps to speed document loading significantly, although you will of course not see any other images that arrive using the `<img src...>` tag.

Hexadecimal colour codes can be difficult to remember, so Table 3.1 lists the most popular colour codes for use in your hypertext documents. Refer to the *Hex Code* column to see the

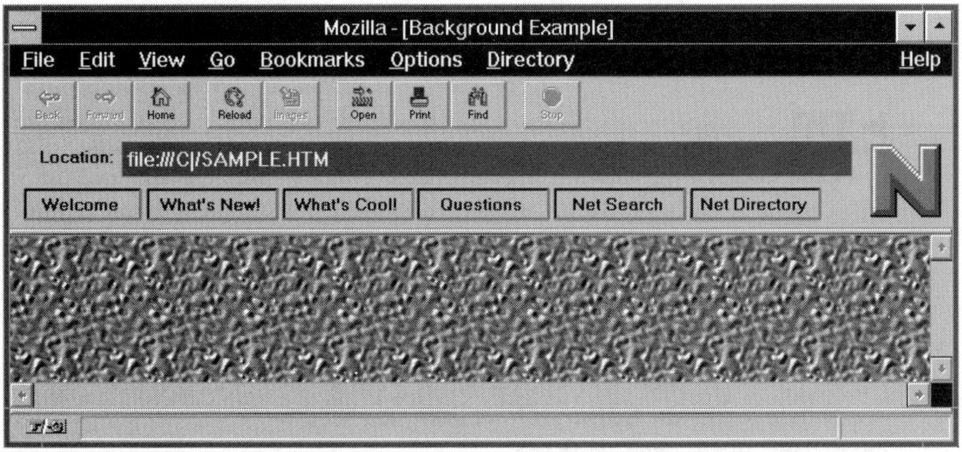

Figure 3.48 The background pattern (only) in Example 3 as seen through Netscape.

Table 3.1 Hexadecimal colour codes for use in the `<body..>` tag.

Red	Green	Blue	Hex Code	Colour Description
191	000	000	#BF0000	Red (Dark)
255	000	000	#FF0000	Red
191	191	000	#BFBF00	Yellow (Dark)
255	255	000	#FFFF00	Yellow
000	191	000	#00BF00	Green (Dark)
000	255	000	#00FF00	Green
000	191	191	#00BFBF	Blue (Medium)
000	255	255	#00FFFF	Blue (Bright)
000	000	191	#0000BF	Blue (Dark)
000	000	255	#0000FF	Blue
191	000	191	#BF00BF	Magenta (Dark)
255	000	255	#FF00FF	Magenta
128	128	128	#808080	Grey (Dark)
192	192	192	#C0C0C0	Grey
000	000	000	#000000	Black
255	255	255	#FFFFFF	White

code required for a particular colour (the *Red*, *Green* and *Blue* columns show the relative amounts of each colour to obtain the final colour effect rendered by Netscape).

▶ TIP

You can dazzle the reader by placing multiple `bgcolor="#RRGGBB"` tags into your document, each with a different colour. The result will be a screen that changes colour rapidly – good for an introductory sequence to your page, perhaps.

▶ TIP

Using the `<body>` tag with the 'background' keyword to load a background image can delay matters while the image is being fetched. Therefore it is a good idea to precede such `<body>` tags with a `<title>` tag informing the user of the short delay that is about to happen; for example:

```
<html>
<title>Loading page and background. Please wait ...</title>
<body background="back.gif" vlink="#FFFF00">
<title>My Home Page</title>
...
```

This will allow users to see a message informing them of the delay caused while the background image is being loaded. The main page title can then be shown accordingly, as illustrated in the small HTML excerpt above.

▶TIP

When specifying background images using the BACKGROUND keyword, it is recommended that you also specify a background colour using the BGCOLOR keyword at the same time as well. This colour should be as similar as possible to the colour of the background image. In the case that the person viewing your page has Netscape's image loading feature disabled, or is unable to load your background image, the page will still resemble the original effect you intended to provide.

Font control

The HTML dialect used by Netscape 1.1 also introduces changes that allow font size selection. Netscape can now display characters in a variety of different sizes. Two main font tags have been provided to facilitate this, namely `<font size=size>` and `<basefont size=size>` both of which are described in detail below.

Basic font size control tags

Syntax:

```
<font size=+size>
```

Changes the size of a font within the current hypertext document. Font sizes range from 1 to 7 (smallest to largest), and can be prefixed with an optional **+** or **–** sign, which changes the size of the font *relative* to the current *base font* size. The default base font size is set using the `<basefont size=size>` tag (see below).

Main use: As a text enhancement feature, and to improve text readability (see examples).

Example 1: Changing the sizes of characters at the beginning of each word (Figure 3.49).

```
<font size="+4">F</font><font size="+2">ont sizes can be
changed</font>
```

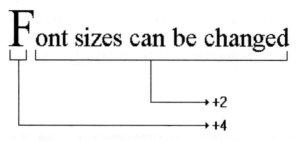

Figure 3.49 The result of Example 1 as shown in Netscape (with size annotations).

Changing the base font size

Syntax:

```
<basefont size=size>
```

Changes the default font size (the default font being the font used for the main text in your hypertext documents. The default is 3 and all `<font...>` tags used after this with the **+/–** characters will be sized *relative* to this base font setting. There is always a default base font in place, with a value of 3.

Base font sizes also range from 1 (smallest font) to 7 (largest font). The base font setting will also dictate the number of font sizes that you can use since Netscape only has seven font sizes, all of which are relative to the current base font; i.e. selecting a base font of 4 means that you effectively have access to only three larger font sizes.

Main use: To change the default size of all body text within a hypertext document.

Example 1: A simple comparison of font sizes with base font set to 1 (Figure 3.50).

```
<basefont size=1>
Default,
<font size="+1">1</font>,
<font size="+2">2</font>,
<font size="+3">3</font>,
<font size="+4">4</font>,
<font size="+5">5</font>,
<font size="+6">6</font>,
<font size="+7">7</font>
```

Default, 1, 2, 3, 4, 5, 6, 7

Figure 3.50 The marked-up version of Example 1.

Line centring

Netscape can now centre (horizontally) lines of text, images and tables using a dedicated centring tag.

Syntax:

```
<center>CenteredText</center>
```

Main use: To centre a portion of text on the current line within the dimensions of the current window.

The text may run onto more than one line just as long as you include a line break (`<br>` tag) in the appropriate place (UK users: note the spelling of `center`). The `<center>` tag can also be used to centre other objects, such as tables and in-line images, when the tag encapsulates the object in question.

Example 1: A simple example showing the centring of a text portion.

```
<center>This text will be centred</center>
```

Example 2: Centring two lines of text.

```
<center>Both of these lines<br>
will be centred.
</center>
```

In Example 2, the `<br>` (line break) tag has been used to break the line after the word *lines*. Remember that HTML ignores any white space, so without the `<br>` tag all of the text would appear on just a single line.

Example 3: Centring an in-line image.

```
<center><img src="image.gif"></center>
```

Blinking text

Another new tag found in Netscape allows text to blink on and off. This can be a useful visual effect in order to catch the user's attention. The blinking effect is slow, occurring approximately once a second, and does not start until the document has been loaded (or interrupted).

Syntax:

```
<blink>BlinkText</blink>
```

Makes the text **BlinkText** flash on and off. Any text can be made to blink in this way, although images, forms and other such objects cannot share this effect.

Main use: Visual effects, e.g. urgent messages, or messages required to 'catch the user's eye'.

Example 1: Simple use of the <blink> tag with some text.

```
<blink>
 Urgent Message! - This site has moved to:
 <a href="http://www.newsite.com">here</a>
</blink>
```

Embedding file objects within a hypertext document (MS Windows)

Netscape 1.1N for Microsoft Windows has a non-standard <embed> tag that allows a file to be embedded within the current hypertext document, just as long as an external image viewer (or helper application) is available for that particular file format. If the embedded file is not a bitmap and cannot be rendered directly onto the page, Netscape inserts an icon for the file to allow it to be loaded. This facility uses Windows' OLE (Object Linking and Embedding) capability.

Syntax:

```
<embed src="FileName" width=x height=y>
```

Embeds an image (or other file) into the current document, and optionally scales the size of the file. The embedded file can be double-clicked on to call up the helper application associated with that file format, as specified in Netscape. All icons are taken from the helper application itself. The WIDTH and HEIGHT specify an alternative size for a bitmap image (both measured in pixel units).

Main use: To embed files as clickable objects within the current hypertext document, and to make these files available without first having to load them into Netscape.

Example 1: Embedding a Windows bitmap file (.BMP) literally on the hypertext page as an object.

```
<embed src="demofile.bmp">
```

This <embed> tag simply places the file demofile.bmp on the hypertext page, rather like an <img src> in-line image tag with a GIF or JPEG file. This capability is useful, since Netscape can now deal with a wider range of image formats (depending on whether or not a suitable viewer is installed).

Example 2: Embedding a Windows Write (.WRI) file within a hypertext page (Figure 3.51).

```
Here is an embedded <i>Write</i> file: <embed src="test.wri">
```

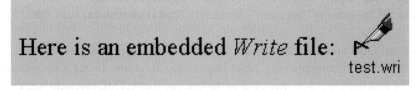

Figure 3.51 Example 2 as rendered by Netscape.

▶**TIP**

After creating your Web pages, why not publicize them via the Internet? The *Submit It!* service interfaces to the registration screens of the main Web URL databases, Web Robots and other Web Crawlers. The URL you need is simply:

http://www.cen.uiuc.edu/~banister/submit-it

Now watch that hit-count soar! See Chapter 5 for more information.

3.4 **Creating dynamic documents**

Netscape have proposed a new tag for HTML 3.0 called the `<meta>` tag, which allows for the creation of *dynamic* hypertext documents. An open standard known as *client pull and server push* has been implemented which allows documents to be automatically updated. *Client pull* is by far the easiest technique to use, since it can be demonstrated through Netscape, and requires no server-end programming. With client pull, the Netscape browser updates the current document at a regular interval, re-loading it in its entirety. Real-time data such as financial data and weather information (data that constantly changes) can thus be fetched from a server automatically without the need for you to press the *Reload* button.

In *server push* an HTTP connection is kept open for an indefinite amount of time, either until the server has finished sending its data to the client, or until the client interrupts the connection, whichever happens first. In contrast, *client pull* connections are never kept open. Instead the client is specifically told when to open a new network connection, and what URL to load when it does. The *server push* technique is achieved by using a variant of the MIME (Multimedia Internet Mail Extensions) format named `multipart/mixed`, which allows a single data transmission to contain many individual items of data.

Syntaxes:

```
<meta http-equiv="Refresh" content=UpdateSeconds>
<meta http-equiv="Refresh" content="UpdateSeconds; url=URL">
```

NB: Note the case of the word `Refresh`, the first letter of which must be capitalized. Quotes are optional in the first syntax only. More importantly, the `<meta>` tag must appear on the *first* line of your hypertext document, unless the first line is an HTML comment (i.e. a `<!...>` tag).

Main use: To allow dynamic document updating, document-chaining, dynamic image updates.

Client pull

In the first form of the `<meta>` syntax, a document can be *refreshed* after a predetermined number of seconds, as set by the numeric **UpdateSeconds** value. This is known as a *client pull*, since the client (Netscape) is pulling data from the network, i.e. from a Web server. You could use this feature to provide a document update service. The **UpdateSeconds** value can in fact be set to zero (0), in which case the document will be reloaded as quickly as possible, i.e. immediately after the document has been retrieved from the network.

Once a document is being continuously loaded, it can be hard to stop it. The *Stop* button and ESCAPE key will stop the reloading, although if the document being loaded is very small you may not get the chance to click on the *Stop* button since it only activates when the document is loading. Keeping the ESCAPE key pressed down a for a couple of seconds, or longer, will normally stop the document from being reloaded. The only other way of stopping a document from continuously loading is to load a new screen, i.e. a new URL which does not contain the `<meta>` tag entry that is carrying out the reload operation. If you have caching enabled, even a very large document will load slowly the first time around, although on all subsequent occasions it will seem to load much faster. One approach to allow the user to exit the page is to place a hyperlink in the document for a new URL to be loaded in order to stop the page reloading.

▶TIP

As an introduction to a home page, you could load a successive series of screens to display a simple animation. If you intend to do this, keep the images small and make them non-interlaced so that they load in one pass. See the `<meta>` examples given below.

Example 1: Loading the current document continuously.

```
<meta http-equiv="Refresh" content="3">
This document will be re-loaded every 3 seconds<br>
```

In this example, the current hypertext document is reloaded every three seconds. Press the ESCAPE key and hold it down a for a few seconds in order to stop the page, or place an `<a href..>` hyperlink to load a new page (URL), which will also stop the document from reloading.

Example 2: Loading the current document continuously with stop button.

```
<meta http-equiv="Refresh" content="3">
```

This document will be re-loaded every 3 seconds<hr>

```
<a href="index.htm">Stop and return to Home page</a>
```

This example assumes that the file `index.htm` exists, although any valid filename could be used, just as long as it takes you somewhere meaningful. A blank page, for example, would stop the document from reloading, although it would also confuse the user. Try to make your dynamic pages subordinate to an earlier home page, so that you can provide a hyperlink to take you back to that page. Alternatively, you can use the URL= keyword (second syntax) of the `<meta>` tag to invoke a different URL automatically, as Example 3 illustrates.

Example 3: Document reloading via file chaining.

The `<meta>` tag also has a `URL=` keyword which allows the current hypertext document to invoke a new uniform resource locator after a specified period. Documents can thus be *chained* together, facilitating visual effects such as simple animation, and of course to stop automatic reloading of documents (in the case of the latter, the final document called would not have a `<meta>` tag, and would thus not reload itself, or another document). In the hypothetical example below, assume that there are three separate hypertext documents called `file1.htm`, `file2.htm` and `file3.htm`. In the example the first file will call the second, and the second will call the third file, which in turn will stop the reload operation. This is made possible because the third file does not have a `<meta>` tag.

The HTML for `file1.htm` resembles:

```
<! file1.htm>
<meta http-equiv="Refresh" content="5; url=file2.htm">
This document will call file2.htm in five seconds...
```

And `file2.htm` resembles:

```
<! file2.htm>
<meta http-equiv="Refresh" content="5; url=file3.htm">
This document will call file3.htm in five seconds...
```

Lastly, `file3.htm` (the non-meta file) resembles:

```
<! file3.htm>
Document 3: Re-loading now stopped.
```

Type in and save these files, and load `file1.htm` into Netscape. As soon as the document is loaded and five seconds expire, the second document will be loaded. As soon as another five seconds have expired the final document is loaded and the process is completed. Of course, you could *cycle* pages automatically by making the final file call the first, thus setting up a simple *loop*. Cycling pages are useful for small news items, such as those shown on television-based teletext services, although there are other effects you can create. Since you can now load multiple documents, you could embed an `<img src>` tag into each file to load a small image and effect a simple animation (assuming each image was slightly different). Images can be slow to load (until a duplicate that has been cached is called), so make them as small as possible to achieve the best effects. You can of course animate other objects, such as table structures – try creating a series of files with `<table>` tags that alter the cell-padding sizes in order to expand and contract the table's dimensions.

Client pull has the disadvantage that multiple network connections need to be opened. Server push does not have this drawback, since it keeps open a single connection, and then uses this to transmit multiple items of data, e.g. images, hypertext chunks and audio files. Another major advantage is that the server is in complete control, and you have much more control over *what* data is sent from the server because you can interface to the server using a variety of programming languages, using a standard known as the Common Gateway Interface (or CGI). With a CGI program in operation, you can make your hypertext documents interface to databases and other stores of data, and then have the server push whatever is required to the client at the other end of the network connection.

Server push

Server push is a slightly more difficult technique to use, since it requires some programming (or *scripting* as it is often referred to), plus some knowledge of Web server software. You will also have to learn about the Common Gateway Interface (CGI) – a standard way of interfacing Web servers with third-party programs, or *scripts* as they are known. You can experiment with server push techniques on your own local machine without an Internet connection by obtaining a suitable Web server program, such as the NCSA Windows HTTPD server (see Appendix C for its FTP location on the Internet). If you install this software and have access to a language such as C or Icon (both are freely available in the public domain in one form or another on the Internet, e.g. through the GNU free software foundation archives) you can run a Web server and client (Netscape) on one machine, thus simulating both sides of an Internet connection. This will allow you to use some server push techniques with Netscape as the client program. Programmers will want to read the sections below; the topic of CGI and scripting is covered in great depth in my earlier book, *The World-Wide Web, Mosaic and More.*

The program below has been coded in the language Icon (which is not unlike the C programming language, and which should be understood by even the most novice of programmers. Indeed, C can be used if you have access to a suitable compiler and linker). Icon can be found at the FTP site `cs.arizona.edu` in the `/icon` directory, and is available for the DOS (PC) and UNIX platforms. The program in the example is serving three individual files to the client (Netscape) – hence the name server push, i.e. it is *pushing* the file(s) to the client in a *controlled* way, control being the key word here, since a program is dictating what data is actually being sent and when. Server push requests can also be interrupted very easily, simply by pressing the *Stop* button on the Netscape toolbar (or of course by pressing the ESCAPE key).

Each object of data has an associated MIME header – this the `Content-type:` line – which is followed by the MIME subtype code, e.g. `text/html` for HTML formatted (tagged), or `image/gif` for a GIF image. MIME is used by HTTP to encapsulate the data returned from a Web server in response to a client request. In nearly all cases an HTTP response consists of just a single item of data; however, MIME can deal with multiple items. A *boundary marker* is used to break up each segment of data, such as an image or hypertext file, as set in the `boundary=` keyword in the first `Content-type:` line. Notice the conventions used for boundary markers between data segments. Each segment is encapsulated with a marker starting with two hyphens (– –) – a *segment id* – whereas the very last marker has two hyphens at both the start and end in order to mark the end of the entire segment (an *end-of-segment id*). The first content-type line uses a special MIME type known as `multipart/x-mixed-replace` (a variant of the MIME type `multipart/mixed` which allows a single HTTP response to contain a collection of data items, or *segments*). The important concept to bear in mind is that the most recent data item replaces the previous one, so you do not receive multiple pages (as in client pull) and the updates tend to happen much more rapidly.

Example 1: Simple server push program to animate some text.

Program overview: the `write()` functions in the program simply output a line of text; the #s are comments, and the \ns are *newline* codes, which generate a blank line. The program shown here demonstrates how a line of text can be seen to animate using successive heading sizes (with the `<h1>...<h3>` tags) – in this case the text gets smaller. If this script was named `example.exe` (an executable program) it could be called through a standard `<a href..>` hyperlink tag, as shown here for example:

```
<a href="http://somehost.com/cgi-bin/example.exe">Run the script!</a>
```

Here is the Icon script in its entirety:

```
# Example script 1: Send three HTML files to the client.
procedure main()
 write("Content-type: multipart/x-mixed-replace;boundary=
   ThisRandomString\n")
 write("--ThisRandomString")
 write("Content-type: text/html\n")
 write("<h1>Here is the data for the first object</h1>.")
 write("--ThisRandomString")
 write("Content-type: text/html\n")
 write("<h2>Here is the data for the second object</h2>.")
 write("--ThisRandomString")
 write("Content-type: text/html\n")
 write("<h3>Here is the data for the third object</h3>.")
 write("--ThisRandomString--")
end
```

The string `ThisRandomString` is the *boundary separator* described earlier. Notice how each piece of HTML text is encapsulated with a `Content-type:` header (with a blank line afterwards – note the \n) and is then completed with a boundary separator.

If the data segments you want to send are not HTML text alter the MIME types accordingly, e.g. image/gif for a GIF image. Use Netscape's Options/Preferences/Helper applications menu option to see some further MIME types that are in common use.

Example 2: Simple server push program to animate a horizontal rule.

In this second example the Icon script has been modified to display a horizontal rule (<hr> tag) of increasing size, extending from both sides of the screen out across the page in opposite directions at the same time. This is just one of the many animation effects that can be achieved. The || symbols are the Icon concatenation (*string-joining*) operator. In the example the <hr> tag has been set with a vertical width of 8 and a horizontal width that is increased in increments of 5 units using a simple while loop. Two horizontal rules are used, one with left-alignment and one with right-alignment, thus making each rule appear from both sides of the screen.

```
# Example script 2: Animation of a <hr> tag.
procedure main()
 local n
 n := 1
 write("Content-type: multipart/x-mixed-replace;boundary=
  ThisRandomString\n")
 write("ThisRandomString")
 while (n <= 100) do {
       write("Content-type: text/html\n")
       write("<hr size=8 align=left  width=" || n || "%" || ">")
       write("<center><h2>This is an example
          animation</h2></center>")
       write("<hr size=8 align=right width=" || n || "%" || ">")
             n := n + 5
       write("ThisRandomString")
       }
end
```

If you omit the align= keywords, the rule appears centred and grows in width – another eye-catching effect. You could achieve all of the same effects with client pull techniques, although you would need many individual files, each called in succession, so the whole solution becomes slightly messy. On the other hand, you would not need to use a script of any form, and you could implement such effects from within Netscape without the requirements for a server program. The HTML that calls the above script can be a hyperlink such as:

```
<a href="http://yourhost/cgi-bin/example2.exe">
```

or perhaps just a button within a fill-out-form tag, such as:

```
<! Create a button...>
<form method="post" action="http://yourhost/cgi-bin/example2.exe">
<input type="submit" value="Run Animation">
</form>
```

where `example2.exe` is the executable script (the executable version of the above source code), and `yourhost` is the name of your Web server. If you are using a local server to test these scripts, such as the NCSA Windows HTTPD server, ensure that you use the name **localhost** as a server name. The `/cgi-bin` directory is used by the Win HTTPD program as an alias that points to a directory where all of your DOS-based scripts are held (by default this is `C:\HTTPD\CGI-DOS`). The `method="post"` is redundant if you just require a button to invoke the script, and can be omitted (leave in the posting method if you want to send field values from other `<input type..>` tags, however).

Example 3: Animating images using a server push script.

You can also animate images using server push techniques. The Icon script below opens three GIF files (using the `read()` function) and then simply outputs them using the `write()` function. The `<img src..>` tag can reference a script instead of an actual image file; thus we could call this script using the tag:

```
<img src="http://yourhost/cgi-bin/example3.exe">
```

where `example3.exe` is the executable (compiled) icon program, and `yourhost` is the name of the HTTP server. Note again that if you are using a local server to test these scripts, e.g. the NCSA Windows HTTPD server, make sure that you use the special name **localhost** as a server name (so that the tag above becomes: `<img src="http://local-host/cgi-bin/example3.exe">`). As mentioned, `/cgi-bin` is a directory alias used by the Win HTTPD program to point to the directory where all of your DOS-based scripts are held (`C:\HTTPD\CGI-DOS` by default). Another point worth noting for Win HTTPD users is the use of the `HSCRIPT.PIF` file (a Windows Program Interchange File that resides in the `\HTTPD` directory). This file should be modified before running any script that references external files – such as the GIF files in Example 3. Change the `%TEMP%` to the name of the directory where your GIF images are held, otherwise the program will not be able to locate them. By default, the Win HTTPD server looks in your temporary directory for such files, as defined by the DOS `TEMP` variable.

```
# Example script 3: Animation of some GIF-image icons
procedure main()
  local fd1, fd2, fd3, line
```

```
fd1 := open("httpd1.gif", "r")
fd2 := open("httpd2.gif", "r")
fd3 := open("httpd3.gif", "r")
write("Content-type: multipart/x-mixed-replace;boundary=
  ThisRandomString\n")
write("--ThisRandomString")
# Image 1:
write("Content-type: image/gif\n")
while line := read(fd1) do
      write(line)
write("\n--ThisRandomString")
# Image 2:
write("Content-type: image/gif\n")
while line := read(fd2) do
      write(line)
write("\n--ThisRandomString")
# Image 3:
write("Content-type: image/gif\n")
while line := read(fd3) do
      write(line)
write("\n--ThisRandomString--")
end
```

The important point that Example 3 demonstrates is that it is not a requirement that the script be invoked by a person – it is loaded automatically from the server. Indeed, the server could serve different portions of a file at certain intervals, and not necessarily immediately, or after a certain number of seconds, as in client pull. So, for example, your script could feed the client data every half an hour. The client can quite easily break the client/server connection at any time simply by pressing the *Stop* key or by moving the changing the window/URL.

Example 4: An extended image animation script.

Example 3 could be made more compact by a simple program loop. This would avoid having the same code repeated for every file or image segment that you want to send. The example below shows how this can be implemented. The variable MAXIMG controls how many segments (in this case we can assume they are images) you want to send, and the variable PREFIX stores the name of the files in question – assume that the filenames end with a number, e.g. icon1.gif, icon2.gif,..., icon6.gif (six images in all).

```
# Example script 4: Image animation using program loop
procedure main()
```

```
local fd, line, counter, MAXIMG
counter := 1
MAXIMG  := 6
PREFIX  := "icon"
write("Content-type: multipart/x-mixed-replace;boundary=
  ThisRandomString\n")
while (counter <= MAXIMG) do {
# Join together the prefix, counter and extension
# to make a filename e.g. icon1.gif
        fd := open(PREFIX || counter || ".gif")
        write("--ThisRandomString")
        write("Content-type: image/gif\n")
        while line := read(fd) do
                write(line)
        write()
        if (counter != MAXIMG) then {
          write("\n--ThisRandomString")
            }
        counter := counter + 1
  }
write("--ThisRandomString--")
end
```

▶ TIP

For some excellent examples of dynamic push/pull documents in action, see the URL below for a real-time demonstration:

http://www.homepages.com/tools

The actual scripts for the server-side activity are also available for you to view and download from this site (these are written in the Perl language).

3.5 And finally... publishing your work

After you have actually written your HTML documents, you may of course want to actually publish them on the Internet to a global audience. In order to do this you must first have rented some hard disk space on an Internet Web server, such as your service provider's Internet host, and then uploaded your HTML and other files (such as images and sounds) to the server, thus allowing the rest of the Internet community to access these files. By far the most common way of providing access to a Web server is via FTP (File Transfer Protocol).

Using a username and password allocated to you by your service provider you can access the disk drive of the machine where your pages are stored, and then up- and download the files you require, as well as performing general housekeeping tasks, such as deleting files. Nearly all Internet service providers rent out hard disk space (or *Web space* as it is known in Netspeak) to their customers for a fee – depending on the space required.

Netscape 1.1N only provides one-way FTP access at the time of writing, allowing files to be downloaded from an FTP site, not uploaded. You will therefore have to obtain an FTP client that allows file uploads, and many freeware and shareware Internet tools are available for this task, e.g. the simple Trumpet FTP client. Graphical FTP client programs exist, as well as the simpler command-line interfaces. In all cases you will simply log in to your Web server and then upload any file(s) that you want to publish. It is then a case of publicizing these files to the Internet community.

Chapter 5 discusses a number of search engines that you can submit details to regarding your own pages of information that you want to publish. People searching for information will then find your home page, and will be able to visit it. It makes sense to try out your own pages using Netscape prior to publishing them to ensure that everything is working (such as hyperlinks to other pages). For example, my own service provider is called `www.gold.net`, and their home page is stored at the URL address `http://www.gold.net`. They have an FTP interface to that machine at the address `ftp.gold.net` which allows authorized users to upload files and generally maintain their information on the Web server of the same name (`www.gold.net`). My own home page is stored on the Internet at the URL `http://www.gold.net/users/ag17/index.htm`. Many other people have their home pages and other associated files stored at this site under the `/users` directory, according to their username (mine being `ag17` in this instance).

Useful FTP commands to remember (for interactive client programs that use a command-line interface) include **put** *file* (to upload a file); **mput** *files* to upload multiple files (e.g. mput `*.htm`); **del** *file* to delete a file; **get** *file* to download a file; **mget** *files* to download multiple files (e.g. `mget*.htm`); **quit** to end the FTP session; **binary** to enable binary file up/downloads; and **ascii** to enable ASCII (plain text) up/downloads. Enabling binary mode is required for image files (e.g. GIFs, JPEGs and other non-text files), although binary mode will also upload ASCII files in the vast majority of cases, so a good rule-of-thumb is just to enable binary mode immediately when you have both ASCII and non-ASCII files to upload to the FTP server. You can navigate directories using the **cd** *dir* command (as in DOS and UNIX systems). Probably the most important command is **lcd** (*local* cd) which is used to point to the directory on your local hard disk where the source files are actually coming from in order to be uploaded. Graphical FTP clients do not require such commands to be employed and are generally easier to use, although personally I prefer the text-based clients, (such as the *Trumpet FTP* client).

Shown below is a typical FTP session that I would have to undertake to upload some HTML and GIF files to my own FTP server (the `ftp>` is the FTP command-mode prompt). The commands in **bold** type are the commands typed into the system:

```
ftp> lcd c:\webfiles
ftp> prompt
ftp> mput *.htm
ftp> mput *.gif
ftp> quit
```

which would upload all of the GIF and HTML files in the `C:\WEBFILES` directory on my hard disk to the server situated at site `ftp.gold.net`. The `prompt` command simply stops the FTP program from asking whether or not I want to upload each file, since `mput` requests conformation for each file before it is uploaded otherwise (a useful feature where you may want to exclude certain files from being uploaded). Remember that you can use `put` instead of `mput` to upload individual files. The exact FTP client commands may differ between programs, although the commands briefly described here are commonly accepted. Try typing `help` to summon a full list of commands.

Lastly, a hyperlink tip. Remember that if your HTML pages simply refer to files in your own area of the provider's disk, the `http://` prefix in a hyperlink (i.e. in an `<a href>` HTML tag) can be omitted. Once a person has actually typed your full URL into their Web browser to access your home page, all other pages are assumed to exist *relative* to this. If, however, you need to access a hypertext page or other file from another Internet host, then you will of course need to provide the full URL for that particular resource within your HTML file. If files are stored in other directories of your area of the disk, it is quite valid to have entries such as:

```
<a href="..\directory\filename.html">A hyperlink</a>
```

where the '`..`' refers to the parent directory (a notation used in DOS and UNIX systems), thus enabling you to refer to files in other directories of the disk. Note also that Netscape uses the `\` and `/` characters interchangeably as directory separators.

C H A P T E R

4

Netscape: the news browser

4.1 Using Netscape as a USENET newsreader

A major advantage of Netscape over many other browsers is its ability to be used as a fully-fledged USENET *newsreader*. USENET, or USErs' NETwork, is a vast collection of electronic mail messages from users all over the world that are categorized into different forums, or *hierarchies*. Just about any subject known is discussed on USENET, and apart from simple text messages, many USENET groups even carry software and computer imagery (or *binary* files, as they are more commonly known). One important distinction to remember is that USENET is not the Internet; rather, it is information transmitted over the Internet and stored on thousands of computers for people to access. All USENET messages get transmitted across the Internet via electronic mail (email) – a principal application of the Internet. Such messages only really differ from their email counterparts in that they contain the name of a *newsgroup* rather than a human recipient name. Newsgroup names are formed into hierarchies by separating each part of the name with a full stop (`.`). For example, `rec.sport.golf` is a recreational (`rec.`) newsgroup dealing with sport (`sport.`) and the game of golf (`golf`). Likewise, you will also find a related group called `rec.sport.hockey`, and so on. While the entire USENET system comprises many thousands of newsgroups (over 15 000 currently exist), the number of *top-level* hierarchy names is very small – an example being `rec`, as we have already seen, for recreational newsgroups. Only a dozen or so mainstream top-level hierarchy names exist, including `alt` (alternative lifestyle), `comp` (computing hierarchy), `news` (all matters relating to USENET itself), `sci` (science-related issues), `soc` (social and cultural issues), and `misc` (miscellaneous). Hierarchies for individual countries also exist, for example `uk.jobs.offered` deals with employment positions offered in the United Kingdom, while `fr.rec.humour` deals with French humour, for example.

4.2 Configuring Netscape for USENET: news server basics

A few things have to be done before diving into USENET with Netscape. The main thing to decide upon is a *news server* that will handle your news requests. The Internet provider you finally join up with will have its own news server that you can use with Netscape. In addition, there are a number of public news servers, although not all will allow the posting of messages, i.e. only *read-only* access is enabled. USENET news is stored on news servers all over the world, and not in any central Internet repository. It is left to the discretion of individual system administrators as to which newsgroups are actually carried on their systems. As mentioned before, you would be highly unlikely to find a news server that carries every USENET group in existence, simply because the disk space required would be too large (around 60–100 Mbyte of USENET news could be delivered in a single day from the mainstream groups). It clearly makes sense to link into a news server situated more locally to yourself in order to speed things up (although this itself is also debatable, since traffic loads on different portions of the Internet will dictate just how fast news can be delivered to a site – an Internet site in Japan may actually be faster than a site in your own country, simply because more people are accessing the server and are therefore slowing the entire system down). As a general rule of thumb, however, it is generally best to equate greater speeds with shorter distances in this context. The name of your news server will be mentioned in the `netscape.ini` file. This plain text file contains many other configuration items, which are dealt with in Appendix E, although you can locate the USENET entry by searching (using an ASCII editor, such as DOS's `EDIT.COM`) for the word

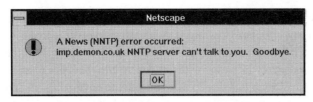

Figure 4.1 'No permission to talk' warning.

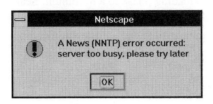

Figure 4.2 News server 'too busy' warning.

NNTP, an acronym which stands for Network News Transfer Protocol, the principal communications protocol for delivering news over the Internet network. Alternatively, search for the [Services] section of the file. A typical entry could therefore resemble:

```
[Services]
NNTP_Server=news.cityscape.co.uk
```

which in this case uses the NNTP server at the host `news.cityscape.co.uk` (CityScape is a popular Internet service provider based in the United Kingdom), and the name of the news server in this case is just *news*, which has been added onto the front of CityScape's own Internet hostname. You could in theory place any NNTP news server name here, although you have to remember that at an earlier stage you will have logged into your service provider to gain access to the Internet, and thus to the USENET system. In this process your identification to the system will have given you permission to use a news server. Specifying the server name of another host may therefore result in a news error, along the lines of 'You have no permission to talk', which basically translates to: 'Push off – you are not a valid user of this system!', as Figure 4.1 illustrates with one NNTP server chosen at random.

In the case that a news server will respond to you, you may find that its user limit has been reached. User limits are commonly set at between 10 and 30 users, depending on the server. In the case that the server load is too high, Netscape responds with the warning message shown in Figure 4.2.

4.3 **Telling Netscape which newsgroups to track**

Finally, you should also tell Netscape which USENET newsgroups you want to access; after all, you wouldn't want to keep loading Netscape and then go through the continuous rigmarole of telling it which newsgroups to load on every occasion! In order to make Netscape keep track of the newsgroups that you are interested in (and make it keep track of the articles that you have read) you must supply Netscape with a `newsrc` file. This is a plain text ASCII file that consists of the name of each newsgroup that you want to have access to. You could in theory mention the name of every valid newsgroup, although this is not advisable since Netscape formats the file as a hypertext page, and this can take some time to display. It is therefore best to keep the initial newsgroup loading phase to a minimum. Search the `netscape.ini` file for the `[Main]` section and then modify your `News RC=` entry to point to the `newsrc` file that you want to use (you can modify the actual file afterwards). For example:

```
[Main]
News RC=c:\netscape\newsrc
```

which uses the file `c:\netscape\newsrc` as the newsgroups file. A typical `newsrc` file can be seen below. You do not have to create this file if it does not already exist, since Netscape can maintain newsgroups quite easily, although you may as well modify this now, since it will save you time on-line (remembering that you must connect to the Internet in order to make use of Netscape's USENET facilities).

```
alt.books.reviews: 0
alt.books.technical: 0
uk.jobs: 0
```

The numbers after each newsgroup show the articles that you have read. Netscape will alter these as you read articles from each group. It will also use this information to change the colour of the entries you can see on the screen in order to show the article(s) that you have already read while on-line. All articles on a news server are numbered to allow your newsreading software (here, Netscape) to keep track of what you have read. Article numbers are arranged in two different ways, namely: (i) *individual* articles; and (ii) *ranges* of articles. These can be combined together as well, so for example if you had read a range of articles, say articles 1278 to 1287 (10 articles) Netscape would modify the `newsrc` file for the group concerned so that it contained `1278-1287`, and if you had read any individual articles, these would be placed in the file as well, so for example an entry of:

```
alt.books.technical: 1211, 1212, 1278-1287, 1300
```

shows that in the group `alt.books.technical` you have read articles 1211 and 1212, and the articles 1278 through 1287, and finally article 1300. Most newsreading programs maintain their `newsrc` file in this way. When initially creating a `newsrc` file you clearly cannot tell which articles you have read, so the number 0 should be placed as an initial article number. Netscape will change this as soon as you start to read some articles. You may also see some newsgroups with an exclamation mark (!) after them. These are *unsubscribed* news-groups – groups in which you are no longer interested. Netscape does not delete the entry, just in case you want to reinstate it at a later stage (thus keeping all details of the articles you have read etc.). If you ever subscribe to a non-existent group, Netscape will make the group an unsubscribed group also. From time to time you may want to edit out such entries manually with an text editor.

▶TIP

Because there are so many newsgroups, you may want to use your newsreading software to look at the USENET group `news.lists` which lists all of the current newsgroups that exist. However, no news server receives every news-group, rather a subset of the most popular groups, so you may have to check with your local systems administrator to see which groups are available (or ask for an up-to-date `newsrc` file).

4.4 **Reading 'The News'**

Now that we have configured Netscape for use with the USENET system, we can actually start to read some articles. Articles themselves are made up of two parts, namely a *header* and a *body* part. The header contains all of the addressing information for the article, such as the newsgroup name, the person posting the message, and additional details for the news server, such as a unique message-id code etc. Some of these items are made into hyperlinks so that you can access other messages and follow links to related articles etc. All of this will be demonstrated in this section. In order to make Netscape enter newsreading mode, you can do one of two things. Firstly, you can enter a `news:` URL along with the name of the group that you want to examine. Do this by opening the Netscape File menu and selecting the option Open a Location. You can then enter a URL such as

```
news:alt.books.technical
```

into the screen's main *Location:* field, and Netscape will read in the newsgroup accordingly. You can also click on the

    Newsgroups

button in the Directory toolbar – the last button. If you have used a variety of news servers with Netscape already this button will load up a list of such servers which you can choose from accordingly – this button thus provides the equivalent of a `newsrc:` URL. In addition,

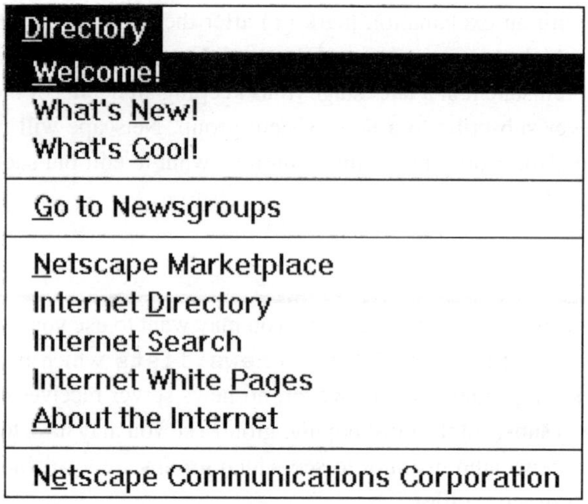

Figure 4.3 The Directory menu (Netscape 1.1).

you can also use the Directory menu and choose the option Go To Newsgroups, as shown in Figure 4.3.

▶**TIP**

If you want to see a listing of all the current newsgroups, enter the special URL as follows into the *Location:* field on the screen:

`news:*`

although be warned: the list is likely to be *very* long indeed. The `*` is a *wildcard* name, which matches all of the current newsgroups. Alternatively, you can specify the group list as `comp.*`, which will load all of the `comp` hierarchy newsgroups (computing subjects).

Figure 4.4 demonstrates a typical subscribed newsgroups screen (the word *subscribed* refers to the fact that these newsgroups exist in the `newsrc` file). The example includes only five newsgroups, namely `alt.books.reviews` (book reviews), `alt.books.technical` (technical book reviews and commentary), `alt.journalism` (journalism forum), `uk.jobs` (UK jobs forum) and `comp.text.sgml` (a group discussing the SGML standard and mark-up language). The salient parts of the screen to note are:

■ *Newsgroup hyperlinks*
These are coloured blue by default, and allow you to see the article(s) in that particular group. The numbers in brackets that precede each newsgroup represent the number of

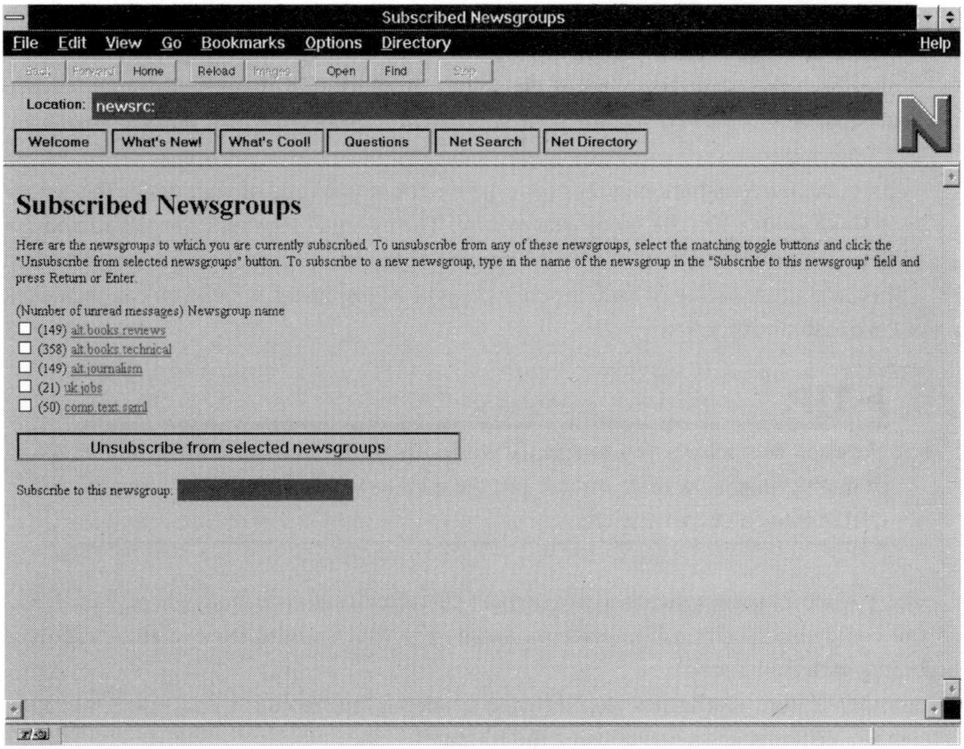

Figure 4.4 A typical subscribed newsgroups screen (v1.0N).

unread articles that exist. You will also notice the check-boxes at the start of each newsgroup line – these are used in conjunction with the *Unsubscribe* button, which removes a particular group from the `newsrc` file (the page is updated automatically when you remove a group).

■ *Subscribe newsgroup field*

Subscribe newsgroup is a data entry field that allows you to subscribe to a newsgroup. Simply enter the name of the newsgroup and a reference for it will be added in the `newsrc` file. The screen will also be updated so that you can start to read articles from that group. Netscape will not validate the name of the group you enter. A tell-tale sign that a group is invalid can be seen if you click on the group and receive the error message 'News Error', or if there are zero articles in the group (the latter could of course be a valid outcome if no articles were available, although the main groups are hardly ever without articles unless your service provider has temporarily cleaned out the server for some reason).

■ *View all newsgroups button*

This button, when pressed, simply shows every newsgroup that is currently available on the news server that you are using. Netscape can obtain a list of every newsgroup carried on your news server by sending it the special URL `news:*`, which uses the * wildcard to match the name of every newsgroup name. This can take some time to download, so press the red *Stop* button in the Netscape toolbar if you tired of waiting for this list, or if you have reached the group you require. The eventual list that is displayed will not have any article numbers or check-boxes, as in the main subscribed list shown earlier. Instead, a bare listing of each group name will be displayed, which you can then click on to call up accordingly.

▶TIP

Netscape now allows you to specify wildcards *within* newsgroup names. For example, you may want to browse just the `alt` news hierarchy by entering the URL `news:alt.*` by itself.

The * wildcard (which matches zero or more characters) can appear anywhere in the URL, so you could also specify a URL such as `news:c*`, which would retrieve all newsgroups beginning with the letter 'c'.

Another feature that is new to Netscape concerns the `news:` URL, which can now reference a different news server using the format:

```
news://server-name/usenet-group
```

So, for example, we could enter a news URL such as:

```
news://news.somewhere.com/alt.books.technical
```

which would use the NNTP server `news.somewhere.com` and make it load the articles for the USENET group `alt.books.technical`. USENET messages do tend to propagate across the Internet relatively slowly; it may be the case that articles on one server take longer to reach another, depending on the up/downloading arrangements between network administrators etc. It is easy to miss messages that may have been posted to another country in this way, especially when many news servers purge their articles more quickly than others. For this reason, I would advise browsing more than one news server (perhaps in different countries). Many external news servers will deny you access. Public news servers are still available, although they are a dying breed simply because they become heavily over-used.

▶TIP

A good technique for finding public news servers is to examine the *bang-path* in a typical USENET article. This is the entry with the names of news servers with a ! character (*bang* character) in-between them. The purpose of the bang-path is to trace the route that the current article took in order to arrive on the current news server, remembering that USENET news propagates across the network from server to server. By trying a `news:` URL with the name of one of the host names here, you may be lucky to find a site where public access has been granted – or accidentally left enabled `;-)`.

Another good technique you may want to use makes use of the * wildcard when using the `news://server-name` URL syntax, which makes Netscape present a list of all the USENET hierarchies that exist on the news server being referenced. For example, typing the URL:

`news://news.funet.fi/*`

would result in a screen containing all of the USENET hierarchies carried by the news server `news.funet.fi`, all organized in an A to Z fashion. You can now click on an appropriate hierarchy and have it expanded so that all of the individual newsgroups can be accessed. The actual hierarchies available will depend on the news server being accessed. This feature requires that Netscape must download the details for each hierarchy, which can be time-consuming (a message will enable you to stop at this stage, although you can of course click on the *Stop* icon in the Netscape toolbar to halt the download, although you will lose the complete list if you do this). Also, no progress display will be shown, other than the number of bytes that have been downloaded. This is because Netscape must query the server to build up a list of groups from scratch.

The Netscape USENET article screen

Once you have clicked upon a newsgroup that interests you, Netscape will contact the news server and request that all the articles currently available from that group be downloaded. Netscape will used the `newsrc` file to see which articles you have already read, so that they can be coloured differently from the default blue, to show those articles already examined on previous visits to the group in question. Netscape formats the articles as a hypertext page, and indents articles according to the responses that they have generated from other users. Articles that share the same subject are termed *threads*, and Netscape has the necessary facilities to follow article threads if you require (something Mosaic did not have). A typical articles screen for the group `alt.books.reviews` can be seen in Figure 4.5.

The first thing to notice is how the *Location:* fields URL has changed to `news:alt.books.reviews`. This is what you could have typed in order to reach this newsgroup without using any mouse clicks. The bulleted list on the screen represents individual articles posted to this group from users all over the Internet. The *Earliest articles* and *Earlier*

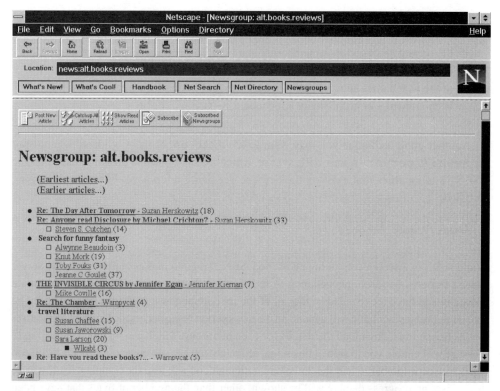

Figure 4.5 An article screen for the USENET group `alt.books.reviews`.

articles hyperlinks allow you to retrieve articles that were posted at an earlier date (the article numbers will be shown when you move to the link before clicking on it in the status bar). Notice how some articles are indented. These represent responses to an article, a *thread*. Such threads can continue to many layers of indentation, as different people respond to particular articles. Netscape makes each article a hyperlink (coloured blue) so that you can click on an article in order to see it on the screen. In addition, Netscape adds the name of the person posting the message and the number of lines that make up the message. You can use this number to see how extensive an article is, and thus whether or not to download it at this moment. Netscape has one considerable advantage over Mosaic in this respect, namely the ability to invoke *background tasks*, that is to say, that you could click on a large article, and then while it is being loaded you could click elsewhere, perhaps to load another article, or to move back a screen etc.

You will have also noticed a new *toolbar* that has been inserted into the hypertext version of the article selection screen, as shown in Figure 4.6.

Figure 4.6 The Netscape article toolbar.

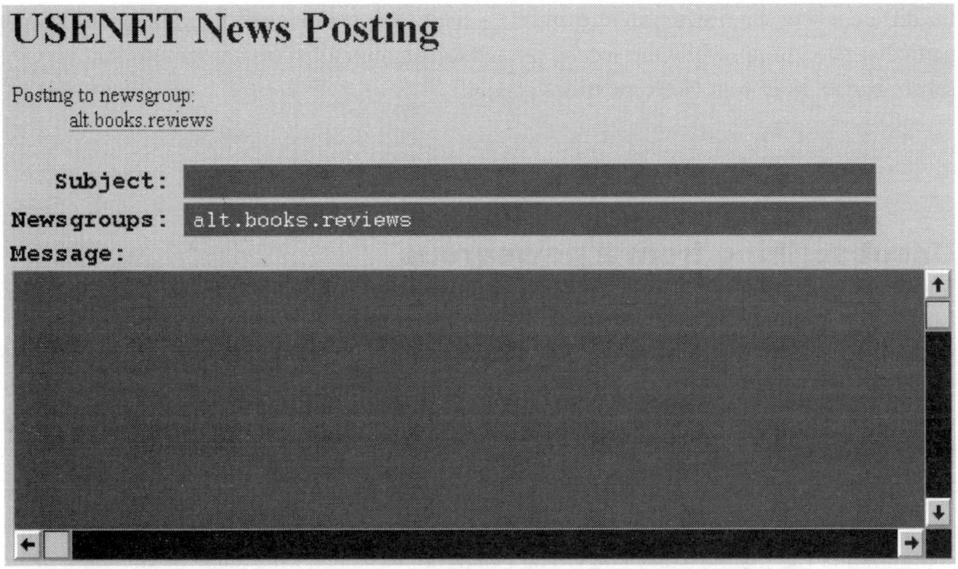

Figure 4.7 Posting a new message to the USENET forum `alt.books.reviews`.

Posting an article onto USENET

The *Post New Article* option, as the name suggests, allows you to post a USENET article to the current group. When clicked upon, Netscape opens up a window for you to type in your message, as shown in Figure 4.7. You should click on the *Post Message* button to send the message to your news server. You must have a news server configured in the Options/Preferences menu in order to post a message via Netscape.

▶TIP

To abandon a typed message, you should simply click on the *Back* icon to move back a screen. This option can be found on Netscape's main toolbar, or alternatively you can click on the Go menu and press *B* instead.

The *Catchup All Articles* option scans for any new articles that have been posted since your last visit to the group (taking you back to the main newsgroup screen in the process); the special `newscatchup:` URL is used for this purpose – watch the status bar for the exact command.

The *Show Read Articles* button, when invoked, simply reloads the entire newsgroup from scratch (this button changes to *Hide Read Articles* when selected, although in Netscape 1.1N the effect seems to be unchanged, making this a rather superfluous option it seems).

The penultimate button, *Subscribe*, allows you to subscribe to the current group, i.e. add it to the main list of newsgroups in your `newsrc` file. The *Subscribed Newsgroups* option simply returns you to the main list of newsgroups using the `newsrc://news server` URL. Notice the different between `news:` and `newsrc:` – the first is mainly used for gaining access to a particular newsgroup, while the second is used to summon a list of newsgroups that you are subscribed to, as in your Netscape `newsrc` file.

Unsubscribing from a newsgroup

This option is found in the main newsgroups screen. The *Unsubscribe* option simply *disables* a particular group by flagging it with an exclamation mark (`!`) in the `newsrc` file. You can manually change newsgroups in this way also. Figure 4.8 illustrates how we can unsubscribe from the `uk.jobs` forum – the check-box to the right of the group is simply enabled (note the cross in the small white square) and the *Unsubscribe from selected newsgroups* button is then clicked on.

Simply type `newsrc:` followed by your news server name to get to the *Unsubscribe* option shown in Figure 4.8 (this will use the current news server as defined in the Netscape configuration file `netscape.ini`). You can of course specify the name of any valid news server on the Internet, if you have one available, in which case the same newsgroups will be scanned, although a different selection of articles may be forthcoming – bearing in mind that different news servers can carry more or fewer articles depending on their configuration (some servers keep older articles longer, for example).

▶ TIP

Using the `newsrc:` URL by itself will make Netscape provide a list of news servers that you have visited in the past. Clicking on a particular news server

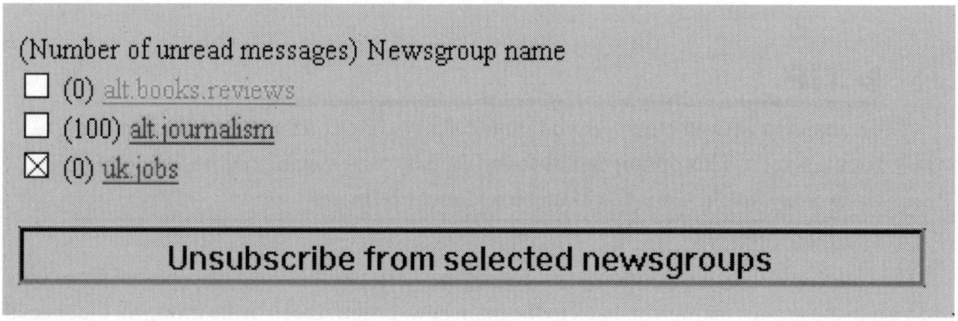

(Number of unread messages) Newsgroup name
☐ (0) alt.books.reviews
☐ (100) alt.journalism
☒ (0) uk.jobs

Unsubscribe from selected newsgroups

Figure 4.8 Unsubscribing from the newsgroup `uk.jobs`.

will then lead to the main newsgroups screen, which you can then browse at your leisure.

▶TIP

You can re-subscribe to a group by removing the exclamation mark (!) from the group name in the `newsrc` file. Alternatively, you can use Netscape's *Subscribe* option, as discussed below.

Subscribing to a newsgroup

Also seen on the same screen, and on the main newsgroup selection screen, is a field allowing you to subscribe to a particular newsgroup, as illustrated in Figure 4.9.

All newsgroups that are entered into this field will be validated by your news server. You can use the `newsrc` file to see which groups are valid, or you can type `news:*` in the main *Location:* field in the Netscape window – which will load all of the current newsgroups.

Reading an article

Once you are reading articles in the article selection screen, you are free to click on any hyperlink in order to read the text of that particular article (Figure 4.10). Newsreading can be quite fast in Netscape since only the headers are loaded and marked up into HTML; a unique message-id field in the message allows the actual article to be located from the news server. For example, clicking on the article entitled *Bugs in Writing*, i.e. the hyperlink:

```
news:jkiernanD8sqnu.729@netcom.com
```

would load up the screen shown in Figure 4.11. The speed at which an article is loaded depends on the size of the article and the speed of your connection, although Netscape will show you

Subscribe to this newsgroup:

Figure 4.9 The main newsgroup subscription box in Netscape.

● THE INVISIBLE CIRCUS by Jennifer Egan - Jennifer Kiernan (7)

Figure 4.10 A typical USENET item shown as a hyperlink under Netscape.

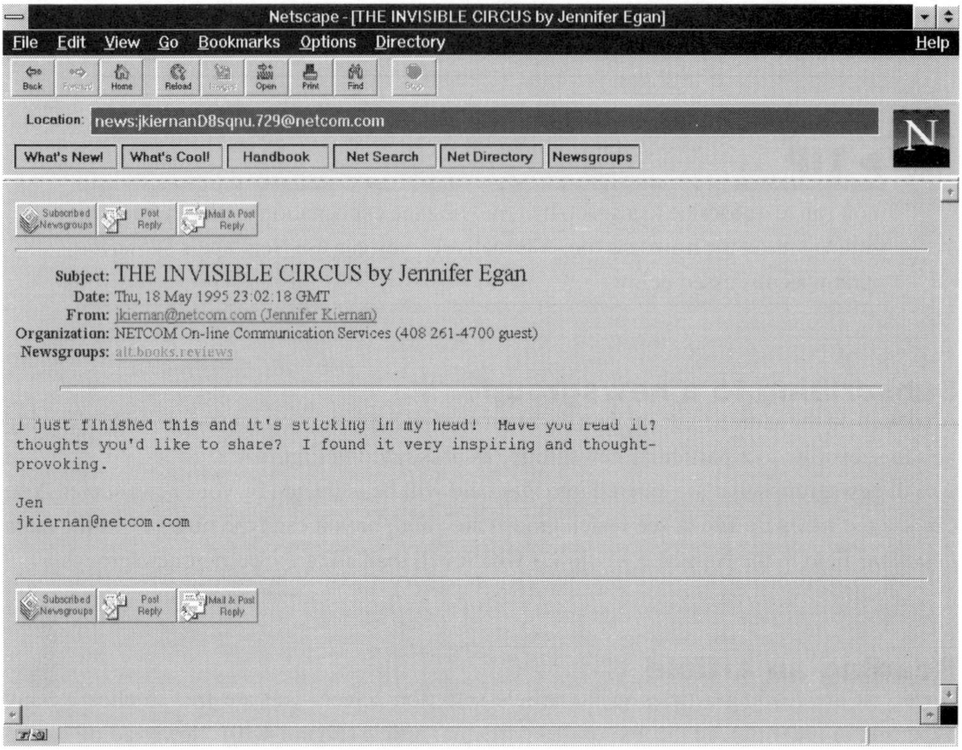

Figure 4.11 A typical USENET hypertext article as seen through Netscape.

its progress at the bottom of the screen, and you can of course stop article loading at any point using the *Stop* button in the main Netscape toolbar. Alternatively, press the ESCAPE key to halt the current download.

▶ TIP

The best way to save an article is to Shift-Click on the hyperlink for the article in question, i.e. rather than clicking on a hyperlink with the mouse, hold the SHIFT key down first and then click the left mouse button.

Figure 4.11 shows an actual article, marked up by Netscape into an HTML hypertext page. The article's `Subject:` line is shown first, in the larger emboldened font, followed by four lines from the message's header, namely:

- `From:` field – the person posting the article, with their *friendly*, or human name, in brackets

Figure 4.12 The Netscape article toolbar (shown when in an article).

- `Date:` field, showing the article's date and time of posting onto the USENET system (notice the time zone factor at the end of this field)

- `Organization:` field, which shows the name of the company and/or organization who sent the message (most email and newsreader packages allow a value for this field to be specified)

- `Newsgroups:` field – this specifies the name(s) of newsgroups into which the current article was posted. The `Newsgroups:` field is also made into a hyperlink to allow movement directly into the newsgroup in question. The article then follows in its entirety.

You will also have noticed that another article toolbar has also been inserted into the screen, as shown in Figure 4.12.

Many of the buttons in this toolbar deal with *articles* and *article threads* – the latter are articles that share the same `Subject:` field, or to put it another way, responses from other users discussing the same article. The last five button options allow navigation to various newsgroups and for the posting of an article directly to the sender, or to the entire newsgroup.

The ⬚⬚ buttons allow movement between different articles in the current news-group. For example, take the portion of a hypothetical article's screen, as shown in Figure 4.13. The bulleted entries indicate each of the main articles that these buttons will jump back and forth between. In Figure 4.13 a number of different articles are shown, totalling seven in all. The first six have the same subject line (*Male Writers v. Female Writers*) and are thus classed as a *thread* of articles. The very last article (the seventh hyperlink) is a non-threaded article, since it is the only article with its own unique subject line (*Writers as speakers*). If we were currently reading article three (the article with 46 lines) and clicked on the right-arrow button to move to the next article, we would in fact move to article seven (the last article in the list), and not to one of the threaded articles.

The ⬚⬚ buttons must be used if you want to navigate within (up and down) between a thread of articles, as with articles one to six shown in Figure 4.13.

If we were to click on the sixth (penultimate) hyperlink article we would call up the article and see the header information, as illustrated in Figure 4.14.

Notice how Netscape has now inserted a `References:` field into the article header, which is itself a hyperlink (the numbers **1**, **2** and **3**). These refer to articles in the current thread that have had replies sent back concerning the original article. We could therefore click on these

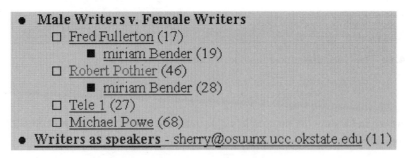

Figure 4.13 Six threaded articles and one non-threaded article.

Figure 4.14 The header information in a threaded article.

references to bring up the appropriate document. Netscape will insert as many references as are required, according to the number of threaded articles that exist.

Then we have the ![Mark Thread Read] icon, which is used to mark all of the current thread as being examined, i.e. read. Once this icon is clicked upon, all new subject threads are loaded.

The ![This Newsgroup] button simply reloads the current newsgroup (i.e. all articles associated with it), and the ![Subscribed Newsgroups] button jumps back to the main newsgroups screen.

Posting follow-up articles and replying to individuals

These options allow feedback to be sent to individuals or to the entire USENET community.

The last two icons on the article toolbar are ![Post Reply] and ![Mail & Post Reply] (*Post Reply* and *Mail & Post Reply* icons). One of the main reasons for Netscape's popularity is its read/write

USENET mode. Some browsers, notably the earlier versions of Mosaic, could only read USENET articles. Netscape allows articles to be posted into existing newsgroups, and even allows personal email to be sent to individual recipients via a preconfigured email server. In keeping with Netiquette (*net etiquette* – the correct way of behaving on the Net) only post unsolicited messages when they have wide appeal to the entire newsgroup community. Separate email messages can be sent to a person when discussing a subject on a on-to-one basis. *Spamming* is the term given to people who send unsolicited messages to multiple newsgroups (mainly to advertise goods or services).

The *Post Reply* icon allows a new article to be sent back to the newsgroup, thus following on from the original (a *threaded* article). This will then appear in the Netscape item selection screen as an indented article, as we have seen earlier with other threaded messages. Netscape retains the `Subject:` line for this purpose, although you could change this, thus making the article non-threaded. When using this option to post a reply article, Netscape copies the text of the current article into a window to which you can then add your own comments. It is useful to include the actual article which you are posting a follow-up to, since other USENET readers will be able to see the context of the message. Netscape also places a right-facing chevron (>) in front of the follow-up article so that the original message can be distinguished from any new text you are about to add. For example, we could see the screen in Figure 4.15 after responding to a published article using the *Post Reply* button:

It is also possible to place a follow-up to a follow-up article, in which case Netscape will simply nest each message within the previous. You should then of course see two levels of chevrons (>>), indicating both the original messages. Netscape will also have filled in the `Subject:` field for you. This field is a standard addition to all Internet email messages. You can alter the field if you wish. By default, Netscape will place the characters `Re:` (*Regarding*) in front of the original subject in order to indicate to readers that this is a follow-up message. Readers will also know that the message is a follow-up article because their own newsreader (perhaps Netscape, although not necessarily) will indent the article. Netscape also provides a single line of text saying who originally posted the follow-up article to indicate to readers who posted the original message onto USENET (this appears at the very top of the article).

Now we can type in our response and then click on the *Post Message* button to post the article into the current group. In order to move between fields, use the keyboard's TAB key (SHIFT+TAB will move backwards), or of course use the mouse to click on the field concerned. Because of the way in which USENET functions, your message will not be accessible to the entire Internet community immediately. Instead, your message will first arrive on your Internet provider's news server, and will then filter out across the Internet between cooperating news servers accordingly. You can expect your message to have reached most of the Internet in around a working week.

Exactly the same concept as the above is undertaken for using the *Mail & Post Reply* button, except that the message is also delivered via electronic mail to the actual person who posted the USENET article that is currently selected, thus ensuring that the recipient will get email regarding that article, as well as allowing the USENET community to see your response. Be

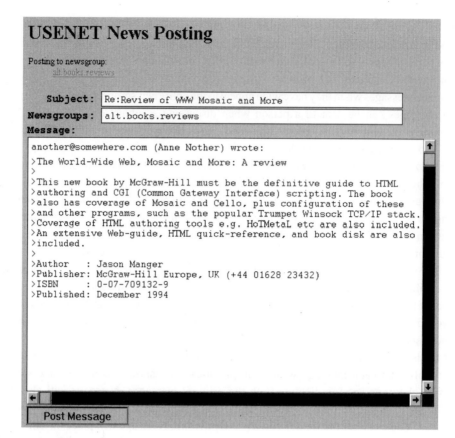

Figure 4.15 Posting a follow-up message using Netscape.

sure that you are replying to the correct person, since you may be located within a thread of articles. After selecting the option, Netscape presents you with a blank article screen, and an empty `Subject:` line. You can then compose your message, i.e. type it in. Click on the *Post Message* button to send the article to the recipient. In order to use this option you must have specified the name of an email server in the `netscape.ini` file. You can use Netscape to specify such a name rather than editing the file manually. In fact, you should not even have to edit the main initialization file at all now, since this is all handled via the Options/Preferences menu. Notice how Netscape fills in the *Mail to* and *Post* fields on the screen when using this option (this facility is new to Netscape 1.1N).

▶**TIP**

If you want to save articles just click on the File menu and select the Save As option to save the file to disk. You can save the file as an HTML-formatted file, or you can save it as a plain text file using this option. If you save the file as plain text, all of the HTML tags will be stripped out, making the document more readable.

C H A P T E R

5

Searching the Web: directories, robots, spiders and crawlers

5.1 Introduction

A major problem with the Internet for its users must be the overwhelming size of this vast resource. Netscape is undoubtedly a very good tool for browsing sites and visiting URLs, but when it comes to finding a specific item of information Netscape must rely on third-party sources of information, such as databases of URLs (e.g. the CERN Virtual Library). Such resources are notoriously difficult to keep up-to-date, given the pace at which new sites come on-line. Enter the *Robot* (also known as a *Crawler* or *Spider*), a new approach in resource discovery that uses a program to *crawl* around the Web seeking out relevant URLs. A number of useful programs have sprung up in recent months to deal with the problem of cataloguing and indexing the many thousands of Web sites and corresponding URLs that now exist. This chapter considers a number of on-line databases and robots, including *AliWeb*, *Yahoo*, *Nikos*, *The World-Wide Web Worm*, *WebCrawler* and *Lycos*. Each program considered in this chapter has been awarded two ratings, the first for its search options and the second for the overall speed, interface and ease-of-use. It makes sense to use more than one resource to locate that elusive fact. Different tools have a variety of searching methods at their disposal, and of course, a much-wanted resource may not have been registered with every on-line database that exists. The URL of each service is listed, along with any *mirror sites* that also exist. Mirror sites are basically duplicate services which are provided to lessen the load on a single server, and may be geographically nearer, thus speeding up searches.

▶TIP

Why not register your own Web pages via the services discussed in this chapter? Many of the services covered allow on-line registrations, whereby you provide a short description of your service, your email name (for contact purposes) and the URL of your home page. Some services may require slightly more information (e.g. AliWeb), although the extra effort is worth it bearing in mind that you will probably want as much publicity as possible. Alternatively, point your Web browser at the *Submit It!* service at the URL:

```
http://www.cen.uiuc.edu/~banister/submit-it
```

Robots, spiders and other Web-crawlers work in a number of ways. Algorithms to scan USENET newsgroups and other 'announcement' pages are commonly employed, as are URL link trails, whereby hyperlinks from a page are continually followed to see where they lead, and whether or not they have already been visited etc. Apart from Web crawlers, expect to find a number of on-line databases of URLs. These include the massive CERN Virtual Library, The EINET Galaxy and Global Network Navigator (GNN) Web sites. A confusing aspect of many services is that they seem to use a combination of automated robot programs and dynamic databases. In fact, this is true of the vast majority of services on offer. Allowing a robot (or other program) to conduct a real-time search for every user enquiry would severely impact on the underlying network. Thus, robots are used at low-peak periods, and their results are then stored in a database which you interrogate directly. Some databases are stored in proprietary formats, which are then converted to HTML so that they can be browsed through a program such as Netscape. Other databases are made up hierarchies of HTML pages from scratch.

Apart from information on general topics, Internet users also need to find software, i.e.

computer programs and other documentation that specifically reside in software archives. A number of Archie Web gateways are therefore also explored in this chapter.

5.2 Searching for general information

This section considers a number of search engine programs that are accessible via the World-Wide Web. These tools are mainly used for finding Web resources that deal with specific topics; for example, you could use a search engine to seek out any Web-based resources that deal with law, agriculture or physics for example. It is also possible to refine your searches with some of the tools described in this section using Boolean operators, e.g. AND and OR-style operators. For example, a search-term such as 'Law AND Computer' would search for documents that deal with law and computing.

AliWeb

Name	AliWeb (Archie Like Indexing of the Web)
Location (URL)	`http://web.nexor.co.uk/public/aliweb/aliweb.html`
Search system	Searchable dynamic database of URLs
Update period	Daily
Mirror sites	`http://www.cs.indiana.edu/aliweb/search`
	`http://www.leo.org/www_index/aliweb.html`
	`http://www.traveller.com/aliweb`
	`http://sunsite.nus.sg/inet/aliweb.html`
	`http://www.singnet.com.sg/staff/gmlim/mirror/form.html`
	`http://www.fh-wolfenbuettel.de/rz/service/aliwebform.html`
	`http://www.met.nps.navy.mil/form.html`
Search methods	URL/Case-sensitive/Regular expression/Category/Country
Rating	★★★★
Statistics	4000 unique URL entries (as of May 1995)
Overall rating	★★★★

AliWeb is described as a *resource discovery* tool by Nexor, the company that runs the AliWeb service. It is a public service that requests people to send them details of their Web pages, such as subject coverage and address details (e.g. URL). AliWeb then combines the details of these files into a searchable database that is updated daily (which is not unlike the Internet's Archie service – a file indexing tool that facilitates searches of anonymous FTP sites). AliWeb requires that you create an IAFA index file that should be placed in the same directory as your main home page on the Internet. The file (`site.idx`) is required in order that AliWeb is informed about all of the documents in your Web pages. A portion of Nexor's own `site.idx` file is shown below:

```
Organization-Email:     info@nexor.co.uk
Organization-Postal:    PO Box 132, Nottingham, NG7 2UU
City:             Nottingham
State:            Midlands
Country:          United Kingdom
URI:              /nexor/nexor.html
Description:      NEXOR is an OSI X.400/X.500 software company.
Keywords:         NEXOR, OSI, X.400, x400, x-400, X.500, x500, x-500

Template-Type:    USER
Title:            Martijn Koster
Handle:           m.koster@nexor.co.uk
Email:            m.koster@nexor.co.uk
Work-Phone:       +44 602 520576
URI:              http://web.nexor.co.uk/mak/mak.html

Template-Type:    DOCUMENT
Title:            List of Hypertext Archie Servers
URI:              /archie.html
Description:      A list of Hypertext Archie Servers in the World
                  Wide Web.
Keywords:         Archie, Hypertext, World Wide Web
Author-Handle:    m.koster@nexor.co.uk
```

As can be seen from the final entry, above, a template-type of DOCUMENT indicates that an HTML-formatted file is being indexed (the indexed resource that someone may be searching for – in this case a list of hypertext-based Archie servers around the world). The `Keywords` line presents a series of terms that describe the resource and which the user may type as a search term. You will have to create your own entries for your own Web service if you want to be included in Nexor's AliWeb database. Once you have created a `site.idx` file in the format specified (all details are on Nexor's server, if you need further information) and have placed it in the home directory where your main home page resides, you can fill in the Nexor registration form. Figure 5.1 illustrates the opening screen of the AliWeb service.

AliWeb also requires that you provide a URL to the `site.idx` file that you eventually create. This takes the format `http://yoursite/yourpath/your-file.html`. You can have more than one entry in the AliWeb database simply by entering multiple DOCUMENT templates, as shown earlier. Figure 5.2 illustrates the registration screen (a form interface) to my own Web pages at the URL

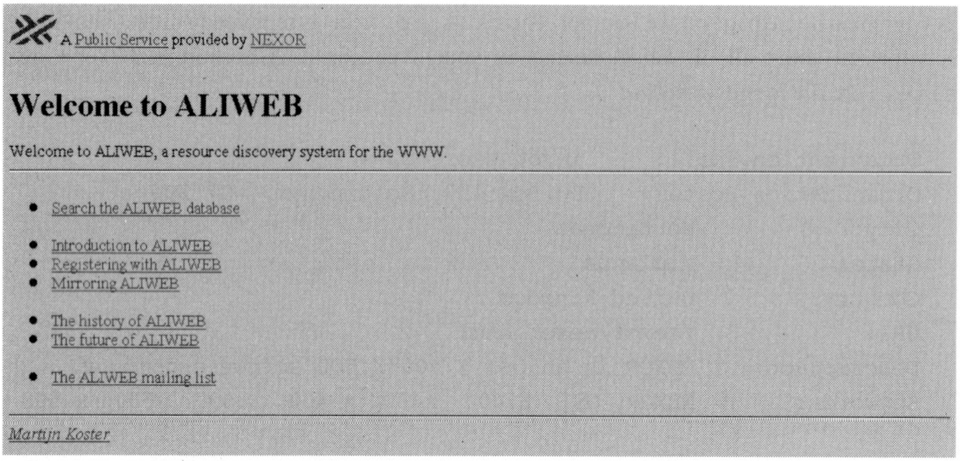

Figure 5.1 The AliWeb opening screen.

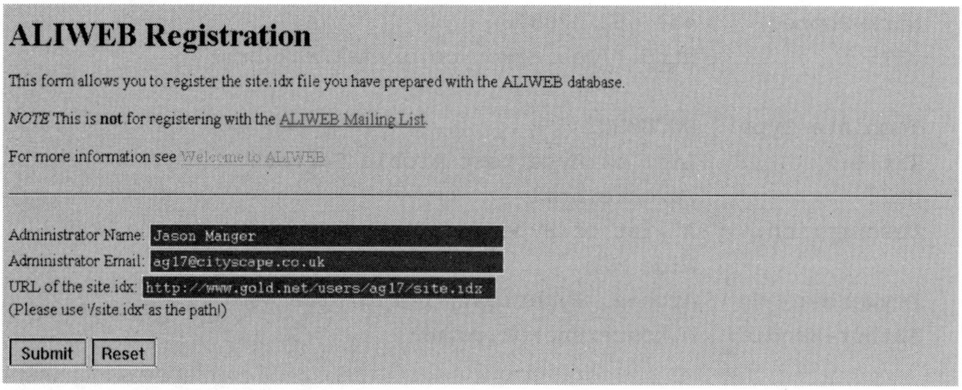

Figure 5.2 The AliWeb registration screen.

```
http://www.gold.net/users/ag17/index.htm
```

The `site.idx` file resides at `http://www.gold.net/users/ag17/site.idx` and resembles the following in my own case:

```
Organization-Email:     ag17@cityscape.co.uk
Organization-Postal:    CityScape UK
City:           Cambridge
State:          Midlands
Country:        United Kingdom
```

```
URI:              http://www.gold.net/
Description:      CityScape is a UK Internet service provider
Keywords:         Cityscape


Template-Type:    USER
Title:            Jason Manger
Handle:           ag17@cityscape.co.uk
Email:            ag17@cityscape.co.uk
Work-Phone:       Omitted
URI:              http://www.cityscape.co.uk/users/ag17/index.htm


Template-Type:    DOCUMENT
Title:            McGraw-Hill's Essential Internet Pages
URI:              /index.htm
Description:      Details of McGraw-Hill's Internet books by Jason
                  Manger
Keywords:         Manger, McGraw-Hill, Internet, Web
Author-Handle:    ag17@cityscape.co.uk
```

The `site.idx` entry above contains the filename URI (Uniform Resource Indicator) `/index.htm` that points to the main home page on the Web server that stores my files. The keywords I have supplied include my own surname, as well as my publisher's name and the two additional keyword `Internet` and `Web`.

AliWeb's requirement for a *site index* pays off in the long-term, since its searches are very comprehensive. For example, it is possible to conduct a search on certain organizations and countries only (although admittedly a URL will indicate the country location of a particular service also). AliWeb's search interface is also very impressive, with options to search URLs, conduct case-sensitive searches, substring searches, regular expressions and much more besides, as illustrated in Figure 5.3. The overall speed of AliWeb is also impressive, and search results can be shown in a variety of formats according to the information provided in the site index file. The only downside to AliWeb remains the need for a site index file at all. Many organizations may have second thoughts about submitting details because they may be too long-winded to enter. In the main, people probably prefer to submit just a URL and one-line description, and this is the technique employed by many registration schemes. Personally, I favour the site index feature, since the structure of each entry can be controlled more flexibly. The presentation of search results is also more attractive.

Figure 5.4 illustrates a substring-search with the keyword 'Africa'.

Ultimately, the success of any Web database, such as AliWeb, depends on people taking the time to promote their creation and to submit the necessary details for their site's inclusion in the database. AliWeb has achieved a good spread of sites, and its mirror sites are also well established.

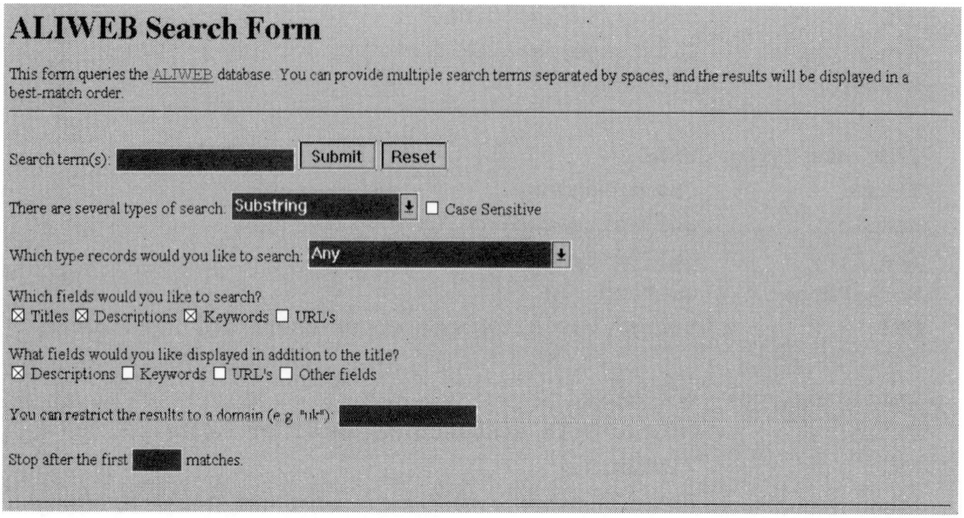

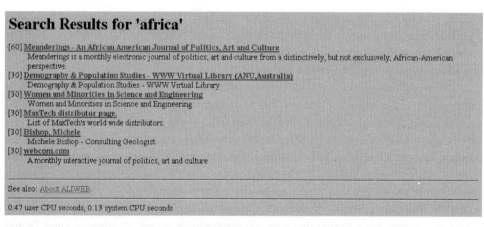

Figure 5.3 The AliWeb search (form) interface.

Figure 5.4 An AliWeb search result (substring search for term 'Africa').

 **CERN WWW Virtual Library**

Name	CERN World-Wide Web Virtual Library
Location (URL)	`http://info.cern.ch/hypertext/DataSources/` `bySubject/Overview.html`

Search system	A truly vast collection of URLs stored in HTML files, organized in an A–Z fashion by subject and/or topic
Update period	Daily
Mirror sites	None known
Search methods	Hyperlink interface according to topic. There is no form interface as such. Hyperlink navigation is provided
Rating	★★★
Statistics	100 Subject categories
Overall rating	★★★★

The CERN Virtual Library (CERNVL) is vast resource containing many thousands of URLs, all organized by subject in an A–Z fashion using clickable hyperlinks. The CERNVL is a popular resource because it is logically organized. You can quickly see what topics are available, and then click on one of these for a further breakdown of topics. Since there is no option to specify a search term the CERNVL can be slightly daunting to navigate at a first glance. Unlike other Web database services, such as CUI W3 and Yahoo, entries are not searched for using any known algorithm, but instead are broken down into topic hierarchies as individual hypertext files. Figure 5.5 illustrates the main subject listings you can expect to find.

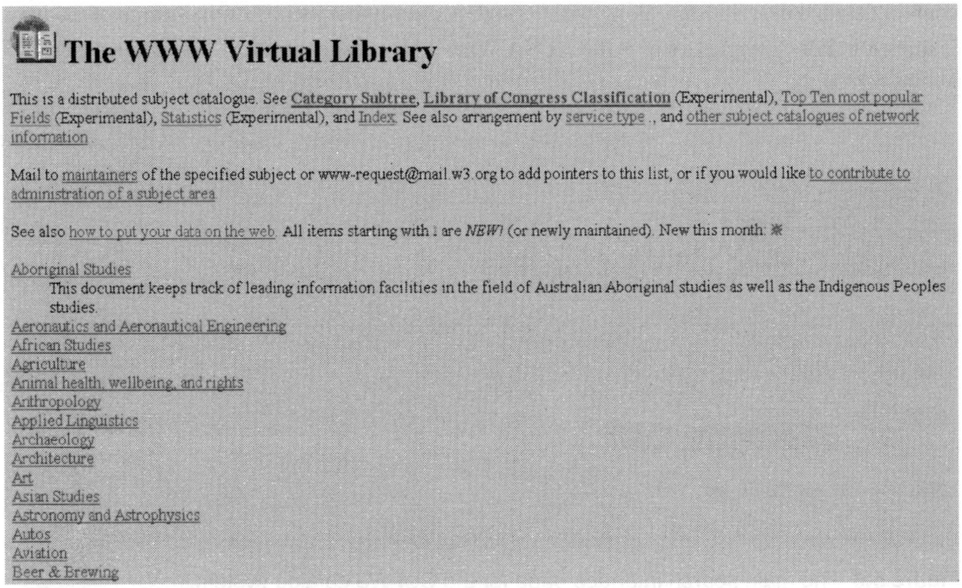

Figure 5.5 CERN's Virtual Library (A–Z subject list).

CUI W3 Catalog

Name	CUI World-Wide Web (W3) Catalog
Location (URL)	`http://cuiwww.unige.ch/cgi-bin/w3catalog`
Search system	An amalgamation of URLs from existing Internet resource listings (e.g. The Yanoff List, December List, NCSA What's New Pages and CERN's WWW Virtual Library)
Update period	Daily
Mirror sites	`http://www.winc.com/W3catalog.html` `http://www-resus.univ-mrs.fr:80/W3catalog`
Search methods	A limited interface is offered. Single field provided. Perl/`grep` regular expressions are accepted for search terms
Rating	★★
Statistics	100 000+ entries (as of May 1995)
Overall rating	★★★★

The CUI service maintains a database of URLs that are updated from a series of existing URL databases, such as the CERN Virtual Library and the NCSA's What's New Web pages, as well as many others. The search interface is very simple, consisting of a single field that facilitates case-insensitive regular expressions (based upon the Perl and `grep` tools). Figure 5.6 illustrates the main home page of the CUI W3 Catalogue. While the search interface is poor, the results produced are extensive.

The results returned from a typical CUI search are very comprehensive. All items returned contain detailed descriptions, along with a small acronym that identifies the source of the item in question. For example 'nwn' is the NCSA What's New page. Figure 5.7 illustrates a typical results screen.

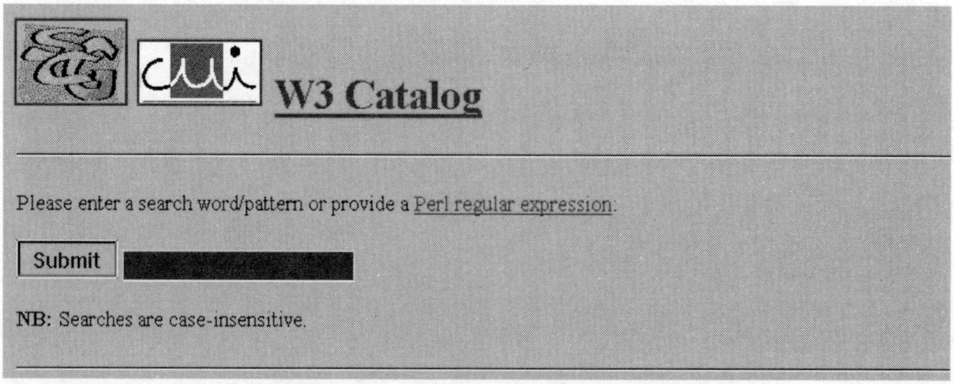

Figure 5.6 The main search interface page for the CUI W3 catalog system.

Result of search for "africa":

: Wesgro
Southern Scientific, South Africa
Wesgro is pleased to announce it's WWW pages to provide potential investors in the Western Cape, South Africa, with substantial assistance and information. (nwn)

: Lehman College Art Gallery
Bronx, NY, US
Wake up and add your itch, your niche, your passion, your theory, your critique to the World's First Collaborative Sentence growing now before your eyes. The sentence began in New York a few days ago, placed there by Douglas Davis, the artist who pioneered global satellite video, sponsored by the Lehman College Art Gallery in the Bronx, fed to date by Americans, Russians, South Africans, Haitians and next by you. (nwn)

: Impex Connect - Global Network Trading
Impex Connect, Cape Town, Western Cape, ZA
Information on marketable products and crafts of South Africa. (nwn)

: Kwanzaa Information Center
New Perspective Technologies, Norfolk, VA, US
The Kwanzaa Information Center, from the MelaNet Information and Communications Network, provides information concerning Kwanzaa, the African-American holiday, including symbols, principals, and a schedule for Kwanzaa celebration. (nwn)

Figure 5.7 A typical results screen from the CUI catalogue (search term: 'Africa').

 # EINET's Galaxy

Name	EINET's Galaxy
Location (URL)	`http://galaxy.einet.net/fixed.html`
Search system	Searchable dynamic database of URLs
Update period	Daily
Mirror sites	None known
Search methods	Boolean phrases/Stemming/Web link and Gopher URLs/WAIS-like hit-list
Rating	★★★★
Statistics	Unknown
Overall rating	★★★★

Einet's Galaxy offers an excellent Web searching facility. The search engine was originally based around a freeware version of the WAIS engine, although it has recently been revamped to cope with its increasingly large number of database of entries. Searches can be performed on Web links, Gopher links and, locally, on Einet's own extensive A–Z subject list – the default option, which does not involve a search of any indexes. The option to search Hytelnet, a popular Internet resource location tool, is also provided. All results are presented using a WAIS-like hit-list structure which is marked out of 1000 according to the most relevant document(s) that have been retrieved. The search results also indicate the sizes of the document(s) retrieved – a useful feature to say the least, since you can at least see how large a file is before you decide to download it. The main search interface is shown in Figure 5.8.

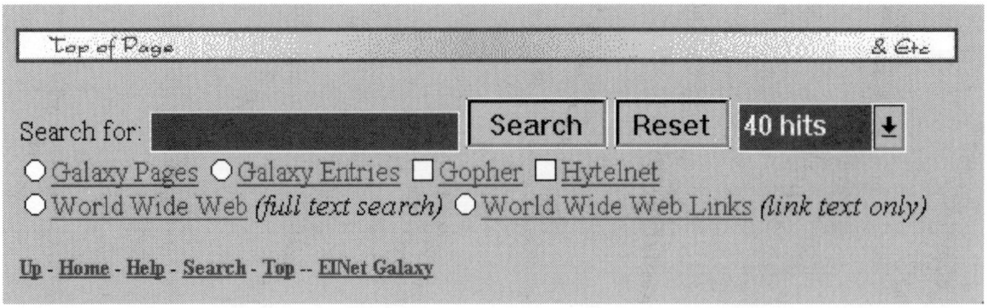
Top of Page
& Etc
Search for:
Search
Reset
40 hits
Galaxy Pages
Galaxy Entries
Gopher
Hytelnet
World Wide Web (full text search)
World Wide Web Links (link text only)
Up - Home - Help - Search - Top -- EINet Galaxy

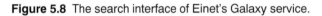

Figure 5.8 The search interface of Einet's Galaxy service.

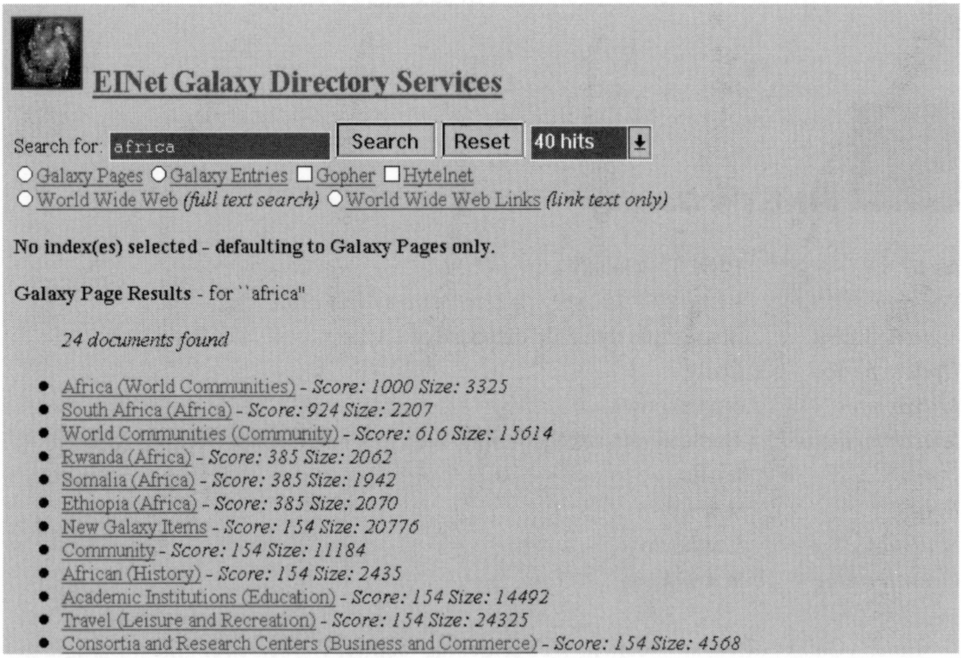
EINet Galaxy Directory Services
Search for: africa
Search
Reset
40 hits
Galaxy Pages
Galaxy Entries
Gopher
Hytelnet
World Wide Web (full text search)
World Wide Web Links (link text only)
No index(es) selected - defaulting to Galaxy Pages only.
Galaxy Page Results - for ''africa''
24 documents found
Africa (World Communities) - Score: 1000 Size: 3325
South Africa (Africa) - Score: 924 Size: 2207
World Communities (Community) - Score: 616 Size: 15614
Rwanda (Africa) - Score: 385 Size: 2062
Somalia (Africa) - Score: 385 Size: 1942
Ethiopia (Africa) - Score: 385 Size: 2070
New Galaxy Items - Score: 154 Size: 20776
Community - Score: 154 Size: 11184
African (History) - Score: 154 Size: 2435
Academic Institutions (Education) - Score: 154 Size: 14492
Travel (Leisure and Recreation) - Score: 154 Size: 24325
Consortia and Research Centers (Business and Commerce) - Score: 154 Size: 4568

Figure 5.9 Results of the search for search term 'Africa'.

Searching for the term 'Africa' resulted in a large number of hits, as shown in Figure 5.9.

WAIS (Wide Area Information Server) is a widely used indexing system for documents. It searches the internal contents of documents (as opposed to URLs and document titles, as with Gopher in the case of the latter), so the results it retrieves should be relevant.

Einet's service is top-notch, being fast, reliable and with links to many esoteric topics and sites.

GNA: Global Network Academy

Name	GNA (Global Network Academy) – Meta Library Search
Location (URL)	`http://uu-gna.mit.edu:8001/cgi-bin/meta`
Search system	Simple pattern matching (*regular expression*) against internal database
Update period	Daily
Mirror sites	None known
Search methods	`rdb` (UNIX) formatted database and UNIX shell script engine. The interface consists of just one field (`<isindex>` tag). Regular expressions can be used
Rating	★★
Statistics	4000 entries; 80 000 individual search words (as of May 1995)
Overall rating	★★

GNA's service uses the UNIX tool `rdb` as the basis of its search engine software. Each entry in the GNA database is structured, rather like CUI's offering discussed earlier, into a series of fields that identify a resource, for example a subject category and URL. Entries are returned in this format also, along with a hyperlink to actually get to the resource. Resources may be Gophers or other Internet resources, although Gophers seem to feature prominently, probably because they interface well with WAIS servers. Since the database is a meta-library, GNA points out that the documents retrieved may well be individual files, although they could also be complete file archives (which you may have to search further). You can quite easily submit your own Web resource to the GNA database, although be sure to read all documentation carefully beforehand, since items need to be categorized accurately. The main search interface to GNA is shown in Figure 5.10.

GNA Meta-Library Search

This script implements a case insensitive initial substring search of the GNA Meta-Library internet reference table. This copy, stored as a /rdb table, has about 4,000 rows containing about 80,000 words.

Search arguments, separated by space, are combined with AND automatically. Don't type the 'and', just the search arguments. The first two hundred hits are returned.

Often a thesaurus (this one is about 80k bytes, almost 9,000 unique words) with frequencies sorted alphabetically or numerically can be helpful. If an entry in the thesaurus has a frequency of 1, then including that keyword in a search will guarantee no more than one hit (unless the keyword is an initial substring of another).

Netscape Communications maintains a comparison of several search engines, using a search for 'surf' as a basis. The number of hits returned by MCOM's surveyed engines ranges from 4 to 266. This GNA meta-library index retrieves 5 hits when looking for 'surf'.

Submit New Entries

ADD your submission to this index or to a variety of other WWW indices.

This is a searchable index. Enter search keywords:  `africa`

Figure 5.10 The interface to GNA's database.

Meta Library Search Results

```
starting script: Tue Apr  4 13:03:17 EDT 1995
load average: 1.98, 1.76, 1.03
Try searching the  alex  database for africa
starting search at Tue Apr 4 13:03:18 EDT 1995
6 hits for africa
ended search at Tue Apr 4 13:03:19 EDT 1995

number          3221
coverage        40
topic           Culture;Africa
authors
maintainers
title           Asa Online
href            gopher://gopher.cic.net:70/11/e-serials/alphabetic/a/asa-online
keywords
descriptions        Electronic journal / Electronic Newsletter on the African Studies
Assocation
format1
format2
indexed_by      Thurs Jul 29 05:19:50 1993 EDT
indexed_from    cic.journals.src
```

Figure 5.11 A typical search item returned from the GNA database.

When a item from the GNA database is matched against the search term provided, the entire entry from the database is retrieved and shown to the user, as illustrated in Figure 5.11, which shows one such item. In general, the GNA service seems to work very well, although the number of database entries is very small. The search criterion is somewhat limited in terms of the competition.

 **GNN Catalog**

Name	GNN (Global Network Navigator) Catalog
Location (URL)	`http://www.gnn.com/wic`
Search system	Extensive hypertext database of URLs broken down by subject type in an A–Z fashion
Update period	Daily
Mirror sites	None known
Search methods	A hypertext interface is provided. Subject categories are provided in an A–Z style guide
Rating	★★★
Statistics	There were 645 individual catalogue entries (e.g. *Art*) as of May 1995, making this a truly enormous resource
Overall rating	★★★

Figure 5.12 The GNN home page and subject directory.

The Global Network Navigator (GNN) is a spin-off from Ed Krol's Internet book *The Whole Internet*. It is an enormous list of Web sites organized by subject into an A–Z guide for easy browsing. A forms-based interface is not provided, implying that this is not a structured database of entries, but rather a series of hypertext *table of contents* pages. Therefore you must navigate the hyperlinks provided in order to find the entries that interest you. The actual entries that comprise the GNN database can be viewed by *category* and by *subject* using the options supplied at the top of the home page (Figure 5.12).

 InfoSeek

Name	InfoSeek
Location (URL)	`http://www.infoseek.com/` *(Full registration required)*
Search system	Database of URLs, most probably updated using an automated robot
Update period	Daily
Mirror sites	`http://home.mcom.com/home/internet-search.html` (under InfoSeek)

Select the box to the left of the Collection you wish to search from the list below. If no box is selected, we'll search the Collection you previously searched. Enter words and phrases likely to appear in documents you seek (syntax and examples):

    africa

☐ Restrict to documents published within ± the last 1 ± day(s) ±

    Run Query | Clear Query Text and Reset Collection

Run my Personal Newswire

Collections with Free Document Retrievals
○ WWW Pages (info)
○ InfoSeek Help (Frequently Asked Questions) (info) *free queries!*

Standard Collections
○ Usenet News (since Sunday): May 21 - May 27 (info)
○ Usenet News (current 4 weeks): Apr 30 - May 27 (info)
○ Cineman Movie, Book and Music Reviews (info)
○ FrameMaker 4.0 Help Notes (info)
○ Hoover's Masterlist of U.S. Companies (brief details) (info)
○ Wire Services (info)
○ MDX Health Digest (info)
○ Computer Periodicals (info)

Premium Collections
○ Computer Select (online version) (info)
○ Hoover's Company Profiles (in-depth details) (info)

Figure 5.13 The main *InfoSeek* search screen.

Search methods	Extensive search-scope available. Interface is limited, although more than adequate
Rating	★★★★
Statistics	200 000 Web documents (URLs) and 2 million USENET postings
Overall rating	★★★★

InfoSeek is the only commercial service to be included in this chapter. A free offer that allows 100 searches is currently available, however. The quality of InfoSeek's results make it a tool well worth considering – it really does uncover some interesting articles. Unlike most Web crawlers and databases, InfoSeek can be made to search USENET articles, Web pages, a selection of news wires and other periodicals (mostly of American origin). You should really register with InfoSeek in order to obtain a free demonstration account. All this can be done on-line and you will obtain immediate access to the system after this has been completed. You are under no obligation to sign up after your allotted number of queries has been used up (at which point you can re-subscribe under a new alias, at least until the trial service is available). Registration is not compulsory, however. Netscape Communications Corporation's server has a direct link into the InfoSeek system which will bypass the registration scheme, which is very useful to say the least. This interface allows the first ten hits to be collected and displayed. Figure 5.13 illustrates the main search screen for the InfoSeek service.

InfoSeek's results are presented with both a hyperlink to the URL for that item and an actual text extract from the item in question (Figure 5.14). This is a useful feature, since you can quickly get the gist of an article to see if it has any relevance. The size of each article (in kilobytes, or thousands of characters) is also shown. Another useful feature within InfoSeek is

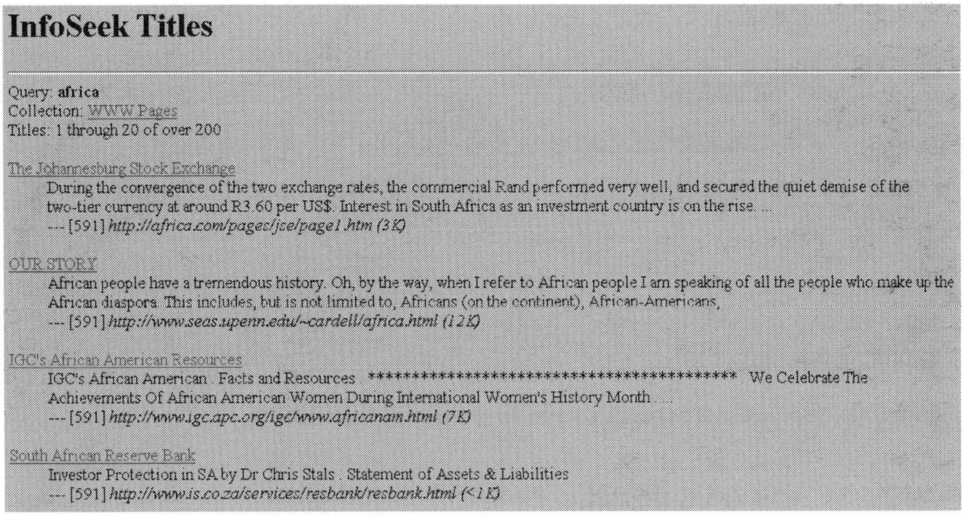

InfoSeek Titles

Query: **africa**
Collection: WWW Pages
Titles: 1 through 20 of over 200

The Johannesburg Stock Exchange
    During the convergence of the two exchange rates, the commercial Rand performed very well, and secured the quiet demise of the
    two-tier currency at around R3.60 per US$. Interest in South Africa as an investment country is on the rise. ...
    --- [591] *http://africa.com/pages/jse/page1.htm (3 K)*

OUR STORY
    African people have a tremendous history. Oh, by the way, when I refer to African people I am speaking of all the people who make up the
    African diaspora. This includes, but is not limited to, Africans (on the continent), African-Americans,
    --- [591] *http://www.seas.upenn.edu/~cardell/africa.html (12 K)*

IGC's African American Resources
    IGC's African American . Facts and Resources ** We Celebrate The
    Achievements Of African American Women During International Women's History Month ...
    --- [591] *http://www.igc.apc.org/igc/www.africanam.html (7 K)*

South African Reserve Bank
    Investor Protection in SA by Dr Chris Stals . Statement of Assets & Liabilities
    --- [591] *http://www.is.co.za/services/resbank/resbank.html (<1 K)*

Figure 5.14 A typical results screen from the InfoSeek service.

the ability to specify a time period for article searching, thus facilitating searches for documents that have appeared within a specified time-frame (very useful for USENET articles, for example).

JumpStation Robot

Name	JumpStation Robot
Location (URL):	`http://js.stir.ac.uk/jsbin/js`
	`http://js.stir.ac.uk/jsbin/jsii`
	(shortly to supersede JS v1)
Search system	Database search
Update period	Weekly update; daily Web-trawl
Mirror sites	None known
Search methods	The JumpStation robot allows searches according to hypertext titles and headers, as well as URLs
Rating	★★★
Statistics	Unknown
Overall rating	★★★

The JumpStation robot maintains an indexed database of Web resources that can be searched on the basis of a URLs or header (e.g. title). A forms-based interface is supplied, and the system is responsive. At the time of writing a new version of the program is being released (note the second URL above). Figure 5.15 illustrates the main search interface.

The Document Search

☐ Check to limit results by title.
    Enter Title Word: ▮▮▮▮▮▮▮▮▮▮
☐ Check to limit results by header.
    Enter Header Word: ▮▮▮▮▮▮▮▮
☒ Check to limit results by subject.
    Enter Subject Word: `africa`

☒ If this box is checked, JumpStation II returns verbose information about each document it finds. If it is unchecked then more terse information is returned.

Press ⎡reset⎤ to clear the form, or ⎡ submit ⎤ it to the search engine.

Contacting the Author

Figure 5.15 The document search screen for the JumpStation Robot.

A search for the term 'Africa' returned some interesting responses, as shown in Figure 5.16.

JumpStation II Results Page

Search for "africa" in document subject

The following list is a verbose list of documents in the JumpStation database that have a high occurence of the word "africa" in their content. Please note that this data is transitory, and not stored on this server.

- http://128.141.201.214/hypertext/DataSources/WWW/Africa.html
  Title: *World-Wide Web servers:Africa*
  Last Modification: *Sunday, 11-Sep-94 09:01:19 GMT*
  Size (bytes): *526*
  Type: *text/html*
  Links: *2*
- http://192.104.1.208/web/washlaw/forint/africa/africa.htm
  Title: *South Africa*
  Last Modification: *Wednesday, 15-Jun-1994 08:05:58*
  Size (bytes): *692*
  Type: *text/html*
  Links: *6*
- http://osprey.unisa.ac.za/
  Title: *UNISA-Computer Science*
  Last Modification: *Friday, 05-Aug-94 13:08:04 GMT*
  Type: *text/html*
  Links: *8*

Figure 5.16 Some typical results using a search term of 'Africa'.

 **Lycos**

Name	Lycos
Location (URL)	`http://fuzine.mt.cs.cmu.edu/mlm/lycos-all.html`
Search system	Web-crawling algorithm and indexed database with over 2.5 million entries. Database has Gopher/FTP/HTTP (Web) entries

Update period	Weekly update; daily Web-trawl
Mirror sites	There are various hosts at `cs.cmu.edu` which handle Lycos requests (with various options/hit levels etc.). Use the main server shown above, since machines change regularly.
Search methods	Lycos maintains a large indexed database of URLs and resource details. The system references titles, headings, URL links and document keywords
Rating	★★★★
Statistics	2.5 million+ unique URLs referenced (as of March 1995); Lycos can pull in (an estimated) 5000 documents per day
Overall rating	★★★★★

Lycos is one of the best-known Web crawlers on the Internet (the name *Lycos* comes from the Latin *Lycosidea*, a predatory spider which, ironically, doesn't use a Web – although this one does!). Based at the Carnegie Mellon University, it is a large system that can reference many hundreds of thousands of Internet URLs. As of March 1995 the system could reference well over 2.5 million unique Internet URLs, and it now also has an automatic URL deletion facility to purge the system. Lycos is a very heavily used system, and has multiple hosts handling search requests. A load average will be shown when conducting a search. Don't be surprised to find that the load is too high and that your request has been rejected. Lycos offers the user a number of search interfaces. The most basic is a single field, as shown in Figure 5.17, although an alternative form interface with further options is also available.

By clicking on the hyperlink to load a form-based interface (Figure 5.18), Lycos will allow you to tailor your searches, indicating whether or not the results should be made more compact, as well as specifying how many hits you would like to retrieve, thus speeding up the search.

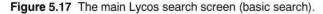

Lycos search:

Load average: 15.62: **Lycos Mar 30, 1995 catalog**, 2687146 unique URLs (see Lycos News)

This is a searchable index. Enter search keywords: `africa`

Enter one or more words or word prefixes in any order. The searcher will prefer documents that match more of your search terms, that match your term more closely, that have more occurrences of any one term, and occurences earlier in the document.

Lycos Search Language description
Form-based search with options (set number of hits, terse mode)
Register your own URLs with Lycos or Delete your own URLs
Lycos Frequently Asked Questions

This indexer is in beta test (see the Lycos Beta Test page). You can also see what features are on the Lycos "To Do" list. Please report any bugs to Michael Mauldin fuzzy@cmu.edu

back to the Lycos Home Page

Figure 5.17 The main Lycos search screen (basic search).

Carnegie Mellon
Lycos™
Lycos search form
Query: africa
Max-hits: 15 Min-terms: 1 Min-score: 0.01 Terse output:
Start search
Reset
Search language help
Back to the Lycos Home Page

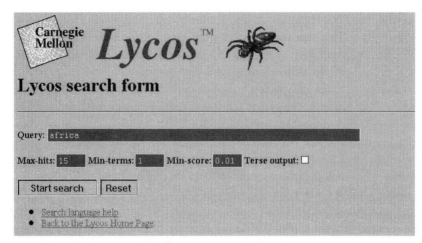

Figure 5.18 The Lycos search form screen.

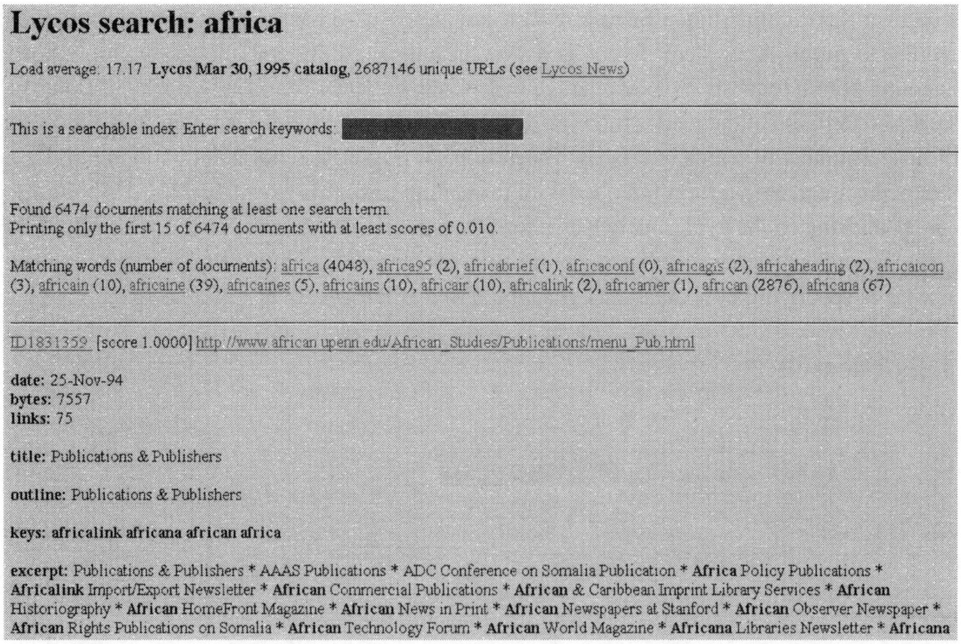

Lycos search: africa
Load average: 17.17 Lycos Mar 30, 1995 catalog, 2687146 unique URLs (see Lycos News)
This is a searchable index. Enter search keywords:
Found 6474 documents matching at least one search term.
Printing only the first 15 of 6474 documents with at least scores of 0.010.
Matching words (number of documents): africa (4048), africa95 (2), africabrief (1), africaconf (0), africagis (2), africaheading (2), africaicon (3), africain (10), africaine (39), africaines (5), africains (10), africair (10), africalink (2), africamer (1), african (2876), africana (67)
ID1831359 [score 1.0000] http://www.african.upenn.edu/African_Studies/Publications/menu_Pub.html
date: 25-Nov-94
bytes: 7557
links: 75
title: Publications & Publishers
outline: Publications & Publishers
keys: africalink africana african africa
excerpt: Publications & Publishers * AAAS Publications * ADC Conference on Somalia Publication * Africa Policy Publications * Africalink Import/Export Newsletter * African Commercial Publications * African & Caribbean Imprint Library Services * African Historiography * African HomeFront Magazine * African News in Print * African Newspapers at Stanford * African Observer Newspaper * African Rights Publications on Somalia * African Technology Forum * African World Magazine * Africana Libraries Newsletter * Africana

Figure 5.19 Some typical results from a Lycos search.

When Lycos returns its search results it displays an excerpt from the actual resource in question, as shown in Figure 5.19 using the search-term 'Africa', which in this instance retrieved a staggering 6474 individual items. Lycos allows you to specify a *score* for your search, thus increasing or decreasing the number of hits that are eventually retrieved (the default score being 0.010). By default, Lycos returns the first 15 matches that fall on or above the default score. Figure 5.19 illustrates a typical results screen with these settings in place.

 **Nikos**

Name	Nikos
Location (URL)	`http://www.rns.com/cgi-bin/nomad`
Search system	Database of URLs
Update period	Weekly update; daily Web-trawl
Mirror sites	None known
Search methods	Nikos maintains a large indexed database of Web URLs. The search interface is currently being revamped, and will eventually be form-driven
Rating	★★
Statistics	50 000+ Web articles referenced (as of May 1995)
Overall rating	★★★

Nikos maintains an index of Web URLs. Well over 50 000 individual entries are indexed, making Nikos a most comprehensive tool. The service will shortly be revamped, so expect a form-driven interface to be made available shortly (with more extensive URL and Boolean options etc.). Some typical results from the service can be seen in Figure 5.20. The search results are rather plain; a simple hyperlink identifies each entry that matches the search term entered, so you just click on the required link to activate the service required.

RBSE URL

Name	RBSE (Repository Based Software Engineering)
Location (URL)	`http://rbse.jsc.nasa.gov/eichmann/urlsearch.html`
Search system	Oracle database of documents indexed via the popular WAIS (Wide Area Information System) standard
Update period	Weekly update; daily Web-trawl
Mirror sites	None known
Search methods	The RBSE project maintains a large indexed database of Web URLs, indexed using WAIS. The single-field search interface currently offers only substring and simple Boolean search facilities

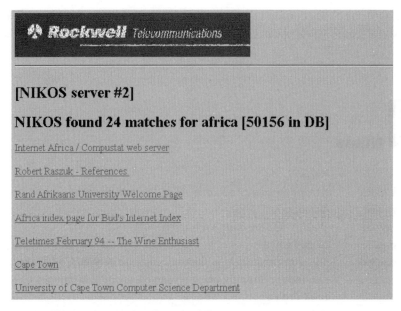

Figure 5.20 A typical results screen from the Nikos server.

Rating	★★
Statistics	36 000+ Web articles referenced (as of May 1995)
Overall rating	★★★

The main RBSE index is a collection of URLs that are collected using a version of WAIS. A Web spider program scours the Web in order to build a list of links, which are then placed in an Oracle database. Over 36 000 documents exist in the index, and since WAIS is used the index can actually reference words and phrases that are embedded within documents, rather than by using the URL or title as in some other schemes. Figure 5.21 illustrates the main search interface of the RBSE system, which is currently just a single field that facilitates substring case-insensitive searches of the RBSE index.

Figure 5.22 shows the results of an RBSE search.

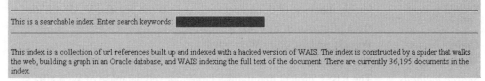

Figure 5.21 The main search interface to the RBSE system.

URL Search Response:

NumberOfRecordsReturned: 100

- Score: 1000, lines: 78 Date: Wed Mar 30 20:43:26 1994 GMT Server: NCSA/1.0a3.1 MIM

- Score: 1000, lines: 30 Date: Wed Mar 30 03:51:43 1994 GMT Server: NCSA/1.0a3.1

- Score: 982, lines: 48 Date: Wednesday, 30-Mar-94 17:53:46 GMT Server: NCSA/1.0 MIME-version: 1.0

- Score: 935, lines: 55 Global Images From GRASS GIS

- Score: 932, lines: 22 1492 -- What Came To Be Called America

- Score: 869, lines: 44 Date: Friday, 01-Apr-94 16:23:56 GMT

- Score: 861, lines: 31 Date: Wed Mar 30 03:48:34 1994 GMT Server: NCSA/1.0a3.1

- Score: 817, lines: 82 Visitors to tbone

Figure 5.22 Some typical results from the RBSE system.

 **WebCrawler**

Name	WebCrawler
Location (URL)	`http://webcrawler.cs.washington.edu/WebCrawler/` `WebQuery.html`
Search system	Database of URLs indexed by an automated Web robot
Update period	Daily update; daily Web-trawl
Mirror sites	None known
Search methods	The Web*Crawler* maintains an index of URLs that it has scanned using an automated Web robot program. The search interface is limited to AND-style Boolean queries and a hit-count, but the results are extensive.
Rating	★★★
Statistics	100 000 + documents referenced; 900 000 documents being examined further (NB: unindexed) as of May 1995
Overall rating	★★★★

The WebCrawler has constantly popped up in the 'top 25' Web-sites list in recent months. It uses an automated robot program that follows URLs from one document to the next, building a searchable index as it proceeds. Indexing is handled by a WAIS (Wide Area Information Server) engine – search entries receive a score (out of 1000) to indicate their relevance. Expect

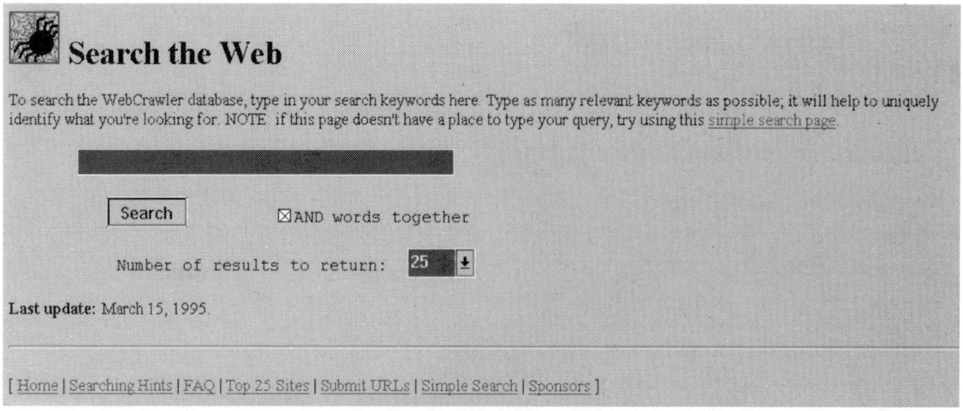

Search the Web

To search the WebCrawler database, type in your search keywords here. Type as many relevant keywords as possible; it will help to uniquely identify what you're looking for. NOTE: if this page doesn't have a place to type your query, try using this simple search page.

[Search]   ☒ AND words together

Number of results to return: 25 ↕

Last update: March 15, 1995.

[Home | Searching Hints | FAQ | Top 25 Sites | Submit URLs | Simple Search | Sponsors]

Figure 5.23 The search interface to the WebCrawler program.

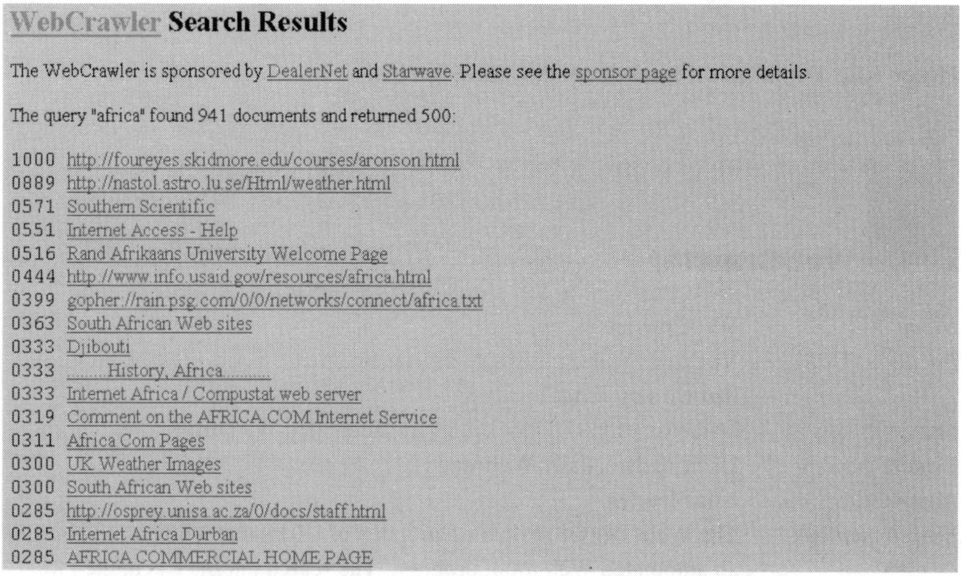

WebCrawler Search Results

The WebCrawler is sponsored by DealerNet and Starwave. Please see the sponsor page for more details.

The query "africa" found 941 documents and returned 500:

```
1000  http://foureyes.skidmore.edu/courses/aronson.html
0889  http://nastol.astro.lu.se/Html/weather.html
0571  Southern Scientific
0551  Internet Access - Help
0516  Rand Afrikaans University Welcome Page
0444  http://www.info.usaid.gov/resources/africa.html
0399  gopher://rain.psg.com/0/0/networks/connect/africa.txt
0363  South African Web sites
0333  Djibouti
0333  ......History, Africa........
0333  Internet Africa / Compustat web server
0319  Comment on the AFRICA.COM Internet Service
0311  Africa Com Pages
0300  UK Weather Images
0300  South African Web sites
0285  http://osprey.unisa.ac.za/0/docs/staff.html
0285  Internet Africa Durban
0285  AFRICA COMMERCIAL HOME PAGE
```

Figure 5.24 A typical WebCrawler results screen (search term: 'Africa').

the site to be slow to respond, since it is very popular. You may also want to read the on-line documentation that explains how the robot works – it is one of the best written guides to the searching algorithm employed by a robot program. Figure 5.23 illustrates the search interface screen.

The WebCrawler returns a list of results in the descending order of their relevance. A WAIS index engine is used which ranks every result document according to the number of occurrences of the search term that occur within the document, as shown in Figure 5.24.

World-Wide Web Wanderer (Wandex)

Name	WWWW Index (Wandex)
Location (URL)	`http://www.netgen.com/cgi/wandex`
Search system	Database of URLs
Update period	Weekly update; daily Web-trawl
Mirror sites	`http://www.mit.edu:8001/cgi/wandex`
Search methods	Wandex maintains an indexed database of URLs. Its search facilities are limited to Boolean (AND-type) searches and case-insensitive substring searches
Rating	★★
Statistics	25 000 + Web documents referenced; 6000 home pages referenced (as of May 1995)
Overall rating	★★★

Wandex is the name of the World-Wide Web Wanderer program. It is an extensive database of URLs that have been collected from the Web using a robot program known as The World-Wide Web Wanderer (WWWW). The WWWW updates the main Wandex database on a regular basis. Wandex currently knows the addresses of over 6000 home pages. Figure 5.25 illustrates the main Wandex screen.

Wandex's search-results are comprehensive, and contain the URL, home page title and a relevance score, which is calculated by the WWWW algorithm when searching the main index. Figure 5.26 illustrates some typical search results (using the search term 'Africa', as before).

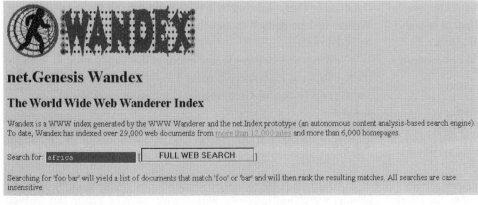

Figure 5.25 The opening search term screen of the Wandex service.

Wandex search for africa

Best Matches

- AFRICA COMMERCIAL HOME PAGE
  (http://www.africa.com) Score: 150
- Comment on The University of South Africa's WWW Server
  (http://www.unisa.ac.za/0/docs/comment-form.html) Score: 150
- UNISA-South Africa
  (http://osprey.unisa.ac.za/0/docs/south-africa.html) Score: 150
- Social Science:African-American Studies
  (http://www.yahoo.com/Social_Science/African_American_Studies) Score: 150
- World-Wide Web servers: Africa
  (http://www.w3.org/hypertext/DataSources/WWW/Africa.html) Score: 150
- African Studies
  (http://gnn.com/gnn/wic/african.01.html) Score: 150
- South African Broadcasting Corporation Welcome Page
  (http://www.sabc.co.za) Score: 150
- Black/African Related Resources
  (http://gnn.com/gnn/wic/african.02.html) Score: 150
- African-Americans for Humanism
  (http://freethought.tamu.edu/aah/) Score: 150

Figure 5.26 A typical results screen returned from the Wandex service.

World-Wide Web Worm

Name	World-Wide Web Worm (WWWW)
Location (URL)	`http://www.netgen.com/cgi/wandex`
Search system	Database of URLs indexed by a Web crawler that follows URL links
Update period	Weekly update; daily Web-trawl
Mirror sites	None known
Search methods	WWWW has an extensive search interface that can be used to search titles, URLs and even specific countries. Case-insensitive searching and `egrep` (extended Grep) regular expressions are allowed.
Rating	★★★★
Statistics	350 000+ multimedia objects (URL documents) as of May 1995
Overall rating	★★★★

The World-Wide Web Worm (WWWW) won a *Best of the Web* award in 1994, making it one of the Internet's premier search tools, ranking with services such as Yahoo and AliWeb. WWWW follows URL links in hypertext documents and then places these in an indexed database that can then be searched accordingly. The UNIX tool, `egrep` (extended global

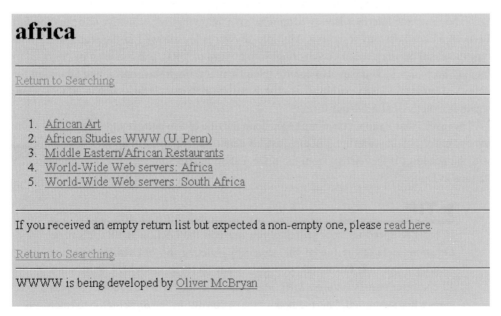

Figure 5.27 The form interface to the search facility of the WWWW.

regular expression print) is used to conduct comprehensive searches – a large list of examples are provided on the home page for the WWWW service. Figure 5.27 illustrates the main search interface, which is structured as a fill-out-form, and Figure 5.28 shows a typical search result.

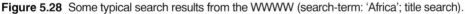

Figure 5.28 Some typical search results from the WWWW (search-term: 'Africa'; title search).

Yahoo

Name	Yahoo (Yet Another Hierarchical Organized Oracle)
Location (URL)	`http://www.yahoo.com`
Search system	Database of URLs indexed by a Web robot that scans sites for new announcements etc.
Update period	Weekly update; daily Web-trawl
Mirror sites	None known
Search methods	An A–Z style subject list is provided, as well as a search-engine/ interface. A random URL link is a nice addition, and the site is well documented
Rating	★★★★
Statistics	36 000+ unique entries and growing (as of May 1995)
Overall rating	★★★★

Yahoo is another well-known Web robot and resource guide rolled into one. At the time of writing, this service referenced over 36 000 individual Web documents, half of which are made up from submissions and the other half by its automated Web robot program, which scans the Web for new sites. The main Yahoo home page has both a subject breakdown and a search interface, which makes it particularly attractive. Yahoo gathers its information in a number of ways. A robot program is used that examines many existing Web resources, such as the NCSA What's New page, as well as examining any relevant Web USENET groups (such as the newsgroups `comp.infosystems.www.[users.misc.providers]`) for new page announcements. Figure 5.29 illustrates the main home page for the Yahoo service.

Yahoo's search interface is very comprehensive, allowing case-sensitive searches and full Boolean and/or keyword searching. Multiple keywords are allowed in the search field. The type of search conducted can be substring, whole-word or URL, and can even be confined to Internet host names. You can also control the hit-count though this screen, and an option for unlimited hits is provided via a pull-down list. Figure 5.30 illustrates the search interface screen, which is structured as a fill-out-form.

The results that Yahoo returns are based upon the title of a hypertext page. Individual items are not ranked by any scoring scheme; instead items are displayed in an A–Z fashion, some with subheadings if they arrive from the main Yahoo index. Some typical search results can be seen in Figure 5.31.

▶TIP

In order to speed up your searches you can edit the URL in Netscape's main *Location:* field at the top of the screen by deleting the old search term and entering a new one. Ensure that you replace any literal spaces with + signs, since all character strings within a URL that contain spaces will be encoded as plus signs when submitted. This method will save you hitting the *Back* button to enter

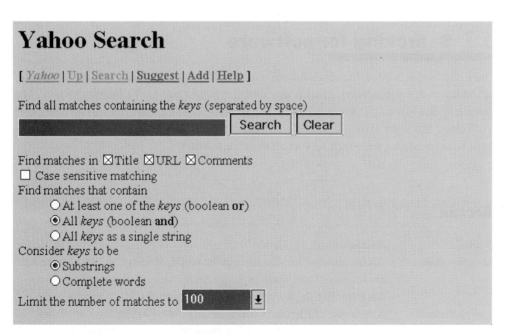

Figure 5.29 The Yahoo home page.

Figure 5.30 The Yahoo search screen interface.

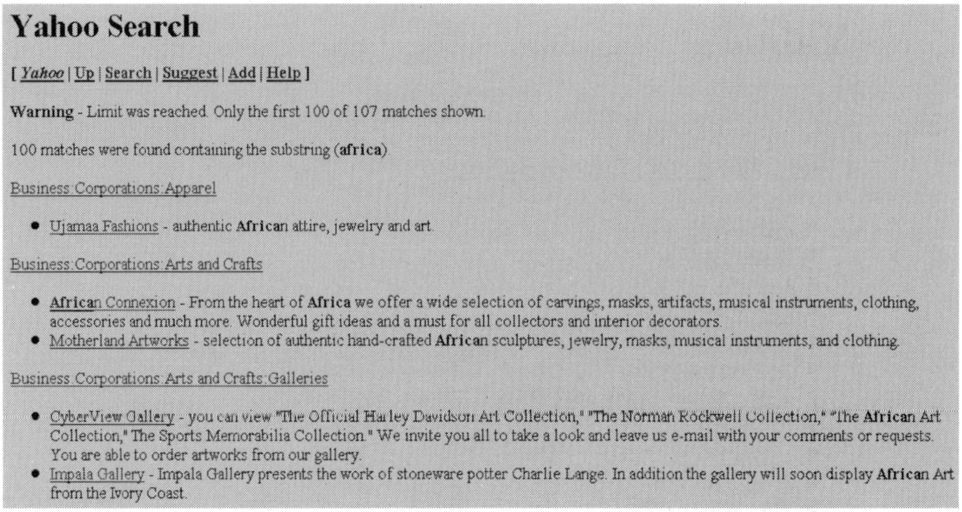

Yahoo Search

[*Yahoo* | Up | Search | Suggest | Add | Help]

Warning - Limit was reached. Only the first 100 of 107 matches shown.

100 matches were found containing the substring (**africa**).

Business:Corporations:Apparel

- Ujamaa Fashions - authentic **African** attire, jewelry and art.

Business:Corporations:Arts and Crafts

- African Connexion - From the heart of **Africa** we offer a wide selection of carvings, masks, artifacts, musical instruments, clothing, accessories and much more. Wonderful gift ideas and a must for all collectors and interior decorators.
- Motherland Artworks - selection of authentic hand-crafted **African** sculptures, jewelry, masks, musical instruments, and clothing.

Business:Corporations:Arts and Crafts:Galleries

- CyberView Gallery - you can view "The Official Harley Davidson Art Collection," "The Norman Rockwell Collection," "The **African** Art Collection," The Sports Memorabilia Collection." We invite you all to take a look and leave us e-mail with your comments or requests. You are able to order artworks from our gallery.
- Impala Gallery - Impala Gallery presents the work of stoneware potter Charlie Lange. In addition the gallery will soon display **African** Art from the Ivory Coast.

Figure 5.31 Some typical results from the Yahoo database (search term: Africa).

another search phrase in the form or field provided. Press RETURN to submit the URL afterwards.

5.3 **Searching for software**

Only one tool is needed to search for software: Archie. Archie is the Internet's software searching tool, a public service that is distributed around a number of Internet servers. The Archie system started out life as a character-based service, and was (and still is) accessible via Telnet. Since the arrival of the World-Wide Web, a number of Archie search engines have been interfaced with Web servers all over the Internet.

Archie

Name	Archie
Location (URL)	Archie sites are located all over the world, although not all of these sites are mirrors of one another. Some Archie servers maintain their own database. See the list below for actual locations
Search system	A database of filenames that exist on public FTP servers, which are spread all over the Internet (i.e. those accessible via `ftp://` URLs)
Update period	Daily update
Alternative sites:	`http://www.nexor.co.uk` `http://www.lerc.nasa.gov/Doc/archieplex.html`

```
http://www.csi.nb.ca/archgate.html
http://hoohoo.ncsa.uiuc.edu/archie.html
http://www.sco.com/Third/archie.html
http://http2.sils.umich.edu/utility/archie.html
http://src.doc.ic.ac.uk/archieplexform.html
http://www.funet.fi/funet/archie/
    archieplexform.html
http://www.twi.tudelft.nl/Local/archieplex/doc/
    form.html
http://www.th-darmstadt.de/archie/
    archieplex.html
http://www.gae.unican.es/archie.html
http://cuiwww.unige.ch/archieplexform.html
http://www.pvv.unit.no/archie
http://www.tubitak.gov.tr/archieplex/
    public-form.html
http://archie.ac.il/misc/archie.html
http://www.tansu.com.au/Services/ArchiePlex/
    archieplex.html
http://www.gh.cs.su.oz.au/Utils/
    archieplexform.html
http://peacock.tnjc.edu.tw/NEW/archie/AA.html
```

Search methods	Search is carried out using a simple string match against the file or directory concerned. Any part of a filename can be matched in this way
Rating	★★★
Overall rating	★★★★

Figure 5.32 illustrates a typical Archie interface at the Web server www.nexor.co.uk, whose Archie interface and database is mirrored extensively on the Internet. In the diagram, we have entered the search-string pkzip.exe, which is the name of a popular file compression utility. Notice the search options that are available, including the ability to restrict searches to a particular country and to sort the results by date or by host order. The search string itself can match any part of a file, so you could search for file extensions or directory names, as well as actual filenames or parts of filenames etc. You can also control the number of hits (i.e. matches) returned, in order to speed up searches (an option is even provided to allow you to control the impact of the search on other Internet users – something not found in conventional Archie client interfaces). Figure 5.33 illustrates some typical search results. As can be seen, the Archie server archie.doc.ic.ac.uk has been used for the search. Notice how the results are marked up into an HTML document with all the embedded hyperlinks to the FTP server(s) that have the file(s) you require. For example, you could click on the second link in Figure 5.33, which would then download the file pkzip.exe from the popular HENSA

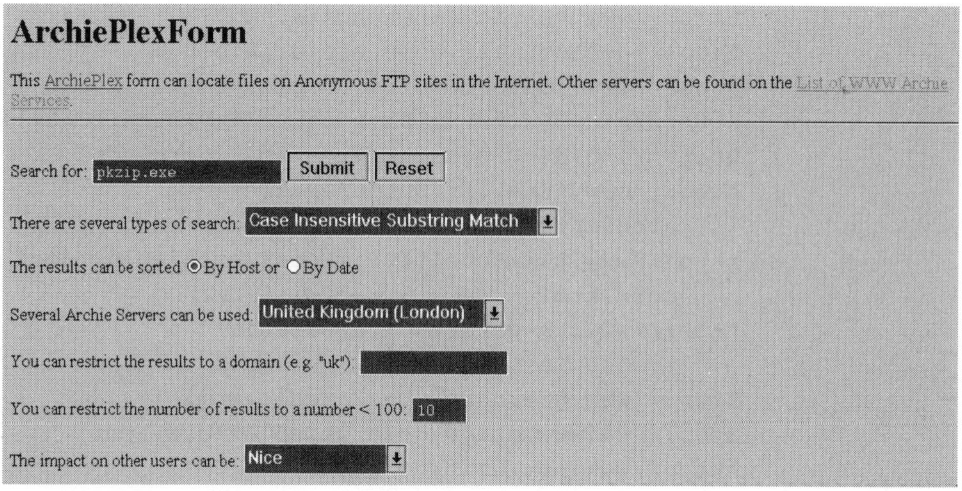

Figure 5.32 The ArchiePlex interface at `www.nexor.co.uk`.

Figure 5.33 Some typical search results from the ArchiPlex server.

archive at the FTP site `unix.hensa.ac.uk`. Remember to shift-click on the filename in order to download the file under a filename and/or directory of your choice.

As a rule of thumb, always retrieve more than one hit because some FTP servers can be badly congested. A problem with Archie is its assumption that you know the filename or part-filename that is required, although this problem can usually be overcome by using substrings or by entering a generic name (e.g. *winsock* for WinSock compatible packages, or *gopher* for Gopher-related tools). Such terms will normally match a directory or other filename which will then lead to the software you require. Remember that once you have found an FTP site you can browse its file system for the files you require using the `ftp://` URL (Chapter 2). It is also a good idea to get hold of an index or contents list, which most directories will have stored as the very first file in each particular directory.

A P P E N D I X

A

HTML quick reference

This appendix provides a reference guide to all of the most common HTML tags. All entries are ordered in an A–Z fashion. The tags in this appendix cover HTML versions 1.0 through 3.0. Any new Netscape tags that have been introduced, including proposed tags for HTML 3.0, are also included for completeness. All of the tags in this appendix work with the Netscape 1.1N browser.

<! CommentText>

Provides the HTML author with a commenting mechanism. Analogous to REM in BASIC, or /* and */ in C etc. Comments are ignored by the HTML parser. Text may run onto more than one line.

`<address>`**AddressText**`</address>`

Provides details of the current document's author, typically the email address of the author.

`<a href="`**URL**`">`**LinkText**`</a>`

Creates a hyper-reference to another Internet resource. **URL** can be the name of a local HTML file (e.g. `file:myfile.htm`), a URL to a remote server, such as a gopher (e.g. `gopher://info.brad.ac.uk`), or it can be the name of an image or audio clip for which Mosaic has the necessary viewing utility installed.

`<a name="`**myref**`">`**Word**`</a>`

Creates an *anchor* for the string **Word** in a document. The `<a href>` tag is used to index the anchor. For example, the tag `<a href="#mytag">Click here</a>` would create a hyperlink to the `<a name>` tag with the name '`mytag`', thus moving the user to that entry accordingly. If the anchor entry is in another document, the form of the tag is changed to `<a href="document.htm#anchorname">Click here<a>`, where `document.htm` is the remote document in question and `anchorname` is the name of the `<a name>` tag in the remote document.

`<b>`**BoldText**`</b>`

Emboldens the text **BoldText**. See also `<emp>`, `<strong>`.

`<blockquote>`**QuoteText**`</blockquote>`

Inserts a portion of text that is a quote from another source (e.g. from a speech). No quotes (") are placed around the **QuoteText**. Text may run onto more than one line.

`<body background="`**ImageFileURL**`"`
`bgcolor="#rrggbb"`
`text="#rrggbb"`
`link="#rrggbb"`
`vlink="#rrggbb"`
`alink="#rrggbb">`

Used to denote the actual *body* (**BodyText**), or part of the HTML document that contains all of the text and associated tags that the reader will actually view on screen (as opposed to the document *header*, which contains tags such as `<title>`, which are not used as body text). Netscape has enhanced this tag to allow the background and text colour (foreground) to be altered. Hyperlink colours can also be changed. All colour codes are specified as hexadecimal (*red*, *green* and *blue*, ranging from 0–FF in hexadecimal; 0–255 decimal). Refer to

Chapter 3 (Table 3.1) for more information on colour codes. **ImageFileURL** is a URL that points to an image in the GIF or JPEG format, typically with use of the http:// URL.

`<br>`

Inserts a line break at the current position (like a carriage return code), making the next string after the `<br>` code appear on a new line.

`<code>`**PrefText**`</code>`

Inserts some preformatted text. Analogous to `<pre>`, although `<code>` does not insert a carriage return afterwards, so it is perfect for embedding monospaced text within an existing sentence made up of proportional font characters, without breaking the line.

`<dd>`

See `<dl>`.

`<dir>`**Text**`</dir>`

Directory text (similar to pre-formatted) although typically for entries fewer than 20 characters (computer directory listings etc.).

`<dl>`
`<dt>header`
`<dd>text`
`</dl>`

Inserts a series of tabbed items, known as a *descriptive list*, where `<dt>` marks the heading and `<dd>` the subheading (tabbed in from the left margin accordingly).

`<dt>`

See `<dl>`.

`<embed src="`**FileName**`">`

Inserts an embedded object into the current hypertext document, so that it can be double-clicked upon to load it. If **FileName** is a bitmap, Netscape loads it on the page directly, as long as an appropriate viewer is available.

`<form method="`**Method**`" action="`**URL**`">`
`<input type="`**Type**`" size=`**Size** `name="`**cName**`">`
`<input type="submit" value="Send details">`
`</form>`

Inserts a fill-out-form (FOF) into the document. Forms are used to send data to a remote Web server, and to facilitate two-way communication over the Web. The server interfaces to the form using a script file (named by the client in the **URL**, e.g. `http://hostname/dir/script.bat` – a DOS batch file script). **Method** controls how the form is encoded by the client; GET and POST are the most common posting methods currently used. The `<input type>` tag allows input fields to be defined in order to receive user input. A wide variety of data types are supported, including TEXT and NUMBER plus some others called RADIO and CHECKBOX, which allow the user to provide *yes/no* type answers. The `submit` input type is a special attribute that creates a user-defined button, which when clicked upon, sends the data in the form to the server identified in the `action=` part.

`<h1>`**Header1**`</h1> ... <h6>`**Header6**`</h6>`

Denotes a header. Headers are numbered 1 to 6 in HTML (decreasing in size as the header number gets larger). Use headers for chapter and section headings, or for titles etc. Headers are the only way of controlling the size of characters.

`<head>`**HeadTags**`</head>`

Denotes the header part of a document, where tags such as `<title>` and `<isindex>` should ideally be placed within a document. See also `<body>`.

`<hr>`

Inserts a horizontal rule (and paragraph break afterwards). Useful for breaking up text into sections, and to underline headings etc. See also `<u>`.

`<html>`**Document**`</html>`

Top-level document element. Denotes that the document that follows is in the HTML format. Used to encapsulate the entire HTML document, and should ideally be the first tag used (by convention).

`<i>`**ItalicText**`</i>`

Italicizes the text **ItalicText**.

```
<img align=left|right|top|texttop|middle|absmiddle|
    baseline|bottom|absbottom
src="URL-Imagename"
width=w-pixel height=h-pixel
border=value
vspace=value hspace=value
alt="Text">
```

Inserts an in-line image into the current HTML document, where the name of the image is **ImgName**. The image can be aligned with the text surrounding it using the align **type** keywords shown. The ALT= keyword allows some alternative text to be displayed when Netscape's image-loading feature is disabled. Refer to Chapter 3 for examples of the <img src> tag in action.

<isindex prompt="**PromptText**">

This tag makes an HTML file into a *search document*, providing a field within the Mosaic window for a search string, allowing user input. This input is encoded (as with a <form> tag) and is sent to a server script to interface with a *back-end* program (e.g. to facilitate a search). Netscape has a prompt keyword which allows some alternative text to be displayed instead of the default text ('*This is a searchable index. Enter search keywords*'.

<meta http-equiv="Refresh" content="**n**">
<meta http-equiv="Refresh" content="**n**; url=**URL**">

A newly proposed Netscape tag (for HTML 3.0) and available since the Netscape 1.1 beta. Creates a *dynamic* document which is updated every **n** seconds, i.e. the document is automatically reloaded after this interval expires, allowing new information from the server to be brought to the user automatically. In the second form of the syntax, a different URL can be called, thus allowing documents to be chained together in succession (this can be used for animation effects, for example).

<nobr>Text</nobr>

Specifies some text where a line break should not be employed by Netscape.

<ol type=A|a|1|I start=**number**>
<li type=ol|ul>Item-name
</ol>

Inserts an ordered list, rather like a bulleted list (see <ul>), although using ascending letters or numbers instead. The new **type** keyword facilitates this (A for an A, B, C... list; a for an a, b, c... (lower case) list; 1 for a 1, 2, 3... list; and I for a Roman numeral list, e.g. I, II, III, IV...). The start keyword allows the ordering to start at a specific point (this applies to letters as well, e.g. 5 = E).

<p>
<p center>
<p>**ParaText**</p>

Inserts a paragraph break (implied carriage return) and inserts an empty line after the tag. Netscape has a center keyword which simply centres the last line in the paragraph. HTML also introduces the <p> and </p> pair to encapsulate paragraphs of text, although <p> by itself will suffice.

`<pre>`**PrefText**`</pre>`

Inserts preformatted text (e.g. a monospaced font, by default `Courier`). This tag will break the line at the point where the closing element `</pre>` is placed. See also `<code>`, `<tt>`.

`<strong>`**BoldText**`</strong>`

Emboldens the text **BoldText**. See also `<b>`.

`<title>`**TitleText**`</title>`

Provides a title on the Netscape screen, which is used to tell users about the current document that they are reading. Only one title per HTML document should be used.

`<tt>`**PrefText**`</tt>`

Inserts some preformatted text (or *teletype* text) (i.e. with a monospaced font). See also `<code>`, `<pre>`.

`<ul type=disc|circle|square>`
`<li type=disc|circle|square>Item-name`
`</ul>`

Inserts a series of bulleted items. A new `type` keyword allows the bullet type to be changed. Use as many `<li>` tags to define each item of the list. You can also nest bulleted lists within one another.

A P P E N D I X

B

The URL directory

This appendix lists a few of the most popular home pages found on the Internet. Entries are shown using their URLs (uniform resource locators). The only entries that find their way into this section are true *hypertext pages* – not services such as Gophers and FTP servers. Those entries whose URL ends in a '/' (for example `http://www.cityscape.co.uk/`) will load a *default* home page automatically. In fact, you can omit any directory and/or filenames from a URL in order to access that machine's *default* home page. This can be a good technique to use, especially if a home page no longer responds or if it has been renamed or moved etc. (which is frequently the case on the Internet). Entries are marked out of 5 stars (★★★★★) for their information content and general usefulness, on the following scale:

★	You aren't missing much here.
★★	Worth a look. *Under construction* perhaps.
★★★	A good resource. Worth revisiting.
★★★★	A very good resource. Bookmark material.
★★★★★	A truly *net-tastic* Web-resource!

URLs for hypertext pages are structured as: `type://site-name:port/directory/html-filename`, although default home pages will be loaded by all hosts if you specify just the `type://site-name:port` part of the URL. Note that with Netscape 1.1, the `http://` prefix is now optional when entering Web page URLs. The actual case of URLs is also important, since many services are located on UNIX-based, rather than DOS-based, machines (e.g. '*HomePage*' is not the same as '*homepage*').

No paper-based resource can keep up to date with the Web's rapid growth; Chapter 5 examines a number of *Web-robots* and searching tools that will help you locate information on just about any topic known, however esoteric. There is now so much information on the Web that it is becoming impractical to maintain paper-based lists. However, this mega-list documents many of the most prominent sites that are currently on the Internet. Chapter 5 details a number of Web search engines that can be used to find Web-based information (e.g. InfoSeek, Yahoo and WebCrawler).

A

A to Z of Web servers by geographical location (CERN list; around 1 Mbyte in size!) ★★★★★	http://www7.cern.ch/hypertext/DataSources/ WWW/ Geographical.html
Abekas Video Systems ★★	http://www.abekrd.co.uk/
Aberdeen University ★★★	• http://www.abdn.ac.uk/ • http://www.biochem.abdn.ac.uk/ • http://www.csd.abdn.ac.uk/index.html
About the Internet (historical hotlinks) ★★★	http://www.internic.net/infoguide/gopher/ about-internet.html
Acronym List (*Cyberese*/technical acronyms) ★★★★	http://wombat.doc.ic.ac.uk/
Adam Curry's (formerly of MTV) MusicServer ★★	http://metaverse.com/vibe/index.html
Addison-Wesley (book publishers) ★★	http://aw.com/
Adobe's Web server (home of PostScript format and the *Acrobat* software) ★★★	http://www.adobe.com/
Adult Video Conferencing (a *pay and see* scheme using live models – software available) ★★	http://www.cts.com/~telon
Africa Commercial (African commerce on the Net and beyond) ★★	http://www.africa.com/
Algorithmics Ltd UK ★★	http://www.algor.co.uk/

ALIAN (sic) Nation Web Site (3D imagery; lots of images) ★★★	http://www.alias.com/
ALIWEB (an Archie-like indexing service for the Web) ★★★	http://web.nexor.co.uk/aliweb/doc/aliweb.html
`alt.sex.pictures` (USENET) Web page. In-depth discussions about adult flicks ★★	http://www.xmission.com/~legalize/asm/asm.html
Amdahl's Web server ★★	http://www.amdahl.com/
America's Library of Congress ★★★	http://lcweb.loc.gov/homepage/lchp.html
AM/FM – UK radio industry news ★★	http://www.tecc.co.uk/public/tqm/amfm/index.html
Amiga Mosaic home page ★★	http://www.commerce.digital.com/palo-alto
Amtrak Railroad/transportation company's Web server (with 10% discount for visitors) ★★★	http://www.amtrak.com/
Andy Warhol Web server ★★★	http://www.warhol.org/warhol
Anglia University UK (education) ★★	• http://ultralab.anglia.ac.uk/ • http://www.anglia.ac.uk/
Animate Agent Labcam (another real-time camera view from the Net that you can control!) ★★★	http://www.uchicago.edu/cgi-bin/labcam
Anna Nicole Smith House of Worship (Web erotica) ★★★	http://www.df.lth.se/~micke/annaworship.html
Anne Campbell, MP (Labour Party) home page ★★	http://www.worldserver.pipex.com/home/anne.campbell/
Annie Lennox's Web pages. Details of Medusa album etc. ★★	http://www.webmedia.com/medusa/medusa.html
ANSA (object-based architecture for distributed computing) ★★	http://www.ansa.co.uk/
Antartica WWW server ★★	http://icair.iac.org.nz/
Apollo 11 moon landing server ★★	http://uptime.com:2350/
Apollo Advertising UK (WWW advertisers) ★★★	http://apollo.co.uk/
Apollo airline reservation system ★★	http://www.nando.net/pctravel.html
Apple Computers Web site ★★★	http://www.apple.com/
Archie Web servers (search for files using a graphical browser) ★★★★	• http://hoohoo.ncsa.uiuc.edu/ • http://web.doc.ic.ac.uk/archieplexform.html
Armagh Observatory (Ireland) ★★	http://star.arm.ac.uk/
Artistic Aid for AIDS ★★	http://artaids.dcs.qmw.ac.uk:8001/
ArtNet BBS, Downtown New York ★	http://www.awa.com/
Asia on-line ★★	http://silkroute.com/silkroute
Aston University, UK ★★	http://www.aston.ac.uk/home.html
AT&T 1-800 numbers (US *freephone* telephone numbers) ★★	http://att.net/dir800
Audio Web poems (MPEG recordings on-line) ★★★	http://www.cs.brown.edu/fun/bawp
Australian National Botanic Gardens ★★★	http://155.187.10.12:80/anbg.html

'Awesome List' (to various Web facilities) ★★★★ — http://www.clark.net/pub/journalism/awesome.html

B

Bank of Ireland ★★	http://www.webnet.ie/cust/boo/index.html
Banned Books Web server ★★★	http://www.cs.cmu.edu:8001/Web/People/spok/banned-books.html
Barclaycard (Barclays Bank, UK) Web server ★★	http://www.barclaycard.co.uk/
Bath University, UK ★★	http://www.bath.ac.uk/home.html
BBC 'Big Byte' radio show Web pages ★★★	http://www.bbcnc.org.uk/bbctv/technology.html
BBC Networking Club UK ★★★	http://www.bbcnc.org.uk/
BBC Public Access Server ★	http://www.bbc.co.uk/
Beer Server (Dan's Beer Page) ★★	http://www.eff.org/~brown/beer.html
BellCore Labs' Web server ★★★	http://www.bellcore.com/
Bell Labs' Web server ★★★	http://www.bell.com/
Best of the Web Awards (good for locating the best URLs on the Net) ★★★	http://wings.buffalo.edu/contest
Bianca's Smut Shack (adult entertainment) ★★★	http://bianca.com/shack/index.html
Bible Gateway (a searchable Bible!) ★★	http://www.calvin.edu/cgi-bin/bible
BIDS (Bath Information & Data Services, UK). Part of Bath University ★★	http://www.bids.ac.uk/
Big Red Button (go on, push it!) ★★	http://www.wam.umd.edu/~twoflowr/button.html
Bike Web page ★★	http://seahunt.imat.com/index.html
Birkbeck College, University of London ★★	http://www.bbk.ac.uk/
Birmingham University UK ★★	http://www.cs.bham.ac.uk/
BlowFish (mail order sex catalogue) ★★	http://www.best.com/~blowfish
Body Shop Web pages (environment-conscious/human rights pages etc.) ★★	• http://www.bodyshop.co.uk/ • http://www.the-body-shop.com/
Books on the Net (all tastes & on-line ordering) ★★★	http://www.intertain.com/
Booksellers Web-site ★★	http://www.cs.cmu.edu:8001/web/booksellers.html
BookWeb ★★	http://bookweb.cwis.uci.edu:8042/
BookWire (book information for authors and publishers) ★★★	http://www.bookwire.com/
Bradford University UK ★★★	http://www.brad.ac.uk/
Brazil National Institute of Space Research ★★	http://www.inpe.br/
Brighton University, UK ★★	http://www.bton.ac.uk/
Bristol University, UK ★★	http://www.bris.ac.uk/
British Comedy Web pages ★★★	http://cathouse.org:8000/BritishComedy/
British Computer Society ★★★	http://www.icbl.hw.ac.uk/bcs/bcsmain.html

British Geological Survey ★★	http://ub.nmh.ac.uk/
British Telecom ★★	http://www.bt.net/
Brunel University UK ★★★	http://http1.brunel.ac.uk:8080/
BUBL – *Bulletin Board for Libraries,* UK ★★★	http://www.bubl.bath.ac.uk/BUBL/home.html
Buena Vista Movies Server ★★★	http://bvp.wdp.com/BVPM/
BundyLand (of *Married With Children* fame) ★★	http://www.eia.brad.ac.uk/mwc

C

Cambridge University, UK ★★★	http://www.cam.ac.uk/
Cambridge University Press (publishers, UK) ★★★	http://www.cup.cama.ac.uk/
Canadian WWW master index	http://www.sal.ists.ca/services/w3_can/www_index.html
Cannes Film Festival ('95) pages ★★	http://www.cannes.zds.softway.wordlnet.net/
Cardiff's movie browser (best on the Net) ★★★★	http://www.cm.cf.ac.uk/Movies
Career magazine on-line ★★★	http://www.jobline.com/jobline
Careers on-line home page ★★★	http://www.britain.eu.net/~idea/main.html
CAT (Centre for Alternative Technology) ★★	http://www.foe.co.uk/CAT
Catalog Central (on-line shopping etc.) ★★★	http://catalog.florida.com/
Cathay Pacific Airlines (US-originating holidays only, so far) ★★★	http://www.cathay-usa.com/
Catholic Resources ★★	http://www.cs.cmu.edu:8001/Web/People/spok/catholic.html
Cello's home page (Cello is a well-known freeware Web browser) ★★★	http://www.law.cornell.edu/cello/cellotop.html
CERN Web server list ★★★★	http://info.cern.ch/hypertext/DataSources/WWW/Servers.html
CERN's WWW Virtual Library ★★★★★	http://info.cern.ch/hypertext/DataSources/bySubject/overview.html
Channel 4 (UK TV) Web pages ★★	http://www.cityscape.co.uk/channel4/
Chess server ★★★	http://www.willamette.edu/~tjones/chessmain.html
Church of the sub-genius ('what happens when computers get into the wrong hands') ★★	http://www.iona.ie/www/hyplan/jmason-data/slack.html
China News Digest ★★	http://cad.ucla.edu/repository/useful/iching.html
ChocNets – chocaholics Web servers on the Web!	• http://mkn.co.uk/HELP+CHOC\CHOC • http://www.godiva.com/
CIA (Central Intelligence Agency, US) Web server ★★★	http://www.ic.gov/
CineMedia film Web server ★★★★	http://www.gu.edu.au/gwis/cinemedia/CineMedia.HOME.html

Cisco Routers home page ★★	http://www.cisco.com/
CityScape (UK provider) Global On-Line home page ★★★★	http://www.gold.net/
City University UK home page ★★	http://web.city.cs.ac.uk/
CIX – Compulink Information eXchange (Internet service provider, UK) ★★	http://www.compulink.co.uk/
CIX – Commerical Internet Exchange (US) ★★	http://www.cix.org/CIXhome.html
Clarinet News ★★	http://www.clarinet.com/
Clean Technologies Web server ★★	http://cct.seas.ucla.edu/
Clip art page (1500+ GIFs!) ★★★★	http://www.cs.yale.edu
CND (Campaign for Nuclear Disarmament) ★★★	http://www.cnd.org/
Coffee server (everything about coffee!) ★★	http://www.infonet.net/showcase/coffee
Coke machine Web server (*why?*) ★	http://www.cs.cmu.edu:8001/afs/cs/cmu.edu/user/bsy/www/coke.html
Colouring book (interactive GIF colouring!) ★★	http://robot0.ge.uiuc.edu/~carlosp/color/
Comdex (*The* US trade show) ★	http://www.comdex.com:8000/
Computer Buyer ★★	http://www.demon.co.uk/buyer/index.html
Computer literacy book server (book search database via forms. Excellent) ★★★★	http://www.clbooks.com/
CommerceNet (commerce and industry on the Net etc.) ★★★★	http://www.commerce.net/
Commercial sites on the Web ★★★	http://www.directory.net/
Company Corporation (*NetBusiness* etc.) ★★	http://incorporate.com/tcc/home.html
Compaq Computer's Web pages ★★★	http://www.compaq.com/
CompuServe's Web server ★★	http://www.compuserve.com/
Computer Games Web server ★★★	http://wcl-rs.bham.ac.uk/~djh/index.html
Computer Manuals on-line home page ★★	http://www.demon.co.uk/compman
Computer Shopper's home page ★★★	http://www.gold.net/cshop/
Condom Country (all about, well, condoms!) ★★	http://www.as.com/Condom/Country
Cool site of the day (updated nightly) ★★★	http://www.infinet.net/cool.html
Cosmetic surgery page ★★★	http://www.surgery.com/body/welcome/html
Cow home page ★	http://netvet.wust.edu/On:\cows.html/
Cranfield University, UK ★★	http://www.cranfield.ac.uk/
Crash course: writing Web docs (PC Mag) ★★★	http://www.pcweek.ziff.com/~eamonn/crash_course.html
Cray Supercomputers Web server ★★★	http://www.cray.com/
Creative Internet (pop culture & TV series) ★★★	http://www.galcit.caltech.edu/~la/creative.html
Creative Labs Web server ★★★	http://www.creaf.com/
CUI's W3 Catalog ★★★★	http://cui_www.unige.ch/w3catalog
Cyberia (The Internet cafe in London) ★★★	http://www.easynet.co.uk/
Cyberpreneurs Guide to the Web ★★★ womenhealth/Cyber.html	http://asa.ugl.lib.umich.edu/chdocs/

CyberSight (for the preservation of the Internet's unconventional nature. Hear hear!) ★★	http://cybersight.com/cgi-bin/cs/s?main.gmml
Cyber Town (arts and lesiure) ★★★	http://www.cityscape.co.uk/cyber-town/index.html

D

Daily Telegraph (UK paper) on-line ★★★★	http://www.telegraph.co.uk/
Data General's Web server ★★	http://www.dg.com/
Date-Line (for people seeking friendship and/or relationships) ★★★	http://www.netmedia.com/date
DEC (Digital) Computers Web server ★★★	http://www.digital.com/
Dell Computers home page ★★★	http://www.us.dell.com/
Demon Internet UK (provider) home page ★★	http://www.demon.co.uk/
Dental Net ★★	http://www.dentalnet.com/dentalnet/
Department of Defense (DoD, US) ★★★	http://www.dtic.dla.mil/defenselink
Department of State Foreign Affairs Network (DOSFAN, USA) – human rights/drugs/terrorism ★★★	http://dosfan.lib.uiuc.edu/dosfan.html
DigiCash (all about the new on-line money equivalent for the future) ★★	http://digicash.com/
Digex (US Internet provider) Web pages ★★	http://www.digex.net/
Disability home page (for people with disabilities) ★★	http://disability.com/
Discovery Channel (Canada) Web pages ★★	http://www.discovery.ca/
DNA to Dinosaurs ★★★	http://www.bvis.uic.edu/museum
DoomGate (for all DOOM addicts!) ★★★	http://www.cedar.buffalo.edu/~kapis-p/doom/DOOM.html
Dow Jones industrial average ★★★	http://www.secapl.com/secapl/quoteserver/djia.html
Drug pages (pointers to drug-related documents etc.) ★★★	http://cyborganic.com/drugz/
Dun & Bradstreet's (financial data) Web server	http://www.dbisna.com/
Dungeon Network Systems (UK provider) ★★	http://www.dungeon.com/

E

Earthquake information (various pointers) ★★★	http://www.msen.com/~emv/kobe.html
Edinburgh University UK map server ★★	http://www.ucs.ed.ac.uk/General/uk.html

Edward Kennedy's (US Senator's) home page ★	http://www.ai.mit.edu/projects/Kennedy/homepage.html
EINET Galaxy home page (index to many Web resources and home of *WinWeb* software) ★★★★	http://galaxy.einet.net/
Electronic News-stand ★★★	http://enews.com/
Elements (chemical) pages ★★	http://www.cchem.berkeley.edu/Table/index.htm
Elf Sternberg's home page (Web erotica. ES is the keeper of the `alt.sex` FAQ!) ★	http://halcyon.com/elf/elf_sternberg.html
Elsevier Science ★★★	http://www.elsevier.nl
Elvis's home page (*The King* lives on...) ★★	http://tamsun.tamnis.tamu.edu/~ahb2188/elvishom.html
Encyclopaedia Britannica ★★★★	http://www.eb.com/
Entering the Web: A guide to cyberspace ★★	http://www.eit.com/web/www.guide/
EnviroWeb ★★★	http//envirolink.org/
Estonia disaster server ★★	http://www.viabalt.ee/News/sos/
Epsilon – ambient music archive ★★★	http://hyperreal.com/ambient
Ernst & Young's Web pages (accountants) ★★★	http://www.ernsty.co.uk/ernsty/
EUNet (European Internet provider) ★★★	http://www.britain.eu.net/
EuroDollar (car-hire) Web server ★★★	http://www.eurodollar.co.uk/
E-Zines list (electronic texts/magazines etc.) ★★	http://www.ora.com:8080/johnl/e-zine-list/

F

Field Museum of Natural History, Chicago ★★★	http://www.bvis.uic.edu/museum
First Mortgage Securities, UK (mortgages on the Net!) ★	http://www.first-mortgage.co.uk/fms
FishCam – fish camcorder (live digitized pictures of an aquarium in real-time. Why?!) ★★★	http://mosaic.mcom.com/fishcam/
FIX – Net-Zine ★★	http://www.easynet.co.uk/pages/fix/frontl.htm
Florists on the Net (UK-based) ★★	http://mkn.co.uk/
FloristNet (a florist on the Net) ★★★	http://mkn.co.uk/HELP+FLOWER\INFO
Focus International Catalogue: sex education and on-line catalogue ★★	http://www.hip.com/focus/catalog.html
Fortean Times (The journal of strange phenomena) ★★★	• http://alpha.mic.dundee.ac.uk/ft/ft.html • http://forteana.mic.dundee.ac.uk/ft
Free computer reference (PC/Mac/Unix information) ★★★	http://ici.proper.com/
Free fax service (fax via the Internet!) ★★★	http://linux1.balliol.oc.ac.uk/fax/faxsend.html
Frequently asked questions (FAQs) about Internet ★★★	http://alfred.econ.lsa.umich.edu:80/FAQs/FAQs.html

Friends of the Earth Web pages ★★★	http://www.foe.co.uk/CAT
Frog dissection server (mainly for biology students – not frogs!) ★★★	http://curry.edschool.virginia.edu/~insttech/frog
Frog server (all about Frogs, basically!) ★	http://www.cs.yale.edu/HTML/YALE/CS/ HYPlans/loosemore-sandra/froggy.html
Frontline Distribution Ltd, UK (trade distributors of hardware and software) ★★	http://www.frontline.co.uk/
FTP '*A–Z Monster List of sites*' (NCSA) ★★★★	http://hoohoo.ncsa.uiuc.edu:80/ ftp-interface.html
FTP Software Inc. Web server ★★★	http://www.ftp.com/
Fujitsu Corporation's Web server ★★★	http://www.fujitsu.co.jp/
Future Fantasy bookstore ★★★	http://www.commerce.digital.com/palo-alto
Future Publishing's Web server (publishers of *Internet and Comms. Today* etc.) ★★★	http://www.futurenet.co.uk/

G

Gallup's Web server (poll info. etc.) ★★★	http://www.gallup.com/
Game for a Laugh (Web links to games, games and more games-related information!) ★★★	http://wcl-rs.bham.ac.uk/GameBytes
GameWave (games-related server) ★★★	http://www.iinet.com.au/~nathan
The Guardian Newspaper, UK. *On*Line computer section (with WAIS search) ★★★	http://www.gold.net/online
Genealogy Web pages (family trees etc.) ★★	http://uts.cc.utexas.edu/~churchh/genealgy.html
General Electric's Web server ★★	http://www.ge.com/
Geometry centre ★★	http://www.geom.umn.edu/welcome.html
Glass Wings sexuality pages ★★★	http://www.aus.xanadu.com/GlassWings/ sexual.html
Global Network Academy ★★★	http://uu-gna.mit.edu:8001/cgi-bin/meta
GNN – Global Network Navigator (a *gold nugget* of a Web server) ★★★★★	http://www.gnn.com/
GNN personal finance center ★★	http://nearnet.gnn.com/gnn/meta/finance/ bio.html
Go Discs (music-related pages) ★★★	http://www.demon.co.uk/godiscs
Golf – '*The 19th Hole*' ★★	http://dallas.nmhu.edu/golf/golf.htm
GolfWeb (all about golf, would you believe?) ★★	http://www.golfweb.com/
Gopher jewels (Net goodies via Gopher) ★★★★	http://galaxy.einet.net/GJ/index.html
Graphics (computer) home page ★★★	http://www.graphics.com/
Graphics for your Web pages ★★★	http://www.rfhsm.ac.uk:70/0/people/gifs/ index.html

Grateful Dead (the group) Web pages ★★★	http://www.cs.cmu.edu:8001/afs/cs.cmu.edu/user/mleone.web/dead.html
Greenpeace home page ★★★★	http://www.greenpeace.org/
Griffin Laundry (a clothes catalogue on the Net!) ★★★	http://www.griffin-corp.co.uk
Grolsch (the lager) pages ★	http://www.intervid.co.uk/intervid/esp/
Guide to Internet mailing lists ★★★	http://alpha.acast.nova.edu/listserv.html
Guide to publishing on the Web ★★★	http://www.webcom.com/html/

H

Harvest (Web-trawler and robot) ★★★	http://harvest.cs.colorado.edu/
HENSA UK Software Archive ★★★	http://www.hensa.ac.uk/
Hewlett-Packard's Web server ★★★	http://www.hp.com/home.html
Hitachi Corporations Web server ★★★	http://www.hitachi.co.jp/
Hitachi Data Systems Europe ★★	http://http://www.hds.co.uk/
HM Treasury (UK) Web server ★★★	http://www.hm-treasury.gov.uk/
Homelessness home page ★★	http://csf.colorado.edu/psn
Homosexuals and the Church ★★	http://vector.casti.com/QRD/religion/
Hong Kong business directory ★★	http://fareast.com/HongKong/directory.html
HotWired – electronic *Wired* magazine ★★★ (see also *Wired magazine*)	http://www.hotwired.com/
HTML icons and imagery ★★★★	• http://akebono.stanford.edu/yahoo/computing/world_wide_web/programming/icons
Human languages page ★★★	http://www.willamette.edu/~tjones/Language-Page.html
HunterSkill (UK IT employment agency) ★★	http://www.demon.co.uk/cyberdyne/hskl/hskindex.html

I

IBM PC User Group (IBMPCUG) ★★★	http://www.ibmpcug.co.uk/
IBM UK Laboratories Ltd ★★	http://www.hursley.ibm.com
IBM's (US) Web server ★★★★	http://www.ibm.com/
Icons and imagery (miscellany) for your HTML Web pages ★★★★	• http://akebono.stanford.edu/yahoo/computing/world_wide_web/programming/icons • http://www.dsu.su.se/~matti-hu/archive.html
Illuminati On-Line (Internet provider and a server about role-playing games) ★★	http://www.io.com/
Information Market Europe (*I'm Europe*) ★★★	http://www.echo.lu/

Informix Web server ★★★	http://www.informix.com/
InfoSeek Web-searching system ★★★★	http://www.infoseek.com/
Innovations – The UK catalogue people's Web server (you must register first to use this service)★★★	http://www.innovations.co.uk/giftpoint.html
Institute of High Energy Physics, Beijing ★★★	http://www.ihep.ac.cn:3000/china.html
Intel Corporation's Web server ★★★	http://www.intel.com/
Interactive stock market quotes ★★	http://www.secapl.com/cgi-bin/qs
InterCon (IBA System Corp's Web pages) ★★	http://www.iba.org/
Interface Group (organizers of the US Comdex exhibition: schedule details etc.) ★	http://www.comdex.com:8000/
Interleaf's (software) Web server ★★★	http://www.ileaf.com/
Internet book information centre ★★★★	http://sunsite.unc.edu/ibic/IBIC-homepage.html
Internet bookshop (750 000+ titles!) ★★★★	http://www.bookshop.co.uk/
Internet business connection ★★★	http://www.charm.net/~ibc/
Internet computer index ★★★	http://ici.proper.com/
Internet and computer-mediated communication (ICMC) ★★★★	http://www.rpi.edu/Internet/Guides/decemj/internet-cmc.html
Internet for Dummies (text from the book) ★★★	http://grfn.org/~topher
Internet group (NetBusiness) ★★★	http://www.tig.com/
Internet phone (details about the real-time phone call system via the Internet. Commerical software is available, as well as a demo) ★★★★	http://www.vocaltec.com/
Internet presence and publishing (a collection of on-line shopping services) ★★★	http://www.ip.net/
Internet resource guide ★★★	http://http2.sils.umich.edu/~lou/chhome.html
Internet shopping network ★★★	http://www.internet.net/
Internet society (net statistics etc.) ★★★★	http://info.isoc.org/
Internet training & consultancy ★★	http://www.itcs.com/
Internet Underground Music Archive (the *IUMA*) ★★★	http://www.southern.com/IUMA/
Internet Web text guide ★★★	http://www.rpi.edu/Internet/Guides/decemj/text.html
InterNic (Net miscellany/stats) ★★★★	http://www.internic.net/
Interpedia Project (an on-line encyclopedia project) ★★	http://www.isacc.exploratorium.edu/
Intertainments on-line sex store (videos etc.) ★★★	http://intertain-inc.com/xxx
InterVid home page (run by journalist Nick Rosen) ★★	http://www.intervid.co.uk/
IP information (Internet Protocol) – specs and more ★★★	http://www.charm.net/pip.html
ISDN page (ISDN information in abundance) ★★★	http://alumni.caltech.edu/~dank/isdn

ISO (International Organization for Standardization) Web pages ★★★	http://www.iso.ch/welcome.html

J

Japanese Prime Minister's Web pages ★★	http://www.kantei.go.jp/
Jazz It Up (the jazz photography of Ray Avery) ★★★	http://bookweb.cwis.uci.edu:8042/Jazz/jazz.html
Jerusalem's WWW server ★★	http://shum.cc.huji.il/jeru/jerusalem.html
JewishNet WWW server (see above also) ★★	http://www.huji.ac.il/www_jewishn/www/t01.html
JobServe Web server with job ads (2000+ subscribers were registered in '94) ★★★★	http://www.demon.co.uk/jobserve/
The Johns Hopkins University WWW pages ★★	http://oneworld.wa.com/htmldev/devpage/dev-page.html
John Wiley & Co (book publishers) ★★★	http://www.wiley.co.uk/
JumpStation (for HTML developers. Also a Web-crawler and robot) ★★★	http://www.stir.ac.uk/jsbin/js
Justin's Links to the Underground (weird and wonderful aspects of the Net) ★★★	http://raptor.sccs.swarthmore.edu/jahall/

K

Kaleida – Joint IBM/Apple venture (all about the Kaleida multimedia player + more!) ★★	http://www.kaleida.com/
Kegan Paul Int. (Educational Publishers) Web pages ★★	http://www.demon.co.uk/keganpaul
Kew Gardens (Royal Botanic Gardens, UK) ★★	http://www.rbgkew.org.uk/
Kid's Web ★★★	http://www.npac.syr.edu/textbook/kidsweb/
Klingon Language Institute (for *Star Trek* fans) ★★	http://www.kli.org/klihome.html
Kylie Minogue Web pages (pictures/lyrics etc.) ★★	http://www.eia.brad.ac.uk/kylie

L

Las Vegas Web server ★★★	http://www.infi.net/vegas/online
LaughWeb (jokes galore + Star Trek info) ★★★	http://www.misty.com/laughweb/
LawNet UK ★★★	http://mkn.co.uk/HELP+LAWNET
Learned Information's LI NewsWire ★★	http://info.learned.co.uk/1s/newswire
Leeds University UK (HTML info etc.) ★★	http://www.leeds.ac.uk/

Lego home page ★★★	http://legowww.homepages.com/
Le Web-Louvre (Paris) ★★★★	http://mistral.enst.fr/~pioch/louvre/
Libido – The Journal of Sex and Sensibility ★★★	http://www.mcs.com/~rune/home.html
Linux (freeware UNIX clone) Web server ★★	http://www.linux.org.uk/
Linux IT catalogue ★★	http://www.fintronic.com/linux/catalog.html
List of Commercial WWW servers (MIT) ★★★	http://tns-www.lcs.mit.edu/commerce.html
ListServs (mailing lists) via the Web ★★★	http://www.clark.net/pub/listserv/listserv.html
Lock-pickers Web server ★★	http://www.lysator.liu.se/mit-guide/ mit-guide.html
London Pub Review ★★★	http://www.cs.ucl.ac.uk/misc/uk/london/pubs/ index.html
London Underground route-mapper ★★★	http://www.cs.ucl.ac.uk/misc/uk/london/tube/ TubeRoute.html
Lotus Cars home page (racing bias) ★★	http://www.netcom.com/pub/lotuscars/WWW/ TeamLotus.html
Lotus Software Web-site ★★★	http://www.lotus.com/
Lycos (Web-crawler and indexing tool) ★★★★	• http://fuzine.mt.cs.cmu.edu/mlm/lycos-all.html • http://lycos.cs.cmu.edu/cgi-bin/pursuit

M

Macintosh (Mac) shareware archive ★★★	http://web.nexor.co.uk/mac-archive/ welcome.html
McAfee's Web server (antivirus software etc.) ★★★	http://www.mcafee.com/
McGraw-Hill Computer and Communication Information magazine (selected on-line articles from *Unix World/LAN Times* etc.) ★★★	http://www.wcmh.com/index.html
McGraw-Hill Publishers catalogue on-line ★★★	• http://www.cityscape.co.uk/mcgraw • http://www.bookshop.co.uk/mcgraw • http://193.133.97.7/mcgraw
McGraw-Hill Publishers US Web server ★★	http://www.mcgraw-hill.com/
McGraw-Hill's *Essential Internet Information Guide* and *The WWW, Mosaic and More* in hypertext format (selected chapters) ★★★ :-)	http://www.quadralay.com/www/Cyb_Pot/ McGraw/index.htm
Macmillan Publishers home page ★★	http://www.mcp.com/
Magellan Space Mission ★★	http://newproducts.jpl.nasa.gov/magellan/
Making money on the INTERNET conference ★	http://cism.bus.utexas.edu/Conf.html
Map browser ★★★	http://pubweb.parc.xerox.com:80/
Maps of the world ★★★	• http://www.lib.utexas.edu/Libs/PCL/ Map_collection/Map_collection.html • http://wings.buffalo.edu/world/
MarketNet UK ★★	http://mkn.co.uk/

MBONE Information – data on the *Mbone* trunk of the Internet (a *backbone* network of the Internet) ★★	http://www.eit.com/techinfo/mbone/mbone.html
MCA/Universal Pictures Web site ★★★	http://www.mca.com/
MecklerWeb (corporate data and news) ★★★	http://www.mecklerweb.com/
Megadeth, Arizona (the group and *much* more besides!) ★★★★	http://bazaar.com/
Metaverse Web server (consumers *Web-mall*) ★★★★	http://www.metaverse.com/index.html
Microfocus (COBOL-related products) ★★	http://mftld.co.uk/
Microsoft Corporation's WWW server ★★★	• http://www.microsoft.com/ • http://www.research.microsoft.com/research/
Microsoft Software Knowledge Base ★★★	http://emwac.ed.ac.uk/html/kb/top.html
Missing Kids Web server (with photos) ★★★	http://www.gems.com/kids/ncmec.html
Monty Python's Web server ★★★	http://www.xs4all.nl/~bigmac/python.html
Mosaic on-line user's guide ★★★	http://www.ncsa.uiuc.edu/SDG/Software/ WinMosaic/Docs/WMosToc.html
Mosaic Communications Corporation (home of Mosaic at NCSA) ★★★★	http://home.mcom.com/
Moscow State University ★★	http://www.npi.msu.su/
Mother of All BBSs – Massive selection of A–Z general information ★★★★	http://www.cs.colorado.edu/home/mcbryan/ public_html/bb/summary.html
Multimedia News-stand ★★★	http://mmnewsstand.com/
MusicBase, London UK ★★★	http://www.musicbase.co.uk/music
Music database (form interface to artists etc.) ★★★	http://www.cecer.army.mil/~burnett/MDB/
Music resources (a real *mega-list*) ★★★	http://www.music.indiana.edu/misc/ music_resources.html
Music Virtual Library ★★	http://www.oulu.fi/music.html

N

NAG™ The Numerical Algorithms Group Ltd ★★	http://www.nag.co.uk:70/
NASDAQ Financial Executive Journal ★★	http://www.ai.mit.edu/stocks/prices.html
NASA space images ★★★	http://images.jsc.nasa.gov/html/home.htm
Natural History Museum, London UK (dinosaurs and more...) ★★★	http://www.nhm.ac.uk/
NCSA (home of Mosaic) ★★★★	http://www.ncsa.uiuc.edu/
NCSA (MS Windows page) ★★★★	http://www.ncsa.uiuc.edu/SDG/Software/ WinMosaic/HomePage.html
NEC (of Japan) ★★★	http://www.nec.co.jp/index_e.html
NetBoy (Internet's comic strip character) ★★	http://www.interaccess.com/netboy.html
NetCom (US Internet Provider) Web pages ★★★	http://www.netcom.com/

Netscape Communications Corporation (home of the Netscape browser) ★★★★★	http://www.netscape.com/
NetMarket Company (shoping mall, with secure server software in operation for CC purchases) ★★★	http://netmarket.com/
NetSurfer E-zine ★★★	http://www.netsurf.com/nsd/index.html
Net T-Shirts (Internet-related T-Shirts, e.g. Anti-Clipper chip, on-line purchases) ★★	http://http.cs.berkeley.edu/~tsph/tshirt.html
NETworth (a resource for individual investors) ★★	http://networth.galt.com/
NEWT*news* (Apple Newton news and views) ★★	http://judith.www.media.mit.edu/SocialWeb/SociableWeb.html
Nikos (Web-crawler and index tool) ★★★	http://www.rns.com/cgi-bin/nomad
Nintendo Web server (video clips of game; press releases etc.) ★★★	http://www.nintendo.com/
Nova-Links Web searching tool ★★★	http://alpha.acast.nova.edu/start.html
Novell's (networking people) Web server ★★★	http://www.novell.com/
NSF (National Science Foundation) Web server ★★★	http://www.internic.net/newsletters

O

O J Simpson Trial (facts and synopses etc.) ★★	http://pathfinder.com/pathfinder/features/oj/central1.html
Olivetti Research Ltd ★★	http://www.cam-orl.co.uk/
One World On-Line (World Disasters – Oxfam, UNICEF input etc.) ★★★	http://www.bbcnc.org.uk/online/oneworld/top/html
On-line books FAQ ★★	http://cs.indiana.edu/metastuff/book-faq.html
On-ramp (business/consumers Web server) ★★★★	http://www.ramp.com/
Open University UK ★★★	http://www.open.ac.uk
O'Reilly and Associates (Publishers) ★★★★	http://www.ora.com/
ORACLE's Web server (with on-line sales) ★★★	http://www.oracle.com/
Origami (paper folding) pages ★★	http://www.cs.ubc.ca/spider/jwu/origami.html
OS/2-related Web servers ★★★	• http://www.mit.edu:8001/activities/os2/os2world.html • http://www.iti.salford.ac.uk/os2power/os2power.html
OTIS (**O**perative **T**erm **I**s **S**timulate) image collection and on-line gallery ★★★	http://sunsite.unc.edu/otis/otis.html
OWL (**O**n-line **W**riting **L**ab) ★★★	http://owl.trc.purdue.edu/
Ozone Campaign home page ★★★	http://www.cyberstore.ca/greenpeace/ozone

P

Paranoia Web page (no, you aren't going crazy, they really *are* coming after you!) ★★★	http://www.paranoia.com/
Paris Information Web server ★★★	http://meteora.ucsd.edu:80/norman/paris
Pathfinder (magazines to browse include *Time*, *Money Watch*, *Vibe* etc.) ★★★	http://www.timeinc.com/
PC Magazine's Favorite WWW sites ★★★★	http://www.pcmag.ziff.com/~pcmag/favehome.htm
Penthouse magazine on-line ★★★	http://www.penthousemag.com/magazine/contents.html
Peter Gabriel's music page ★★	http://geffen.com/gabriel.html
Phrack Magazine (for hackers *et al.*) ★★★	http://freeside.com/phrack.html
Pipex (European Internet Provider) company home pages/client pages etc. ★★★	• http://www.worldserver.pipex.com/ • http://www.pipex.net/
Pizza Hut on-line (and taking orders – in the US only!) ★★★	http://pizzahut.com/
PizzaNet (taking Pizza orders now – in California that is!) ★★	http://www.pizzahut.com/
Planet Earth home page ★★★★	http://white.nosc.mil/info.html
Playboy magazine on-line ★★★	http://www.playboy.com/
Point of no return (Many sex/erotica-related pointers) ★★★	http://zoom.lm.com/
Power PC Web page ★★	http://power.globalnews.com/
Prentice-Hall (book publishers) Web page ★★	http://prenhall.com/
Price Jamieson Group recruitment page ★★	http://www.gold.net/pricejam/
Private Eye (the UK's satirical magazine – visit their *Gnome* page here!) ★★★	http://www.intervid.co.uk/intervid/eye/gateway.html
Profanity & insult server. Bloody rubbish if you ask me! **:**) ★★	http://www.scrg.cs.tcd.ie/cgi-bin/profanity
PSI's (Performance Systems International) Web pages – large US net provider ★★★	http://www.psi.net/
Pulp Fiction Web server (all about the cult film) ★★	http://www.musicbase.co.uk/movie/pulp/

Q

Quadralay Corporation (home of the GWHIS Web browser software) ★★★★	http://www.quadralay.com/
QualComm's Web server site ★★	http://lorien.qualcomm.com/QualHome.html
Quarterdeck's Web server site ★★★	http://www.qdeck.com/
QuoteCom (stock market service) ★★★	http://www.quote.com/

R

Racer archive (Indycar/Formula 1 etc.) ★★	http:/www.eng.hawaii.edu/Contribs/carina/ra.home.page.html
Random URL generator (this picks random URLs for you to visit!) ★★★	http://kuhttp.cc.ukans.edu/cwis/organizations/kucia/uroulette/uroulette
RBSE URL (*Web-crawler*) ★★★	http://rbse.jsc.nasa.gov/eichmann/urlsearch.html
Recommended Reading on the Internet (RRI) ★★	http://www.secapl.com/secapl/seminar/readings.html
RedNet On-line (UK provider) ★★	http://www.red.net/
Reebok (the shoe/trainer people) home page ★★	http://planetreebok.com/
ReliefRock music server ★★★	http://www.earthweb.com:2800/reliefrock.html
R.E.M music server ★★	http://www.halcyon.com/rem/index.htm
Right side of the Web (US political pages) ★★	http://www.clark.net/pub/jeffd/index.html
RockWeb (the world of rock music on the Web) ★★★	http://www.rock.net/
Rolling Stones Web server ★★	http://www.stones.com/
Royal Observatory, Edinburgh UK ★★★	http://www.roe.ac.uk/
RSA encryption server (info/news etc.) ★★	http://www.rsa.com/
Russian information – via the Web ★★	http://solar.rtd.ukt.edu/friends/home.html

S

Safe sex page ★★★	http://www.cmpharm.ucsf.edu/~ntroyer/safesex.html
San Diego – an updated view of this region every half hour (via real-time camcorder! Why?) ★	http://www.cts.com/~jtara/baycam.html
Santa Claus on the Web (told you he exists!) ★★	http://northpole.net/
Schools on the Net ★★★	http://www-bprc.mps.ohiostate.edu/cgi-bin/hpp/langleyji.html
Science Fiction Foundation Collection (SFFC) ★★★	http://www.liv.ac.uk/~asawyer/sffchome.html
SCOPE (formerly *The Spastics Society*). Information on charity activities etc. ★★★	http://www.futurenet.co.uk/charity
Scottish Highlands and Islands server ★★	http://nsa.bt.co.uk/nsa.html
SEGA (the games people) home page ★★★	http://www.segaoa.com/
Sex100 purity test ★★	http://www.circus.com/~omni/purity.html
SexShop (The Internet sex shop) ★★★	http://www.sexshop.com/
ShadowRun (futuristic role-playing game, played via the Web!) ★★★	http://www.oat.ts.astro.it/marcucci/sr2/index.html
Sheffield University UK ★★	http://www2.shef.ac.uk/default.html
Silicon Graphics (SGI) – The workstation people and WebSpace developers ★★★★	http://www.sgi.com/

Silicon Surf (SGI) Web pages ★★★	http://www-europe.sgi.com/
Simpsons Web server (from the TV series) ★★	http://turtle.ncsa.uiuc.edu/alan/simpsons.html
Singapore information ★★	http://www.ntu.ac.sg/intv/intv_www.html
SlipKnot Web page (*SlipKnot* is a Web browser that doesn't need PPP/SLIP access)	http://www.interport.com/slipknot/slipknot.html
Solstice home page (renewable energy etc.) ★★	http://solstice.crest.org/
Sony Corporation's Web server ★★★★	• http://www.csl.sony.co.jp/ • http://www.music.sony.com/
SoundWire (music-related page) ★★	http://soundwire.com/
Space Systems Laboratory (NASA news and space-related material/events etc.) ★★★	http://ssl.umd.edu/
Sport virtual library ★★★	http://www.atm.ch.cam.ac.uk/sports/webs/html
Spry (Mosaic licensers) ★★★	http://www.spry.com/
Spunk Press (anarchists literature) ★★	http://www.cwi.nl/cwi/people/Jack.Jansen/spunk/Spunk_Home.html
SpyGlass (licensers for Enhanced Mosaic) ★★★	http://www.spyglass.com/
Standard and Poor's 500 (stock market) ★★	http://www.secapl.com/secapl/quoteserver/sp500.html
Star Trek (NG) Web page ★★	http://generations.viacom.com/
Starting points for Internet exploration ★★★	http://www.ncsa.uiuc.edu/SDG/Software/Mosaic/StartingPoints/NetworkStartingPoints.html
Star Wars multimedia (SW film buffs page) ★★★	http://bantha.pc.cc.cmu.edu:1138/
Stock market charts ★★★	http://www.ai.mit.edu/stocks/prices.html
Stock quotes (from *QuoteCom*) ★★★	http://www.quote.com/demo-chrt.html
Strange interactions Web server (prints, etchings and lithograph imagery) ★★	http://amanda.physics.wisc.ed:70:/11/show
Subway maps of the world ★★★	http://metro.jussieu.fr:10001/
Sun Microsystems home page (the Workstation people) ★★★	http://www.sun.com/
Symantec's (software company) Web pages ★★★	http://www.symantec.com/

T

Taligent's Web software ★★★	http://www.taligent.com/
Tandem Computers Web server ★★★	http://www.tandem.com/
Tango (the drink) home page ★★	http://tango.hhcl.com/
Tarot information ★★	http://cad.ucla.edu/repository/useful/tarot.html
Teletext for Mosaic (+Singapore Web page) ★★	http://www.ntu.ac.sg/intv/intv_www.html
Textiles home page (needlework, quilting etc.) ★★	http://www.textiles.org/
Thomson International Publishers ★★★	http://www.thomson.com/

Times Educational Supplement on-line (Gopher service included) ★★	http://www.newsint.co.uk/
Time magazine on-line ★★★	http://www.timeinc.com/
Time Warner Inc. Web server ★★★★	http://www.timeinc.com/pathfinder
Timex world-time page ★★★	http://pathfinder.com/vibe/vibeworld/worldmap.html
Today in History ★★	http://mtv.com/misc/todayhistory.html
Toys Web server (and on-line shop) ★★	http://www.toystore.com/
Travel booking (Variety's server) ★★★	http://www.cyberquest.com/variety/welcome.html
Travelling Software's Web-site ★★★	http://www.halcyon.com/travsoft/home-page.html
Trinity College, Dublin, Web server ★★	http://www.tcd.ie/
Trumpet International's home page (home of Peter Tattam's *Trumpet Winsock*) ★★★	http://ftp.trumpet.com.au/wsk/winsock.htm
TVnet (TV/cable-related info) ★★★	http://tvnet.com/TVnet.html

U

Ubique (The *Virtual Places* Company) ★★	http://www.ubique.com/
UK company information (30 000+ companies at the time of writing) ★★★	http://www.milfac.co.uk/milfac
UK Government Web server ★★★	http://www.open.gov.uk/
UK Internet list ★★★	http://www.tardis.ed.ac.uk/~paola/inetuk/
UK media server (A guide to UK magazines, author contacts and much more besides) ★★★	http://www.mcc.ac.uk/~jcridlan/
UK UNIX Users Group (UKUUG) ★★	http://web.dcs.bbk.ac.uk/ukuug/home.html
Ultimate band list (searchable database) ★★★	http://american.recordings.com/wwwofmusic/ubl.html
Unipalm UK Web server (home of the *Mail-It* email software) ★★★	http://www.unipalm.co.uk/
Unisys Web server ★★★	http://www.unisys.com/
University College London UK map server ★★★	http://www.cs.ucl.ac.uk/misc/uk/intro.html
Unofficial Internet book list (maintained by Net-author Kevin Savetz) ★★★	http://www.northcoast.com/savetz/savetz.html
Urban Desires – one of the best general interest e-zines on the Web ★★★	http://desires.com/desires/ud/1.1/urban_toc.html
URL minder (keeps track of URLs/pages that change) ★★★★	http://www.netmind.com/URL-minder/URL-minder.html
US Department of Health on-line ★★	http://www.os.dhhs.gov/

Useless Web page (no star-rating because, well, it's useless!)	http://www.primus.com/staff/paulp/useless.html
USX classified ad service for 2nd hand software ★★	http:/www.hyperion.com/usx/

V

Vampires Web server ★	http://www.wimsey.com/~bmid-diet/vampyre/vampyre.html
Vangelis (the person's music) Web server ★★★	http://bau2.uibk.ac.at/perki/Vangelis.html
Vatican exhibit Rome reborn ★★★★	• http://sunsite.unc.edu/expo/vatican.exhibit/Vatican.exhibit.html • http://www.ncsa.uiuc.edu/SDG/Experimental/vatican.exhibit/Vatican.exhibit.html
Vegetarian Web server page (1000+ recipes on-line) ★★★	http://www-sc.ucssc.indiana.edu/cgi-bin/recipes/
Verity's Web server (software company) ★★	http://www.verity.com/
VideoCam – A video camera whose direction can be controlled via the user through the browser! ★★★	http://vision.uchicago.edu/cgi-bin/labcam
Virtual gallery (modern art on-line) ★★★	http://www.atom.co.jp/gallery
Virtual garden ★★★	http://www.timeinc.com/vg/Welcome/welcome.html
Virtual hospital ★★★	http://indy.radiology.uiowa.edu/VirtualHospital.html
Virtual mirror (Web browser reviews etc.) ★★★	http://mirror.wwa.com/mirror/
Virtual tourist Web server ★★★★	http://wings.buffalo.edu/world
Virtual University (University of London) ★★	http://www.cryst.bbk.ac.uk/PPS/index.html
VISA's Web server (electronic banking etc.) ★★	http://www.visa.com/visa
Visible human project ★★★★	http://www.nlm.nih.gov/extramural_research.dir/visible_human.html
Volcano information site ★★	http://volcano.und.nodak.edu/
Volvo (the car makers) ★★	http://www.volvo.com/
VRML (Virtual Reality Modelling Language). Pointers and documents on the Web ★★★	• http://vrml.wired.com/ • http://www.wired.com/vrml

W

WAIS Inc's server (with access to WAIS – Wide Area Information Server via the Web) ★★★	http://www.wais.com/
Waite Group Publishers ★★★	http://www.waite.com/waite

Walt Disney Studios ★★★	http://bvp.wdp.com/BVPM/
Warner Brothers home page ★★★	http://www.iuma.com/Warner/html
Washington Telecom newswire ★★	http://wtn.com/wtn/wtn.html
WAXWEB – huge multimedia system with a complete movie on-line! ★★★★	http://bug.village.virginia.edu/
Weather maps (up to the minute, nearly) ★★★	http://rs560.cl.msu.edu/weather
Weather server (X-Windows, *imagemap* delivery service to your workstation) ★★★	http://rs560.cl.msu.edu/weather/getmegif.html
Web-Chat (real-time chat with other users via the Web!) ★★★★	http://www.irsociety.com/webchat.html
Web communications home page ★★★	http://www.webcom.com/
WebCrawler (Web search-tool) ★★★	http://www.biotech.washington.edu/WebCrawler/WebQuery.html
Web FAQ (frequently asked questions) ★★★	http://siva.cshl.org/~boutell/www_faq.html
Web Personals page (personal ads) ★★★	http://hamilton.netmedia.com/date/
Web search (via EINET Galaxy) ★★★	http://http/galaxy.einet.net/www/www.html
Webster's Dictionary Web server (word definitions etc.) ★★★	http://c.gp.cs.cmu.edu:5103/prog/webster/
Webster's Weekly (e-zine) ★★	http://www.da.awa.com:80/w2/
WebWorld (interactive city design, rather like *SimCity* to some extent) ★★★	http://sailfish.peregrine.com/WebWorld/welcome.html
West Ham Football Club Web server ★	http://hammers.wwa.com/hammers
West's Legal Directory server (US law) ★★	http://163.231.231.3/
Whitehouse (US President's Web pages) ★★	http://www.whitehouse.gov/
White Sands Missile Base WWW server ★★★★	http://white.nosc.mil/info.html
Whole Internet Catalog (from Ed Krol's A–Z of Internet services) ★★★★	http://nearnet.gnn.com/wic/newrescat.toc.html
Wired Magazine Web pages ★★★	http://www.wired.com/
Women's health pages ★★★	http://asa.ugl.lib.umich.edu/chdocs/womenhealth/womens_health.html
World art treasures ★★	http://sgwww.epfl.ch/BERGER/
World Bank Web server ★★★	http://www.worldbank.org/
World-Wide Web '94 Conference ★★	http://www.ncsa.uiuc.edu/SDG/IT94/IT94Info.html
World-Wide Web '95 Conference ★★★	http://www.igd.fhg.de/www/www95/www95.html
World-Wide Web servers in Russia ★★	http://www.npi.msu.su/RUS-other-WWW.html
World-Wide Web Worm (WWWW).Web-searching tool (form interface) ★★★★	http://www.cs.colorado.edu/home/mcbryan/WWWW.html
Writing on the wall (grafitti server) ★★	http://www.gatech.edu/desoto/graf/index.art_crimes.html
WWW for Instructional Use ★★★	http://www.utexas.edu/world/instruction/index.html

WWW Virtual Library: Communications and Telecommunications ★★	http://www.analysys.co.uk/commslib.htm
WWW Wanderer (Web-*robot*) ★★★	http://www.mit.edu:8001/cgi/wa
WXYC (US student radio station) ★★★	http://sunsite.unc.edu/wxyc/

X

Xerox Corporation's Web server ★★★	• http://www.xerox.com/ • http://pubweb.parc.xerox.com/
X-Open (The UNIX standard-setting body) ★★★	http://www.xopen.org/

Y

Yachting Brokerage (all about yachts, basically) ★★	http://beta.aladdin.co.uk/cpy/
Yahoo Web-crawler (document searcher) ★★★★	http://akebono.stanford.edu/yahoo/
'Yellow Pages' service ★★★	http://www.cityscape.co.uk/gold/
Yellow Silk (Erotic journal) ★★	http://enews.com/magazines/ys

Z

Zambia: Rhodes University Web server ★★	http://www.ru.ac.za/
Zen & The Art of the Internet (book text) ★★★	http://grfn.org/~topher
Ziff-Davies Expo Web server (past and future *Networld* and *Interop* conference information) ★★	http://www.zdexpos.com/

APPENDIX

C

The good Web software guide

This appendix contains the names and locations of popular helper applications that can be used with the Netscape Web browser. Besides helper applications, a wide variety of other Web tools have been included in this appendix. All of the files listed here can be accessed using an appropriate FTP client, or of course, by using Netscape's in-built FTP facility using the `ftp://` URL. Please ensure that you have a suitable decompressor such as PKUNZIP to handle compressed files such as `.ZIP` archives (this is the most ubiquitous format for PCs). Items that are **emboldened** refer to some *core* software tools for use with Netscape. If any of the files listed below have moved, use Archie with any part of the filename to try to locate the entry accordingly. As with all software, new versions are always forthcoming.

Filenames may therefore change also, so you may want to browse around first before downloading any file(s). Each entry in this appendix has been awarded a star-rating (★ = poor, ★★★★★ = excellent) as a guide to help you see at a glance each item's ranking in terms of features, ease-of-use and robustness. Ensure that you virus check all executable files prior to using them on your system.

Name and platform	FTP site location
Cello Win 3.1 (Web browser) ★★★	fatty.law.cornell.edu (/pub/LII/Cello/cello.zip) [a]
Gopher Book (PC Gopher client) ★★★	sunsite.unc.edu (pub/micro/pc-stuff/ms-windows/winsock/apps
GSwin (Postscript file viewer) ★★★★	fatty.law.cornell.edu (/pub/LII/Cello/gswin.zip)
HGopher (PC/Win 3.1 Gopher client) ★★	lister.cc.ic.ac.uk (pub/wingopher/hgopher.exe) [a]
HTML Assistant – Hypereditor software (PC/Win 3.1 + DDE-Cello support) ★★★	fatty.law.cornell.edu (/Incoming/htmlasst.zip) [a]
HTML*Ed* Hypereditor software (PC/Win 3.1) ★★★	src.doc.ic.ac.uk (/computing/systems/ ibmpc/mosaic/util/htmed09a.zip)
HTML HyperEditor (PC/Win 3.1) ★★★	src.doc.ic.ac.uk (/computing/systems/ ibmpc/mosaic/util/hyperdit.zip)
HTMLMapper (shows all the hyperlinks in a document for cross-checking) ★★★	s850.mwc.edu (/pub/pc/htmlmap.zip)
HoTMetaL Editor (HTML hypereditor for DOS/Win 3.1) ★★★	ftp.ncsa.uiuc.edu (/Mosaic/contrib/SoftQuad/ hotmetal) [b]
Hytelnet (Hypertext Telnet for PC) ★★★	ftp.usask.ca (/pub/hytelnet/) a
Lview31 image viewer (PCX/BMP/GIF/ JPEG) ★★★★	fatty.law.cornell.edu (/pub/LII/Cello/lview31.zip)
Mosaic for PC ★★★	• ftp.mcom.com (/Mosaic) • ftp.ncsa.uiuc.edu (/Mosaic)
Netscape Web browser ★★★★★	• ftp.netscape.com (/windows) [c]
PC Gopher – Gopher client ★★★	sunsite.unc.edu (/pub/packages/gopher/ PC_client) [a]
SerWeb (Web Server for PC/Win 3.1) ★★	sunsite.unc.edu (/pub/micro/pc-stuff/ ms-windows/winsock/serweb03.zip [a]
Viewers for Netscape for PC/Windows 3.1 (a miscellaneous selection can be found here, including GIF/JPEG/BMP/MPEG/AVI/Postscript viewers. All work with Netscape et al.) [d]	• www.curtin.edu.au (/pub/internet/mswindows/ viewers) • ftp.ncsa.uiuc.edu (/PC/Mosaic/viewers) • fatty.law.cornell.edu (/pub/LII/Cello)
WAIS Manager (PC/Win 3.1 WAIS client) ★★★	sunsite.unc.edu (/pub/micro/pc-stuff/ ms-windows/winsock/apps) [a]
WFXComm – Windows 3.1 enhanced driver from Delrina software. Replaces Windows `comm.drv` and has better UART 16550 support ★★★	src.doc.ic.ac.uk (/computing/systems/ibmpc/ windows3/misc/wfxcomm.zip) [b]

Wham audio player ★★★	fatty.law.cornell.edu (/pub/LII/Cello/ wham131.zip)
Win32s 32-bit extension for Mosaic (Win 3.1) from Microsoft (license free) ★★★	ftp.microsoft.com
WinGif (GIF image viewer – also BMP/ PCX etc.) ★★★	fatty.law.cornell.edu (/pub/LII/Cello/ wingif14.zip)
WinHTTPD Windows 3.1 HTTP server (run your own HTTP Web server). See also *SerWeb* ★★★★★	unix.hensa.ac.uk (/contrib/winhttpd/ whtp13p1.zip) [a]
Winqvt/net (PC/Win 3.1 telnet/ftp/email/etc.) (sends voice messages across the Net) ★★★★	biochemistry.cwru.edu (/pub/qvtnet) [a]
WinVN (NNTP newsreading software for PC/Win 3.1) ★★★	titan.ksc.nasa.gov (VAX server: [pub.win3.winvn]winvnstd_080.zip) [a,e]
WinWAIS (PC/Win 3.1 WAIS client) ★★★	ridgisd.er.usgs.gov (/software/wais) [a]
WinWeb Web browser (NCSA clone) ★★★	ftp.einet.net (/einet/PC/winweb.zip) [a]
WinSock TCP/IP socket interface for Win 3.1 (Version 1.1+) ★★★★	• info.curtin.edu.au (/pub/internet/mswindows/ winsock) • ftp.utas.edu (/pc/trumpet/winsock/winsock.zip)
WinSock tools, including WinChat, WinFTP, WinPing, and TELW (telnet). Requires the WinSock DLL shown above ★★★	ftp.utas.edu(/pc/trumpet/winsock/winapps.zip) [a]
Wplany (audio player – multiple formats) ★★★★	fatty.law.cornell.edu (/pub/LII/Cello/ wplny09b.zip)

[a]Requires the WinSock TCP/IP socket interface v1.1, or at least an equivalent PC TCP/IP stack.

[b]This file may arrive as a self-extracting PKLITE archive (`.EXE` file). Use the `-D` option with the utility to preserve the directory structure of the archive. Read any documentation that accompanies the file first.

[c]This can be a *very* busy server indeed. You may want to try accessing a mirror site such as one of those shown below in case of difficulties.

[d]See Appendix D for an in-depth list of viewers and filters that can be used with Netscape.

[e]VAX machines use different directory names: `[dir1.dir2.dir3]file.txt` in a VAX environment is analogous to `/dir1/dir2/dir3/file.txt` under UNIX or `drive:\dir1\dir2\dir3` under DOS.

Netscape MIRROR sites:

```
ftp://ftp.cs.umn.edu/packages/X11/contrib/netscape/
ftp://server.berkeley.edu/pub/netscape/
http://mistral.enst.fr/netscape/
ftp.pu-toyama.ac.jp/pub/net/WWW/netscape
ftp.eos.hokudai.ac.jp/pub/WWW/Netscape
ftp.nc.nihon-u.ac.jp:/pub/network/WWW/client/netscape
ftp://ftp.leo.chubu.ac.jp/pub/WWW
ftp.tohoku.ac.jp/pub/network/www/Netscape
```

APPENDIX

D

The A–Z of helper applications

This appendix provides a list of common helper applications (or *viewers*) that can be used
with the Netscape browser. The helper applications in this appendix cover all of the major
image, audio, video and text formats that you are likely to come across in your travels on
the Web. All programs have been awarded a score out of five stars according to their features,
speed and robustness (★ = poor, ★★★★★ = excellent). All of the programs shown run in
the PC Microsoft Windows 3.x environment. Many of the programs here can be found on
alternative FTP sites – simply conduct an Archie search if you need to find a particular file
(using the filename shown, or at least part of the filename, bearing in mind that version
numbers change – see Chapter 5 for more details). Some filenames are wildcarded for this

very purpose (e.g. `wham*.zip` means look for a ZIP archive that starts with the characters *wham*). Many files arrive as compressed archives. The `.ZIP` (PKZIP) format is ubiquitous for the PC platform; some files may be self-extracting `.EXE` files. Ensure that you virus check all executable files prior to using them on your system.

Image/picture viewers

Viewer name/ranking	FTP (URL) address
CompuShow (GIF/BMP/MacPaint/Amiga IFF formats) ★★★	• bongo.cc.utexas.edu (/pub/ibmpc/cshw*.zip) • csn.org (/Unidata/giftools/cshow82b.zip) • nic.funet.fi (/pub/msdos/graphics/gif/cshw*.zip)
CView (JPEG file viewer) ★★★	• wuarchive.wustl.edu (/mirrors/win3/util/CVIEW*.zip) • wuarchive.wustl.edu (/mirrors/win3/desktop/CVIEW*.zip)
DCView (JPEG/GIF/BMP viewer/editor) ★★★	ftp://oak.oakland.edu (/SimTel/msdos/graphics/dcview*.zip)
GifTrans (converts GIF87a to GIF89a transparent) ★★★	ftp://ftp.rz.uni-karlsruhe.de/pub/net/www/tools/giftrans.exe
ImgFun (GIF, PCX, BMP, JPEG viewer) ★★★	wsmr-simtel20.army.mil (/msdos/graphics/ifse100.zip)
JView (JPEG Viewer) ★★★	• ftp.cica.indiana.edu (/pub/pc/win3/desktop/jview*.zip) • oak.oakland.edu (/pub/msdos/windows)
LView31 (GIF/BMP/RLE viewer/editor) ★★★★	• ftp.law.cornell.edu (/pub/LII/Cello) • ftp.uwp.edu (/pub/picture.viewers) • oak.oakland.edu (/pub/msdos/windows3/lview31) • src.doc.ic.ac.uk (/computing/systems/ibmpc/mosaic/viewers/lview31.zip)
LView Pro (GIF/BMP/RLE/JPEG viewer/editor with transparency/interlacing etc.) ★★★★★	ftp://oak.oakland.edu/SimTel/win3/graphics/lviewp1a.zip
WinGif (GIF viewer/editor/interlaced GIFs) ★★★★	• wsmr-simtel20.army.mil (/msdos/windows3/wingif*.zip) • ftp.cica.indiana.edu (/pub/pc/win3/util/wingif*.zip) • garbo.uwasa.fi (/win3/gifutil/wingif14.zip) • nic.funet.fi (/pub/msdos/windows/graphics/wingif14.lzh) • ftp.law.cornell.edu (/pub/LII/Cello/wingif*.zip)

WinJPEG (JPEG/TIFF/PCX viewer/editor) ★★★★	• wuarchive.wustl.edu (/mirrors/msdos/ windows3/winjp*.zip)
	• ftp.cica.indiana.edu (/pub/pc/win3/util/winjp*.zip)
	• oak.oakland.edu (/pub/msdos/windows3/ winjp*.zip)

Note: Windows 3.1 has the `pbrush.exe` program, which will edit/show `.BMP` images (but not GIF), although it can be used to edit images and then to copy these to the clipboard for importation into other editors.

Movie players/animations

Viewer name/ranking	FTP address
AVIPro ★★★	ftp://gatekeeper.dec.com (/pub/micro/msdos/ win3/desktop/avipro2.exe)
MFW (MPEG player) ★★★	ftp.uwp.edu (/pub/picture.viewers/mfw*)
MPEG32w (MPEG player) ★★★★	• wuarchive.wustl.edu/systems/ibmpc/win3/ nt/ [a]
	• gatekeeper.dec.com (/pub/micro/msdos/win3/ desktop/mpegw32g.zip)
MPEGPlay ★★★	• ftp://ftp.cica.indiana.edu
	• ftp://gatekeeper.dec.com (/pub/micro/msdos/ win3/desktop/)
	• src.doc.ic.ac.uk (/computing/systems/os2/ 32bit/unix/mpegplay.zip)
MPEGXing (MPEG player/VT motion scalable) ★★★	• postgres.berkeley.edu (/pub/multimedia/mpeg/ Windows3.x/mpegexe.zip)
	• phoenix.oulu.fi (/pub/incoming/mpeg2_0/ mpegexe.zip)
	• oak.oakland.edu (/pub/msdos/windows3/ mpegexe.zip)
	• gatekeeper.dec.com (/pub/micro/msdos/win3/ desktop/mpegxing.zip)
QuickTime for Windows (`.MOV` file player) ★★★	ftp.sunet.se/pub/pc/windows/winsock-indstate/ WWW-Browsers/Players/qtw11.zip
VidVue (AVI player) ★★★	wuarchive.wustl.edu (systems/ibmpc/win3/ desktop/vidvue*)
VMPEG (MPEG player; very quick) ★★★★	micros.hensa.ac.uk/micros/ibmpc/win/i/i197/ vmpeg16.zip
WAAPlay (FLI viewer) ★★★	• wuarchive.wustl.edu (/mirrors2/win3/ desktop/waaplay.zip)

Note: Windows 3.x has the `mplayer.exe` program that will play `.AVI` format movies.
[a]This software requires a 32-bit capability (such as Windows 3.11, Windows NT, Windows 95 or Windows 3.1 running the Microsoft Win32s software available from `ftp.microsoft.com`).

Audio/sound players

Viewer name/ranking	FTP address
MPLAYER (AU player) ★★★	ftp.sunet.se (/pub/pc/windows/winsock-indstate/ WWW-Browsers/Players/mplayer.zip)
NAPLAYER (AU and AIFF player) ★★★	Arrives with the Netscape browser archive [a]
Wham (WAV and most other formats) ★★★	• ftp.cica.indiana.edu (/pub/pc/win3/sounds/ wham131.zip) • ftp.law.cornell.edu (/pub/LII/Cello/ wham131.zip) • ftp://gatekeeper.dec.com (/pub/micro/msdos/ win3/sounds/wham131.zip)
WPlany (WAV/AU and nearly every other format) ★★★★	• wuarchive.wustl.edu (/systems/ibmpc/win3/ sounds/wplany*)

Note 1: All sounds can be played through the PC speaker with all of the utilities above. The necessary driver is freeware and is available from Microsoft at their FTP site `ftp.microsoft.com` and from numerous other sites, such as NCSA's FTP server at `ftp.ncsa.uiuc.edu` (as `/PC/Mosaic/ viewers/speak.zip`).

Note 2: Windows 3.1 has `soundrec.exe` that can play `.WAV` format files, although since the program cannot take a command-line argument, you must click on the *Play* button first (this also has the advantage that the sound is kept and can be played multiple times). The `mplayer.exe` movie player will also play `.WAV` files (this requires a sound card, however).

[a]This is the default audio player that arrives with Netscape. It runs in both 16 and 32-bit environments.

Telnet launchers

Viewer name/ranking	FTP address
EWAN Telnet client ★★★★	ftp.easynet.co.uk
WinTel (NCSA's Telnet program) ★★	• ftp.ncsa.uiuc.edu (/pub/Telnet) • ftp://gatekeeper.dec.com (/pub/micro/msdos/ win3/winsock/wintelb3.zip)
QVTnet ★★★	wuarchive.wustl.edu (/systems/ibmpc/win3/ util/qvtnt94.zip)
Trumpet Telnet ★★★	ftp://gatekeeper.dec.com (/pub/micro/msdos/ win3/winsock/trmptel.zip)
TELW (see Note below) ★★★	info.curtin.edu.au (/pub/internet/mswindows/ winsock/winapps.zip)

Note: TELW comes as part of the WinSock TCP/IP utilities (`winapps.zip`) and is not normally found by itself.

Text/PostScript viewers

Viewer name/Ranking	FTP address
GSView (Postscript viewer) ★★★	• ftp.ncsa.uiuc.edu (/PC/Mosaic/viewers/ gsview10.zip) • http://www.cs.wisc.edu/~ghost/gsview/ index.html
GSWin (*GhostScript* – Postscript viewer) ★★★	• ftp.law.cornell.edu (/pub/LII/Cello/gswin.zip) • ftp://ftp.cs.wisc.edu/pub/ghost

Note: Windows supplies the `notepad.exe` program as an ASCII viewer (this is an editor as well as a viewer). Any DOS-based ASCII editor/viewer (such as `edit.com`) can be used if you create a PIF file for the application and ensure that it runs within its own window area. Then call the PIF file as the viewer.

APPENDIX

E

Configuring the netscape.ini file

This appendix provides configuration information for the Netscape initialization file `netscape.ini`. Netscape 1.1 allows configuration to be undertaken using the Options/Preferences menu, although it is still possible to make changes to `netscape.ini` to effect larger-scale modifications which would be time-consuming to undertake via Netscape. The `netscape.ini` is placed in the same directory as the main Netscape program when it is first installed. The file itself is split into a number of sections, each of which is described in detail below. Most settings are yes/no-type (binary) answers (**yes** | **no**) which enable or disable certain system features. Other settings specify the names of URLs and the location of various Netscape configuration files. Comments can be inserted into the `netscape.ini` file by starting the line with the word `rem`, which stands for *remark*. A complete `netscape.ini` file is provided at the end of this appendix for completeness. Ensure that you restart Netscape when making changes by hand so that all new settings are properly in force.

The Netscape installation program will add a [`Netscape`] section to the Windows startup file `win.ini`, which specifies the location of the `netscape.ini` initialization file. For example:

```
[Netscape]
ini=C:\NETSCAPE\NETSCAPE.INI
```

You can therefore change the location of this file according to the setting of the Windows variable 'ini'.

[Main] section

Configuration line	Details
`Last Config Menu=`*number*	Specifies the preferences menu that is loaded (Options/Preferences), starting from zero (0).
`Anchor Underline=yes`|`no`	Specifies whether hyperlinks and anchors are underlined (`yes`) or not (`no`).
`Fancy FTP=yes`|`no`	Specifies whether or not additional annotations are displayed for `ftp://` URLs (`yes`=enabled; `no`=disabled).
`Autoload Home Page=yes`|`no`	When `yes`, Netscape loads a default home page URL, as specified in the `Home Page=` setting [a]
`Fancy News=yes`|`no`	Specifies whether or not additional annotations are displayed for `ftp://` URLs (`yes`=enabled; `no`=disabled).
`Home Page=`*URL*	Names a default home page to load. Any valid URL can be used (default is: `http://home.netscape.com/`).
`News RC=`*drive:\dir\newsrc*	Names the `newsrc` file used to maintain all of the USENET newsgroups that you want to read and subscribe to. Specify a valid pathname to the file, e.g. `C:\NETSCAPE\NEWS\NEWSRC` [b]
`Temp Directory=`*drive:\dir*	Specifies the name of a temporary directory, normally a pathname such as `C:\TEMP`.
`Mozilla=`*VersionString*	Netscape (*Mozilla*) version details, e.g. `Good-1.1b3` for Netscape v1.1 beta 3.

`Toolbar=yes|no`	Specifies whether or not to show the main toolbar.
`Starter Buttons bar=yes|no`	Specifies whether or not to show the Netscape directory buttons.
`Location bar=yes|no`	Specifies whether or not to show the main location (URL) bar.
`Display Inline Images=yes|no`	Determines whether or not in-line images are displayed.
`Security Color Bar=yes|no`	Determines whether or not Netscape shows the coloured security bar around a loaded document.

[a]Ensure that if you are using an `http://` request (or other non-local URL) that you have established a TCP/IP (modem) connection first; otherwise Netscape will warn you that it cannot locate the URL.
[b]Netscape 1.1b3/1.1N introduces a new NEWS directory for USENET configuration (`newsrc`) files.

[Viewers] **section**

This section identifies the viewers or *helper applications* that you have installed on your system. Clearly, this section of the `netscape.ini` file will largely depend on the programs you eventually install, although Netscape provides a small number of entries, some of which deal with the audio formats supported by the `naplayer.exe` audio-playing utility. Refer to Appendix D for a list of popular shareware and freeware helper applications that can be used with Netscape.

Configuration line	**Details**
`HTML=`*drive:\dir\file*	Specifies an HTML viewer. Netscape is used for HTML files in nearly every instance, although an HTML file that is downloaded can be viewed using an alternative program if you wish.
`Tn3270=`*drive:\dir\file*	Names a Telnet-3270 (IBM emulation) application for use with the (somewhat obscure) `tn3270://` URL. IBM-3270 mainframes use a different emulation, hence the provision for a different Telnet URL/helper.
`Telnet=`*drive:\dir\file*	Names a standard Telnet application for use with the `telnet://` URL.
`audio/x-aiff=`*drive:\dir\file*	Normally set to the `naplayer.exe` application provided with Netscape to play `.AIF` formatted audio files.

`audio/basic=`*drive:\dir\file*	Normally set to the `naplayer.exe` application provided with Netscape to play `.AU` formatted audio files.

drive:\dir\file   A pathname to a helper application, e.g. `C:\NETSCAPE\HELPERS\LVIEW31.EXE`.

[Settings] **section**

Configuration line	Details
`Background Image=`*URL*	Specifies a URL that points to a background image in the GIF or JPEG formats, for example the URL: `http://somehost.com/images/back1.gif`[a]
`Users Colors Override=yes`|`no`	When `yes`, any custom colour settings will override those set by a loaded hypertext document that attempts to change the screen colours in any way. When `no`, the current document can change the colour settings.
`Custom Background=default`|*rgbCode*	Specifies the page background colour. The setting `default` uses Netscape's default grey background; otherwise a standard RGB colour code must be used in the format Red, Green, Blue, e.g. `255, 255, 255,` where each number ranges from 0 to 255.
`Custom Text Color=no`|*rgbCode*	Specifies a custom text colour (default is black). This must be either `no` or a standard RGB setting, as discussed above.
`Custom Followed Link Color=no`|*rgbCode*	Specifies the colour for a hyperlink that has already been followed, i.e. clicked upon earlier. The options are `no` (no custom colour – use default) or an RGB colour code (see above).
`Custom Link Color=no`|*rgbCode*	Specifies the colour for a hyperlink. The options are `no` (no custom colour – use default) or an RGB colour code (see above).
`Background Color=`*rgbCode*	Specifies the normal background colour using an RGB colour code (default: `192, 192, 192`).
`Followed Link Color=`*rgbCode*	Specifies the colour of a hyperlink that has been followed already (default: `85, 26, 139`).
`Text Color=`*rgbCode*	Specifies the normal text colour using an RGB colour code (default: `0, 0, 0`).

`Link Color=`*rgbCode*	Specifies the normal hyperlink colour using an RGB colour code (default: `0, 0, 238`).
`Blinking=yes`|`no`	Specifies whether or not blinking text can be used.

`yes`\|`no`   Use either of the keywords `yes` or `no`
rgbCode   A red, green, blue colour code, e.g. `0, 0, 255` is blue (values range from 0–255).
[a]This feature is not selectable from within Netscape, it seems, and must be configured externally.

[User] **section**

Configuration line	Details
`Sig_File=`*drive:\dir\file*	Names a *signature file* that is used to hold contact details etc. about yourself, and which is appended to news and email messages. The file should be plain text (i.e. ASCII); 3 lines maximum length.
`User_Organization=`*OrgString*	Specifies the name of the organization you represent, e.g. a company. The name will be placed in the `Organization:` field that all email headers contain (leave blank if non-applicable).
`User_Addr=`*user@host*	Specifies your email address in the format `user@host`, for example the address `ag17@cityscape.co.uk`. This will be used in news and mail messages as a recipient address.
`User_Name=`*NameString*	Your human name. This name will be quoted in outgoing email/news messages, and is used to identify your real name (some email names can be quite cryptic).

[Images] **section**

Configuration line	Details
`Incremental Display=yes`|`no`	Determines whether or not images are loaded incrementally, i.e. in layers. Interlaced images have this capability, and this image format will determine whether or not such a display can be used.

`Dither=yes│no`	Determines whether or not images are dithered, i.e. whether colour substitution is enabled or disabled.

[Main Window] section

Configuration line	Details
x=*number*	Specifies the X position where the Netscape window starts its intercept from.
y=*number*	Specifies the Y position where the Netscape window starts its intercept from.
height=*number*	Specifies the height of the Netscape screen.
width=*number*	Specifies the width of the Netscape screen.

number   All numbers are specified as *pixel* units.

[Bookmark List] section

Configuration line	Details
`Start Menu With=Entire Listing`	Specifies that the bookmark list is shown in its entirety when opened.
`Add URLs Under=Top Level of Listing`│*heading*	Specifies that newly added URLs are placed under the top-level of the bookmark list, or alternatively under the subheading entry *heading* that you have previously created using Netscape's bookmark facility.
`File Location=`*drive:\dir\file*	Specifies the location of the bookmark file. This is an HTML-formatted file named `bookmark.htm`, and by default resides in the same directory as the main program, e.g. `C:\NETSCAPE\BOOKMARK.HTM`.

[Tool Bar] section

Configuration line	Details
`Button Styles=`*number*	Specifies the style of the toolbar used. The value for *number* can be: 1 = Text buttons only 2 = Icon buttons and text

[Services] **section**

Configuration line	Details
SOCKS_ServerPort=*PortNumber*	Specifies a SOCKS server port number, default 1080.
SOCKS_Server=*ServerName*	Specifies a SOCKS server name (e.g. Internet host).
Socks Conf=*drive:\dir\file*	Specifies the location of the socks.cnf Netscape configuration file.
NNTP_Server=*ServerName*	Specifies a NNTP news server, e.g. news.host.com.
SMTP_Server=*ServerName*	Specifies an SMTP mail server, e.g. mail.host.com.

[Fonts] **section**

Configuration line	Details
Fixed Base Size=*fontSize*	Specifies the size of the default monospaced base font.
Fixed Family=*fontName*	Specifies the name of the fixed (monospaced) font used by Netscape (default: Courier New).
Proportional Base Size=*fontSize*	Specifies the size of the default proportional base font.
Proportional Family=*fontName*	Specifies the name of the proportional font used by Netscape, e.g. Times New Roman.

fontSize   The point size of the font concerned.
fontName   The name of the font concerned. Use Netscape's Options/Preferences/Styles menu to see the exact name used for each font installed under Windows.

[History] **section**

Configuration line	Details
History File=*drive:\dir\file*	Specifies the location of the Netscape history file netscape.hst. By default this is stored in the same directory as the main Netscape program.

Expiration=*number*	Specifies the number of days that a hyperlink is marked after it has been visited. After this period, the hyperlink reverts to its default colour (the default is 30).

[Cache] **section**

Configuration line	Details
Cache Dir=*drive:\dir*	Specifies the directory in which Netscape stores its disk cache files, normally an extension of the Netscape main directory named CACHE, for example C:\NETSCAPE\CACHE.
Memory Cache Size=*SizeKB*	Specifies the size of the memory cache (in kilobytes). The default is 600, or just over half of one megabyte.
Disk Cache Size=*SizeKB*	Specifies the size of the disk cache (in kilobytes). The default is 5000, or roughly 5 megabytes.

[Network] **section**

Configuration line	Details
Use Async DNS=yes|no	Specifies whether or not to use asynchronous Domain Name Server (DNS) calls.
Max Connections=*number*	Sets the maximum number of active network connections that can be open at any one time.
TCP Buffer Size=*number*	Sets the size of the network buffer (sizes are in bytes).

[Security] **section**

Configuration line	Details
When Entering=yes|no	Specifies whether or not to issue a warning when entering an insecure server area/document.
When Leaving=yes|no	Specifies whether or not to issue a warning when leaving a secure server area/document.

| When Mixed=yes\|no | Specifies whether or not to issue a warning when moving between a mix of secure and insecure documents/servers. |
| When Insecure=yes\|no | Specifies whether or not to issue a warning when submitting the contents of a fill-out-form to an insecure server. |

[News] **section**

Configuration line	Details
News Directory=*drive:\dir*	Specifies the directory for news related files [a]
News Chunk=*number*	Sets the maximum number of news articles that are loaded into one hypertext document at any one time.

[a]Netscape 1.1b3 introduces a new NEWS directory for this purpose, e.g. C:\NETSCAPE\NEWS, and this is the default directory that will be used by Netscape.

[Suffixes] **section**

The [Suffixes] section contains a list of MIME (Multipurpose Internet Mail Extensions) types which identify a variety of file formats. For example, image/gif is the MIME type for an image stored in the GIF format. See the Netscape Options/Preferences/Helper Applications menu for more MIME types in common use. The suffixes themselves contain one or more filename extensions that identify that file. For example, a typical entry for an audio file could resemble:

```
audio/x-aiff=aif,aiff,aifc
```

which identifies the MIME type audio/x-aiff (an AIFF audio formatted file) as having the filename extensions .AIF, .AIFF or .AIFC. It is important to realize that the same type of file can arrive with a different filename extension. This itself is mainly due to two factors. First, the host operating system may not allow filename extensions to exceed a certain number of characters – DOS is a prime example, which only allows three letters as a filename extension (hence the .AIF entry in the example above). On a UNIX machine the extensions .AIFF and .AIFC would be quite valid. File formats are a very complex area indeed. A variety of standards and software platforms have led to a proliferation of file formats, some of which are extensions of existing formats, and others which are completely different in content. The [Suffixes] section is used in conjunction with the [Viewers] section, which defines the actual helper applications that deal with each type of file format. A typical entry in the [Viewers] section, in the context of the previous example, could resemble:

```
audio/x-aiff=C:\NETSCAPE\NAPLAYER.EXE
```

which tells Netscape to use the `nplayer.exe` utility to play such files, that is to say that every time you reference an `.AIF`, `.AIFF` or `.AIFC` file through Netscape (from a hyperlink, FTP request etc.) the `naplayer.exe` program will load the file and then play it accordingly.

Example `netscape.ini` file

An example `netscape.ini` file is reproduced here for your information. It is important to note that this file can never really be *complete* in the true sense of the word. For example, it is up to users to decide how many helper applications they want to install for use with the Netscape browser. The initialization file reproduced here is sufficient for the most basic Netscape configuration, and does not include helper applications.

```
rem ***
rem *** Sample netscape.ini file
rem ***

[Main]
Last Config Menu=2
Anchor Underline=yes
Fancy FTP=yes
Autoload Home Page=no
Fancy News=no
Home Page=http://home.netscape.com/
Check Server=2
News RC=C:\NETSCAPE\NEWS\NEWSRC
Temp Directory=C:\temp
Mozilla=Good-1.1
Toolbar=yes
Starter Buttons bar=yes
Location bar=yes
Display Inline Images=yes
Security Color Bar=yes

[Viewers]
HTML=
Tn3270=
Telnet=C:\NETSCAPE\TELNET\TELW.EXE
audio/basic=C:\NETSCAPE\NAPLAYER.EXE
audio/x-aiff=C:\NETSCAPE\NAPLAYER.EXE
video/x-sgi-movie=
```

```
application/x-tardist=browser-handle-promptuser
x-world/x-vrml=browser-handle-promptuser

[Settings]
Background Image=
Users Colors Override=no
Custom Background=default
Custom Text Color=no
Custom Followed Link Color=no
Custom Link Color=no
Background Color=192, 192, 192
Followed Link Color=85, 26, 139
Text Color=0, 0, 0
Link Color=0, 0, 238
Blinking=yes

[User]
Sig_File=
User_Organization=YourCompanyName
User_Addr=yourname@your.host
User_Name=YourFullName

[Images]
Incremental Display=yes
Dither=yes

[Main Window]
y=-6
x=-6
height=780
width=1036

[Bookmark List]
Start Menu With=Entire Listing
Add URLs Under=Top Level of Listing
File Location=c:\netscape\bookmark.htm

[Tool Bar]
Button Styles=2

[Services]
SOCKS_ServerPort=1080
```

```
SOCKS_Server=
Socks Conf=c:\windows\socks.cnf
SMTP_Server=mail.somehost.com
NNTP_Server=news.somehost.com

[Proxy Information]
Wais_ProxyPort=0
Ftp_ProxyPort=0
HTTPS_ProxyPort=0
News_ProxyPort=0
Gopher_ProxyPort=0
Http_ProxyPort=0
No_Proxy=
Wais_Proxy=
HTTPS_Proxy=
News_Proxy=
Gopher_Proxy=
FTP_Proxy=
HTTP_Proxy=

[Fonts]
Fixed Base Size=10
Fixed Family=Courier New
Proportional Base Size=12
Proportional Family=Times New Roman

[History]
History File=c:\netscape\netscape.hst
Expiration=30

[Cache]
Cache Dir=c:\netscape\cache
Disk Cache Size=5000
Memory Cache Size=600

[Network]
Use Async DNS=yes
Max Connections=4
TCP Buffer Size=6144

[Cookies]
Cookie File=c:\netscape\cookies.txt
```

```
[Security]
Warn Entering=no
Warn Leaving=no
Warn Mixed=no
Warn Insecure Forms=no

[News]
News Directory=C:\netscape\news
News Chunk Size=100
MIME Posting=no

[Suffixes]
audio/basic=au,snd
audio/x-aiff=aif,aiff,aifc
video/x-sgi-movie=movie

[INTL]
Font0=iso-8859-1,Times New Roman,10,Courier New,10
Font1=x-sjis,élér +Æ_,10,élér +Æ_,10
```

A P P E N D I X

F

Web glossary

This appendix defines the most common terms and acronyms that are currently used in the context of the World-Wide Web, Netscape and the Internet.

BBS

An acronym for **Bulletin Board System**, a service that you dial into with a modem, and which allows access to services such as electronic mail, conference areas and file downloading. Many thousands of BBSs exist around the world, some of which have limited Internet access.

Browser

Synonymous with Web browser, client, or client browser – which all refer to graphical programs such as Netscape or Mosaic. See also Mosaic, Netscape.

CGI

An acronym for **Common Gateway Interface**, a standard defining how client applications (such as Netscape) can interact with a server through an appropriate gateway mechanism, such as using the HTTP protocol. The mechanism is normally a script, or *back-end* program, such as a database interface, so that data can be passed from the client and stored or processed by the server. The CGI interface communicates with a client process through a series of environmental variables that hold details of the client's request, e.g. an encoded query string. See also HTTP, FOF.

Client pull

A *dynamic document* technique used by Netscape that makes use of the proposed HTML 3.0 <META> tag in order to update the request for a document within a specified time period, e.g. every 10 seconds. See also Server push.

DOS

An acronym for **Disk Operating System**. The operating system found on all personal computers, which comes in two flavours: MS-DOS (from Microsoft) and PC-DOS (from IBM).

DTD

An acronym for **Document Type Definition**, a specific implementation of a document description using SGML, and which is contained within a file. HTML is referred to as an SGML DTD. See also HTML, SGML.

Email

Electronic mail. A communication tool that allows users to send textual messages to each other via the Internet (or though a BBS). See also BBS, Internet.

Entities

Entities (or *character escape codes*) are part of the HTML tag language. They allow extended characters to be used within a document, typically those from the Latin-1 character set (e.g. ì, Ô, ê) and are inserted into an HTML document at the point required. Refer to Appendix G for a list of such codes.

FAQ

An acronym for **Frequently Asked Questions**. FAQs are documents that explain Internet fundamentals for new users (although many FAQs are very advanced as well). Many FAQs are distributed via USENET. See also Internet, USENET.

Firewall

A firewall is a security scheme that protects one or more computers with Internet connections from intrusion by external computers which also have Internet connections. A firewall is essentially an *invisible boundary* created through software that distinguishes networked computers within the firewall from those outside the firewall. Those computers within the firewall possess internal access capabilities and shared resources that are not granted to those on the outside. External requests are therefore filtered and examined before they are allowed through the firewall, if at all. See also Proxy, Internet.

FOF

An acronym for **Fill-Out-Form**. FOFs are areas within an HTML document that allow user input to be passed from a client application such as Netscape to a server entity on another Internet host. See also HTML.

FTP

An acronym for **File Transfer Protocol** (or **File Transfer Program**, if referring to the *application* itself). FTP is a tool and protocol that defines how files of information are transferred over the Internet. FTP is the principal tool used for moving files between Internet hosts. The World-Wide Web interfaces to FTP via the `ftp://` URL. See also URL, Internet, World-Wide Web.

GIF

An acronym for **Graphics Interchange Format**, a ubiquitous image format for still pictures used on the Internet. Web browsers such as Netscape use the GIF format for in-line images that appear within HTML documents. The GIF format was originally developed by CompuServe for use over their network. See also HTML, JPEG.

Helper application

A third-party program that can be used with the Netscape browser to view proprietary file formats, such as images, audio files and animations. Examples are *WinGif* and *Lview* for GIF/JPEG images, and *Naplayer* for audio files.

Hot region

A hot region is an area of an in-line image which, when clicked upon (using a mouse) activates a particular URL (or hyperlink). See also In-line image, Hyperlink.

HRREFS

A (partial) acronym for **Hypertext References**, which refers to the hyperlinks embedded within a document that lead to other sources of information. See also Hyperlink.

HTML

An acronym for **HyperText Mark-up Language**. HTML is a mark-up language for documents. It allows authors to design and create hypermedia documents that can be used over the World-Wide Web. HTML is born out of the ISO SGML standard. The HTML language is made up of a series of *tags* that encapsulate parts of the text within a document and provide document mark-up features such as paragraphs, bold/italic/preformatted text, headers, in-line images and so forth. See also SGML, In-line images, Tags.

HTTP

An acronym for **HyperText Transfer Protocol**, the principal protocol used by the World-Wide Web. HTTP is encapsulated within TCP/IP packets for transmission over the Internet. HTTP is responsible for many things, such as interfacing with other Internet tools (e.g. FTP and Gopher) using an appropriate URL, as well as actually making requests for information and carrying the information between the client and server. See also URL, TCP/IP, FTP.

HTTPD

An acronym for **HyperText Transfer Protocol Daemon**, as used in the context of the Windows NCSA HTTPD Web server software. The term *daemon* is used heavily on UNIX-based systems when referring to programs that *listen* for requests in order to process them. The Web server software from NCSA (HTTPD) is classed as a daemon since it waits passively (in the *background*) for incoming HTTP requests. See also HTTP.

Hypereditor

A tool designed for authors that allows HTML mark-up to be automated (albeit to a limited extent). Typically hypereditors allow the insertion of tags and other items via a menu and/or keystroke rather than the user typing them in literally. Some hypereditors also keep track of URLs and other resources so that they can be placed into a document as and when required. Some of the more advanced tools offer WYSIWYG displays so that the mark-up of a document can be seen using a browser of the user's choice. See also WYSIWYG, HTML.

Hyperlink

Hypertext link. Synonymous with hyper-reference. A hyperlink is an item of text (or an image) that the user can click on in order to be led to another item, or source of information. Hyperlinks give the Web its hypertext and hypermedia functionality. See also Hypermedia, Hypertext.

Hypermedia

Hypermedia is similar to hypertext, although bringing together many more forms of media, typically of an audio and visual nature. Hypermedia has been made possible through tools such as Netscape and the World-Wide Web. See also Hypertext.

Hyperspace

A collective name referring to the area in which hypermedia and hypertext documents are circulated. Just as *Cyberspace* is mainly used to refer to the Internet, *Hyperspace* is really only another name for the World-Wide Web. See also World-Wide Web, Internet.

Hypertext

Hypertext is a way of cross-referencing textual information. A hypertext document is made up of many cross-references (hyperlinks) to other, related items of information, perhaps in the same document or located in other external documents. See also Hypermedia, Hyperlink.

Imagemap

An imagemap is an image that has one or more hot-spot regions within it. Each region can be clicked on by the user (using the mouse) in order to activate a particular URL that is associated with that hot region. See also URL, hot region, GIF.

In-line image

An in-line image is a graphics file that is placed within an HTML document. Netscape, for example, can handle GIF, JPEG and X-Bitmap images within documents (as well as any external image format using an appropriate helper application). See also GIF, JPEG, helper application, HTML.

Internet

The world's largest computer network; a network of networks all linked together to form one entity, all of which run the TCP/IP protocol. The Internet is known by many names, including the *Net*, the *Information superhighway* and *Cyber-*

Space. The World-Wide Web now makes up a large proportion of the Internet. See also TCP/IP, World-Wide Web, TCP/IP.

ISO

An acronym for International Organization for Standardization, a major standard-setting body in the computing world.

MIME

An acronym for **Multipurpose Internet Mail Extensions**. MIME defines a number of different internal file formats whose names take the form *filetype/subtype*. For example, HTML text is specified as `text/html`, whereas plain (or ASCII) text is specified as `text/plain`. MIME allows standard email (which is entirely text-based, and 7-bit only) to carry other file formats (typically binary formats that have 8 bits in each byte). All results passed via the HTTP protocol over the Internet are done via MIME formatted messages. See also Internet, HTTP.

Modem

An acronym for **Modulator–Demodulator**. The hardware device that connects you to a destination machine, which also has a modem to answer your call, thus facilitating access to many types of on-line *dial-up* services, such as bulletin boards and of course the Internet itself. Modems use the telephone network as a communications medium. See also BBS, Internet.

Mosaic

The first graphical Web browser available on the Microsoft Windows, X-Windows (UNIX) and Macintosh platforms. NCSA Mosaic, like all graphical Web browsers, is in essence an HTML *parsing* tool that marks up hypermedia documents onto the screen. The original team that developed Mosaic now works for Netscape Communications Corporation (NCC), developers of the Netscape Web browser. See also HTML, NCSA, Netscape.

Mozilla

Another name for the Netscape browser. *Mozilla* is a dinosaur mascot.

NCSA

An acronym for National Center for Supercomputing Applications (at the University of Illinois). This is where those clever people originally developed Mosaic. (Mosaic's full name is normally quoted as *NCSA Mosaic*). See also Mosaic, Netscape.

Net, The

Synonymous with Internet. See also Internet, World-Wide Web.

Netscape

The graphical Web browser program (client) that facilitates access to the area of the Internet known as the World-Wide Web. Netscape is an HTML version 1.0, 2.0 and 3.0 browser with enhanced features such as secure network support and dynamic documents. See also HTML.

Netsite

Netsite is a phrase coined by Netscape Communications Corporation, developers of the Netscape browser, to refer to a Web server that is running their own server software with secure HTTP enabled, i.e. data encryption is enabled for all client/server activity, allowing sensitive information to be transmitted without fear of interception. See also HTTP, SSL.

NNTP

An acronym for **Network News Transfer Protocol**. A ubiquitous protocol used to distribute USENET news over the Internet. Netscape can interface to an NNTP server to gain access to USENET. See also URL.

PC

An acronym for **Personal Computer**.

PPP

An acronym for **Point to Point Protocol**, the more advanced predecessor to the SLIP protocol, which allows TCP/IP to run over serial line connections. SLIP and PPP are the two most common protocols supported for *dial-up* Internet connections. PPP enhancements include an error-correction capability. See also SLIP, Internet.

Proxy

A proxy is an entity, i.e. a server machine (hardware and software), that allows access to the Internet from within a *firewall*. A proxy server runs in conjunction with some suitable firewall software. The proxy server waits for a client-request from inside the firewall, forwards the request to the remote server located outside the firewall, and then reads the response and sends it back to the client. See also Firewall.

PushPull

A term that refers to Netscape 1.1's *dynamic document* capability, whereby the client and server applications (Netscape or a Web server program) can be made to receive or transmit documents automatically (or at least after a specific time period). See also Client pull, Server push.

Render

A term used in the context of many Web browsers to mean *display*, for example *'The image was rendered onto the screen'*. See also Web browser.

Robot

Refers to a program used on the Internet that scours servers for information (commonly based on some criteria imposed by the user, such as a search expression). The term *Robot* comes from the fact that the process is automated and is carried out electronically. Such programs are also known as *spiders* and *Web crawlers*, and use a variety of means to find the information you require. On the World-Wide Web some robots search URLs, and in some case follow these links to other sites to build up an indexed database of Web resources that the user can then search on-line. An example is the Yahoo service. See also Internet.

Server push

A *dynamic document* feature of Netscape 1.1 that allows a Web server entity to send segments of a document, such as an image or hypertext file, to a client browser (such as Netscape). A special MIME type is used to allow data segmentation. Documents are then sent from the server to the client, and they are *updated* by the client, i.e. they are replaced, thus allowing techniques such as simple animation. See also MIME, Netscape, Web server, Client pull.

SGML

An acronym for **Standard Generalized Mark-up Language**. SGML is a meta-language that is used to define a wide range of document types. HTML is an *application* of SGML that is used to create such documents. SGML is itself an ISO standard. See also HTML, DTD.

SLIP

An acronym for **Serial Line Internet Protocol**. A communications protocol used over telephone lines via a dial-up connection from the user's computer. SLIP is essentially an implementation of IP (Internet Protocol) for use over dial-up telephone lines via the serial port on a computer such as a PC, and is a popular way of accessing the Internet. See also World-Wide Web, TCP/IP, Internet, PPP.

SSL

An acronym for **Secure Socket Layer**, an open standard describing an inter-process communication mechanism used by the TCP/IP protocol over the Internet. Secure sockets have extra security features to facilitate secure transmissions over the Internet. See also Internet, TCP/IP.

Tags

Tags are part of the HTML language. They consist of a series of strings enclosed within < and > characters, and are used to control the mark-up of documents when viewed through a browser such as Netscape. For example, a sentence could be set in italics using the tags `<i>This is in italics</i>`. Some tags are structured as two separate parts, known a start-tag and an end-tag (as demonstrated), although some tags do not always have to *encapsulate* the text in this way (e.g. `<img src="mygif.gif">` inserts an in-line image and requires no end-tag). See also In-line image, HTML, SGML, Netscape.

TCP/IP

An acronym for **Transmission Control Protocol/Internet Protocol**. The primary communications protocol used over the entire Internet network. HTTP requests are encapsulated within TCP/IP for use over the WWW. See also HTTP, World-Wide Web, SLIP.

URL

Acronym for **Uniform Resource Locator** (or **Universal Resource Locator**). A URL is basically the address of a resource on the Internet – a way of specifying, in a very compact form, the exact type and location of an Internet resource. URLs allow access into Internet news servers, Gopher servers, WAIS servers, FTP servers and even real-time (Telnet-based) resources. An example URL is `news:alt.books.technical`, a news URL that loads the USENET newsgroup `alt.books.technical` using a default news server. See also Telnet, WAIS, FTP, Gopher, USENET.

URN

An acronym for Uniform Resource Name. An alternative to the URL. There is currently a movement on the Net to introduce URNs . These differ from standard URLs in that they take the user to the nearest resource in order to speed things up, and generally to stop all users ending up at the same point on the Web. See also URL.

USENET

An acronym for **USErs' NETwork**. The Internet's *Bulletin Board*, containing over 15 000 separate subject areas to which users contribute solely using electronic mail. USENET carries text, image and audio content. See also Internet, Email.

Viewer

A utility program used by a browser such as Netscape to handle different file formats. Synonymous with helper application. See also Helper application, Netscape.

VRML

An acronym for **Virtual Reality Mark-up Language**. VRML is an evolving specification for a platform-independent definition of three-dimensional spaces within the World-Wide Web. It will be designed to combine virtual reality (VR) features, networked visualization and the global hypermedia environment of the World-Wide Web. See also World-Wide Web, HTML.

WAIS

An acronym for **Wide Area Information Server**, a searching tool that indexes the contents of public documents on the Internet, and which is available as a Web server at the URL `http://www.wais.com`. See also URL, Web server.

Web

A synonym for the World-Wide Web. The term *Web* refers to the fact that information on the World-Wide Web is linked together in a *matrix*, i.e. all parts of the Internet are accessible from any other point. See also World-Wide Web, Internet.

Web browser

See Browser, Mosaic, Netscape.

Web server

A program that serves hypertext documents to Web browsers such as Netscape. Examples are the NCSA Windows HTTP daemon and the CERN Server (freeware programs). See also Netscape, NCSA, HTTP.

World-Wide Web

A hypertext system used over the Internet for cross-referencing and retrieving information over the Internet. It uses the HTTP protocol. See also Internet, Hypertext, HTTP.

WWW

An acronym for the **World-Wide Web**.

WWWW

Acronym for **World-Wide Web Worm**, a *hypertool* that searches Internet URLs and follows all their links for other information. See also: World-Wide Web, URL, Robot.

A P P E N D I X

G

HTML entity codes

Entity codes allow special characters (many of which are not found on the QWERTY keyboard) to be inserted into an HTML document. Each entity names is prefixed with an ampersand (&) and is suffixed by a semicolon. All characters in the third section are taken from the ISO Latin-1 character set.

1 Common characters with special meanings to HTML

Entity	Description	Literal character
<	The left-facing chevron	<
>	The right-facing chevron	>

&	The ampersand	&
"	The double quote	"

Notes: The " entity is of use where a quoted string must be encapsulated with quotes, for example: `<img src="ebook.gif" alt="Here is a picture from the new &quot;Electronic Book&quot;">`. The " entity does not need to be used in normal HTML text. The < and > entities are used to allow the left- and right-facing chevrons (< and >) to be included literally within an HTML-formatted document (otherwise these characters are interpreted by the HTML parser within Netscape and may not be properly rendered).

2 Netscape entity additions

Entity	Description	Literal character
®	Registered trademark sign	®
©	Copyright sign	©

Notes: The above two entity codes have been introduced with the Netscape browser. Other Web browsers will not render these entities correctly. You can embed the literal character required by using the ASCII code for that character, or by pasting in from an application such as `charmap.exe`, which arrives as part of Windows 3.x.

3 ISO Latin 1 character entities

Entity	Description	Literal character
Æ	Capital AE diphthong (ligature)	Æ
Á	Capital A, acute accent	Á
Â	Capital A, circumflex accent	Â
À	Capital A, grave accent	À
Å	Capital A, ring	Å
Ã	Capital A, tilde	Ã
Ä	Capital A, diaeresis or umlaut mark	Ä
Ç	Capital C, cedilla	Ç
&ETH	Capital Eth, Icelandic	Ð
É	Capital E, acute accent	É
Ê	Capital E, circumflex accent	Ê
È	Capital E, grave accent	È
Ë	Capital E, diaeresis or umlaut mark	Ë
Í	Capital I, acute accent	Í
Î	Capital I, circumflex accent	Î

`&Igrave;`	Capital I, grave accent	Ì
`&Iuml;`	Capital I, diaeresis or umlaut mark	Ï
`&Ntilde;`	Capital N, tilde	Ñ
`&Oacute;`	Capital O, acute accent	Ó
`&Ocirc;`	Capital O, circumflex accent	Ô
`&Ograve;`	Capital O, grave accent	Ò
`&Oslash;`	Capital O, slash	Ø
`&Otilde;`	Capital O, tilde	Õ
`&Ouml;`	Capital O, diaeresis or umlaut mark	Ö
`&THORN;`	Capital THORN, Icelandic	Þ
`&Uacute;`	Capital U, acute accent	Ú
`&Ucirc;`	Capital U, circumflex accent	Û
`&Ugrave;`	Capital U, grave accent	Ù
`&Uuml;`	Capital U, diaeresis or umlaut mark	Ü
`&Yacute;`	Capital Y, acute accent	
`&aacute;`	Small a, acute accent	à
`&acirc;`	Small a, circumflex accent	â
`&aelig;`	Small ae diphthong (ligature)	æ
`&agrave;`	Small a, grave accent	à
`&atilde;`	Small a, tilde	ã
`&auml;`	Small a, diaeresis or umlaut mark	ä
`&ccedil;`	Small c, cedilla	ç
`&eacute;`	Small e, acute accent	é
`&ecirc;`	Small e, circumflex accent	ê
`&egrave;`	Small e, grave accent	è
`&eth;`	Small eth, Icelandic	ð
`&euml;`	Small e, diaeresis or umlaut mark	ë
`&iacute;`	Small i, acute accent	í
`&icirc;`	Small i, circumflex accent	î
`&igrave;`	Small i, grave accent	ì
`&iuml;`	Small i, diaeresis or umlaut mark	ï
` `	blank single space	
`&ntilde;`	Small n, tilde	ñ
`&oacute;`	Small o, acute accent	ó
`&ocirc;`	Small o, circumflex accent	ô
`&ograve;`	Small o, grave accent	ò
`&oslash;`	Small o, slash	ø
`&otilde;`	Small o, tilde	õ
`&ouml;`	Small o, diaeresis or umlaut mark	ö

`&szlig;`	Small sharp s, German (sz ligature)	ß
`&thorn;`	Small thorn, Icelandic	þ
`&uacute;`	Small u, acute accent	ú
`&ucirc;`	Small u, circumflex accent	û
`&ugrave;`	Small u, grave accent	ù
`&uuml;`	Small u, diaeresis or umlaut mark	ü
`&yacute;`	Small y, acute accent	
`&yuml;`	Small y, diaeresis or umlaut mark	

H

Questions and answers

This appendix deals with a number of common questions that frequently arise in the USENET forums concerned with the World-Wide Web and Netscape as a whole. The *Netscape handbook* is also available on-line at Netscape's server (the directory button toolbar also has a new entry for this service, entitled *Handbook*) and also deals with many additional questions and answers.

How do I obtain the latest copy/a copy of Netscape?
Start up Netscape and type in the URL `ftp://ftp.netscape.com` and you can then navigate your way to the appropriate directory to find the executable file required. It is likely to be a large file. Alternatively, use another FTP client program to download the file instead. If you do not have Netscape, use a conventional FTP program to log into the Netscape FTP site.

What is a mirror site?
A mirror site, or mirror, is basically a replication of an Internet host's complete file system. Mirror sites allow easier access to files, since they may be geographically nearer to the user. Mirror sites also disperse the load away from a single server, making it easier for the user to access files. Netscape Corporation has a number of mirror sites that can be used to download the Netscape browser, for example.

What are the licensing arrangements for Netscape?
Download Netscape and look at the file named `license`. When you first start Netscape you will be asked to agree to the terms of the license (the `license` file will be loaded for you automatically at this stage for you to read).

Why do I have two icons on the Windows desktop?
Netscape needs an additional icon so that the program appears in the Windows *task list* (double-click your left mouse button on an open region of the desktop to see the task list). The additional icon will always be named *Netscape* and cannot be activated, although it can be moved. You can tell the difference between the two icons, since the text for the main Netscape program icon will change according to the title of the hypertext page currently loaded.

How can I find information on a general subject/topic?
Use a search engine program, such as Lycos, WebCrawler, AliWeb or WWWW. See Chapter 5 for more information on such programs.

What is a hyperlink?
A *hyperlink* is a clickable region of the screen that invokes a uniform resource locator (or URL – see below) which in turn invokes a particular Internet resource, e.g. to load another hypertext page, or to download a file.

What is a URL?
A URL is a *Uniform Resource Locator*, a compact notation that specifies the address of a resource on the Internet. URLs can be called from a hyperlink (see above), or can be entered directly into Netscape by the user or from a *bookmark* entry.

What is a home page?
A home page is the first hypertext page that is shown when you contact a Web server. Normally it is a glorified index or contents list that introduces a particular service to the user. The name `index.html` is commonly used for home pages, although the exact name is server-dependent.

What is FTP?
FTP is an acronym for File Transfer Protocol, which is used to move files around on the

Internet. You can access a machine known as an *anonymous FTP server* in order to retrieve files. The Netscape `ftp://` URL is used to access FTP sites in this way. For example, the URL `ftp://ftp.netscape.com` would take you to Netscape Corporation's FTP server, where you can browse their system for file(s) to download. Many thousands of anonymous servers are awaiting a visit...

What is a Gopher?

Gopher is a information-searching tool that is widely used on the Internet. The Netscape program has a `gopher://` URL for this purpose. Many hundreds of public Gophers exist on the Internet. The name *Gopher* comes from the University of Minnesota, where the gopher (a small burrowing creature) is their mascot.

How can I access a Gopher/veronica server?

Connect to a Gopher server using the `gopher://` URL, and then follow the links to get to any file(s) you require, or to conduct searches. All veronica searches are normally provided by an appropriate hyperlink to a veronica server. For example, you could connect to `gopher://gopher.ic.ac.uk` at Imperial College London.

How do I stop a document from being downloaded from the Internet?

Press the ESCAPE key, or click on the *Stop* button in the main Netscape toolbar.

How can I save a file to my local disk?

Select Netscape's File menu and then select Save As. You can then proceed to save the file to disk after choosing a name (Netscape will provide a suggestion). For images, see below.

How can I save an image to my local disk?

Simply press the right mouse button while the mouse cursor is over the image. Netscape will then pop-up a menu of options and you can choose the Save Image option accordingly. The image file will then be downloaded to your local disk in its native format. You must have Netscape version 1.1 to achieve this.

How do insert images into my HTML documents?

Use the HTML `<img src>` or `<embed>` tags. Refer to Chapter 3 for more information on such tags.

How do I get a copyright/trademark character into my HTML document?

Netscape introduces two new *entity* codes called `&copy;` and `&reg;` for this purpose (copyright sign and trademark sign respectively). You could insert these non-keyboard characters from an application such as the Windows *Character Map* (`charmap.exe`) also, which is what many non-Netscape HTML dialects do to overcome the problem of viewing them.

How do I use transparent images in Netscape? What are they?

Transparent images are GIF (Graphics Interchange Format) image files whose background colour blends in exactly with the browser, thus giving the impression that the image is *floating* on the page. A number of tools can create transparent GIF images. Refer to Appendix C for a list of such applications.

What is a helper application, or viewer?

A helper application is a third-party program that allows Netscape to deal with proprietary file formats that cannot be handled by Netscape alone. Netscape can view GIF and JPEG images internally, for example, although a PCX (a *PC Paintbrush* file) cannot be viewed. Therefore the image, if referenced, must be viewed using a suitable helper application. Many dozens of helper applications are available as freeware and shareware utilities – see Appendix C for details.

What is the difference between the Internet and the Web?

The Internet is a global collection of computers, some of which run a protocol known as HTTP (HyperText Transfer Protocol). HTTP *traffic* is carried by the main Internet protocol TCP/IP (Transmission Control Protocol/Internet Protocol). All of the computers that run HTTP are collectively known as *The Web*, or *World-Wide Web*. The Internet encompasses many other protocols. Everything on the Web is also located on the Internet, but everything located on the Internet is not on all of the Web. The Web is thus a subset of the Internet.

How can I use Netscape locally?

You can do this in one of two ways. Firstly you can get hold of a suitable WinSock package, such as Peter Tattam's *Trumpet WinSock*. This is a piece of software that allows the TCP/IP protocol (see above) to be run on your personal computer in a Microsoft Windows environment (see the Appendix C for its location on the Internet). Netscape looks for a file named `winsock.dll` when it starts in order to allow you to link into the Internet via your Internet service provider. If you ignore the WinSock completely you can use Netscape locally using `file://` URLs only. Alternatively, obtain the file `mozock.dll` from the Netscape FTP server. This will also allow you to use Netscape locally without the need for any WinSock at all (rename `mozock.dll` as `winsock.dll` and place it in the same directory as the Netscape program).

How do I interface my documents to a Web server, e.g. a database program?

Learn all you can about the CGI standard. See below.

What is CGI and CGI-scripting?

CGI stands for Common Gateway Interface. In a nutshell, CGI is a standard that defines how Web servers interface to *back-end* programs such as databases. HTML forms are used extensively with CGI to allow user details to be submitted to a server, dealt with, and then returned to the client as an HTML-formatted file. If you need to find out more about CGI, read my book *The World-Wide Web, Mosaic and More*, which has a whole chapter devoted to this very subject. *Scripting* is the process of writing CGI-compliant programs that take the information from an HTML form and then process it. For example, a form could submit a search term which would then interface to a database as the basis of a search. Any results could then be returned as HTML-formatted text (just like many of the search engine programs discussed in Chapter 5, for example).

What is the Toolbar in Netscape?
The *toolbar* is a series of buttons arranged horizontally along the top of the Netscape screen. Two types of toolbar are provided in Netscape: the main toolbar (first bar), and the directory buttons toolbar (second bar). The main toolbar allows document navigation, and the directory button toolbar allows connections to be made into specific pages of the Netscape Web server. Chapter 1 discusses the toolbars in more detail.

What is an in-line image?
An in-line image is an image that appears embedded *within* a hypertext document, i.e. an image that appears as part of an HTML <img src> tag. External images (non-in-line images are those which appear in their own window through the help of a suitable *helper application*).

What are GIFs and JPEGs?
GIF (Graphics Interchange File) and JPEG (Joint Photographic Experts Group) are the two main image formats supported by Netscape. Both of these images can be supported as *in-line* images (see above). JPEG images are compressed images and occupy less space than GIFs. Netscape 1.1 can handle in-line JPEGs and GIFs (see question above).

What is HTML?
HTML (HyperText Mark-up Language) is a document mark-up language that was born out of the ISO SGML (Standard Generalized Mark-up Language) standard. HTML is a *tag language* that specifies how a page is marked-up, i.e. how it is rendered when viewed through a Web browser such as Netscape. Many Web browsers support the HTML standard, which arrives in three versions currently, namely 1.0, 2.0 and 3.0. The latter is the most advanced version, supporting tables, font control and backgrounds.

How can I use HTML forms? What are forms anyway?
HTML forms are regions of a hypertext page that allow user-input into a series of *fields*. The HTML <form> tag is used for this purpose. While forms are very easy to create, the actual interfacing of the form to a Web server is more difficult, and requires an understanding of the CGI standard (see above).

What is a WinSock?
WinSock stands for *Windows Sockets*. Sockets are a communications mechanism that allow

information to be transmitted over the Internet. They are a fundamental concept to the TCP/IP protocol. The WinSock standard specifies how TCP/IP applications can be constructed in a Microsoft Windows environment. A suitable *WinSock program* can be used with Netscape to facilitate access to the Internet, e.g. the popular *Trumpet WinSock* for PCs (see Appendix C for the exact location).

How do I connect into the Internet?

A suitable Internet connection will be required. The most popular way of achieving this is via a WinSock package (see above). This implements the TCP/IP protocol on your PC, and also acts as a communications package that dials into your Internet service provider's machine via a modem connected into your computer. Modems use the telephone network to pass TCP/IP *packets* (packets are small units of data sent over the Internet) from your computer to a service provider's machine, and then via their machine to a faster leased line into the rest of the Internet. You can install a much faster leased line directly, e.g. an ISDN (Integrated Services Digital Network) line, although this is a much more expensive option.

What is the DNS?

DNS stands for *Domain Name Server*. A DNS server is contacted when you make a request to access a host on the Internet. The DNS server converts the address (or URL) that you enter (e.g. `http://www.somehost.com`) into a numeric IP (Internet Protocol) address – a process known as *address resolving* allowing the host to be found and then contacted. A *DNS Error* within Netscape may happen if the address you specify does not exist (which in theory is your error, and not that of the DNS, of course).

Why can't Netscape locate a particular URL that I enter?

Because it cannot be *resolved* (see above). Perhaps the address is incorrect. Check it and try again. Remember that some URLs abide to a strict format with some letters in different case. Be sure to enter the name exactly. If you receive a *DNS Error* from Netscape, the host name that you have entered does not exist or is off-line.

How do I save my popular URLs and use bookmarks?

Use the Netscape *bookmarks* feature as covered in Chapter 1. Bookmarks allow you to save the URLs of frequently visited Internet sites, so that you don't have to keep re-entering their details when you want to re-establish contact again. You can create a bookmark entry for a hyperlink by clicking on the right mouse button over the hyperlink and then choosing the *Create Bookmark entry* option.

What USENET groups deal with the WWW and Netscape etc.?

At the time of writing, the main USENET groups are:

- comp.infosystems.www.misc

- comp.infosystems.www.users

- `comp.infosystems.www.providers`

- `cern.www.announce`

- `cern.www.talk`

Most of the `comp.*` groups shown here tend to overlap their subject coverage to a certain extent. You will find coverage of every Web-related topic here. The CERN newsgroups deal with events from the WWW's birthplace in Switzerland. If you want to read one of these groups from within Netscape, enter the URL `news:` followed by the group name, for example: `news:cern.www.talk`. You must have a news server configured for this; otherwise quote the name of the server in the extended news-URL as `news://servername/group`.

Where are Netscape's WWW sites?
They are to be found at the URLs `home.netscape.com` (Web) and `ftp.netscape.com` (FTP server). The FTP server contains all of the Netscape executables (i.e. programs) and much more in the way of downloadable documentation etc. Netscape's Web server, one of the best on the Internet, contains a wealth of information in hypertext form.

How can I access USENET news?
You need to issue a `news:` URL. An NNTP news server must ideally be specified in your `netscape.ini` initialization file, although Netscape can use any news server that you have permission to access. Chapter 3 deals with USENET more extensively. Public USENET servers (news servers) are still available – try searching the Web using Yahoo for a search term such as *public news servers* and a list will be there, somewhere – I found half a dozen recently by doing just this `:-)`

How can I download files from another machine?
Use the `ftp://` URL (file transfer protocol URL). FTP is the main way of moving files around on the Internet. See Chapters 1 and 2. for more information. For example, you could type: `ftp://ftp.somehost.com` to browse the files on the host named `ftp.some-host.com`, or you could specify a route to an actual file to download, for example `ftp://ftp.somehost.com/dir1/file.zip`, which would download the file named `file.zip` immediately.

How can I send and receive electronic mail (email)?
You can only send email using Netscape. Type in the URL `mailto:` and Netscape will display a window allowing you to enter the name of a recipient and the actual text (or *body*) of the message you want to send. You must have pre-configured a mail server first using Netscape's Options/Preferences/Mail & News menu. Public (SMTP – Simple Mail Transfer Protocol) mail servers do still exist on the Internet, although your service provider will of course provide you with such a facility.

How can I change Netscape's colour scheme?
Through the Options/Preferences screen. Some tags in HTML 3.0 also control colour and backgrounds. See the chapter on HTML for more information.

How can I use Netscape's secure transmissions feature?
The ability to use this depends on the server you contact. If the server is a *Netsite*, a term applied to Web servers using Netscape's encryption software, then the server should enable secure transmissions and the `http://` prefix will change to `https://`, indicating that *secure* HTTP is in force. Some servers allow you to connect to a specific `https://` address. Netscape's home Web server has many pointers to *secure sites* on the Web.

I

Netscape 1.2b1 release

Netscape Corporation released version 1.2b1 of Netscape Navigator just before this book went to press. This beta test version makes some small changes to the Netscape interface, specifically in the Bookmarks menu, which now has a nice hierarchical interface with 'drag and drop' facilities. It also does away with the 'two icon' problem (i.e. only one Netscape icon is shown on the desktop, and Netscape still appears in the task list). The Options/Preferences menu is also improved: a folder-like structure now allows selection of the appropriate preferences section (whereas before the user had to navigate a pick-list of options). The program also seems to be faster and more responsive. Minor alterations in the colour scheme have also been implemented – e.g. horizontal rules (<hr> tags) now take the colour of a background bitmap when loaded using the extended HTML tag. Apart from these changes, no other major differences are apparent. Netscape 1.2b1 can be downloaded from the URL:

```
ftp://ftp.netscape.com/pub/netscape1.2b1
```

The user interested in a commercial version of Netscape will be interested in the 'Netscape Navigator personal edition', which has a bundled version of the popular email package Eudora-light. More details are available at the URL:

```
http://www.netscape.com/showcase/personal_edition/index.html
```

Index